The Papers of the
Henry Luce III Fellows
in Theology

Series in Theological Scholarship and Research

The Papers of the Henry Luce III Fellows in Theology
Christopher I. Wilkins, Editor

The Papers of the Henry Luce III Fellows in Theology

VOLUME VI
Christopher I. Wilkins, Editor

 Series in Theological Scholarship and Research

The Association of Theological Schools in the United States and Canada
Pittsburgh, Pennsylvania

The Papers of the Henry Luce III Fellows in Theology

VOLUME VI

edited by
Christopher I. Wilkins

Copyright © 2003 by The Association of Theological Schools
in the United States and Canada

Library of Congress Cataloging in Publication Data

The papers of the Henry Luce III Fellows in Theology / edited by Christopher I. Wilkins
    p. cm. — (Series in theological scholarship and research)
ISBN 0-7885-0297-2 (alk. paper)
ISBN 0-9702-3462-7 (alk. paper) vol. VI
1. Theology. I. Henry Luce III Fellows in Theology. II. Series.
BR50.P24 1996
230—dc20   96-27815
                                         CIP

Printed in the United States of America
on acid-free paper

Acknowledgment

The Association of Theological Schools expresses its profound appreciation to The Henry Luce Foundation, especially Henry Luce III, John W. Cook, and Michael F. Gilligan, for their generous support of the Henry Luce III Fellows in Theology program, the annual Luce Conference, and this volume.

Contents

Contributors to this Volume

Catherine A. Brekus
Assistant Professor of the History of Christianity
University of Chicago Divinity School

Mary Rose D'Angelo
Associate Professor
University of Notre Dame Department of Theology

Stanley J. Grenz
Professor of New Testament
Regent College

Carl R. Holladay
Professor of New Testament
Candler School of Theology of Emory University

Reinhard Hütter
Associate Professor
Duke University Divinity School

Jon D. Levenson
Albert A. List Professor of Jewish Studies
University of Chicago Divinity School

Bonnie J. Miller-McLemore
Associate Professor of Pastoral Ministry
Vanderbilt University Divinity School

Christopher I. Wilkins
The Association of Theological Schools

Introduction

Christopher I. Wilkins, Editor
THE ASSOCIATION OF THEOLOGICAL SCHOOLS
PITTSBURGH, PENNSYLVANIA

The essays of the 1999-2000 class of Henry Luce III Fellows in Theology represent a diverse set of interests, traditions, scholarly methods, and disciplinary and interdisciplinary conversations within theological scholarship as practiced at the end of the twentieth century. Shaped by The Association of Theological Schools as part of its leadership education efforts for theological faculty in the United States and Canada, the Henry Luce III Fellows in Theology program has come to nurture both disciplinary excellence and cross-disciplinary attention in the research projects it supports. The essays in this volume, particularly, contribute to both conversations in a number of ways.

Topically, the essays range from detailed questions concerning ancient Israelite religion and the texts, practices, and traditions of Second Temple Judaism and Late Antiquity to the recent history of, and need for, theological and religious imagination in contemporary western societies. Each writer speaks from a position of authority within biblical studies, American religious history, systematic or moral theology, pastoral theology, or the study of religion in ancient Israel or in Late Antiquity. Academic associations dedicated to making a particular scholarly discipline or subdiscipline thrive should be well pleased with these essays. Yet they, like their predecessors in *The Papers of the Henry Luce III Fellows in Theology*, bring an additional concern for the practical effect that the research and topics at hand will have in communities of faith, and more generally throughout North American society, which should be of benefit in and beyond academic discourse. This additional concern expresses itself in a common theme: the realization that theology *per se* is needed both for adequately reflecting upon, and adequately expressing, the contemporary worth in ancient, modern, and postmodern conceptions not only of God and God's church, but also of value, person, self, freedom, law, death, life, spiritual maturity, and the like.

It is not surprising that theological educators should find their approaches to a wide range of topics linking to this common theme. It should be surprising, indeed disheartening, when they do not. What might surprise is that the theme does not cohere around a set of doctrines or around a series of confessions, but as processes of reflection and expression that prevent one from separating the subjects of theological research from contemporary pastoral and practical concerns. That is, each essay shows how the questions involved in its particular area of academic inquiry have a practical, pastoral valence, and how the questions, needs, and issues that arise in contemporary societies may helpfully be sounded within theological traditions with great richness and a long memory.

Talk of family values, of how to value any family and its members, and of how easily they can be manipulated by the well-intentioned and the cruel, feature prominently in the essays by Mary Rose D'Angelo and Bonnie Miller-McLemore. Yet, in terms of what such talk means for families themselves and for the societies in which they live, such concerns inspire the other five essays as well. Likewise, Stanley Grenz and Reinhard Hütter alone concentrate their energies directly on the anomic theological and cultural fragmentation to which Enlightenment-era philosophies and theologies (and their current heirs) can give rise. These impassioned concerns resonate with Jon Levenson's and Carl Holladay's detailed critical examinations of prior generations' constructs for scholarship on biblical texts and on the religions that made them and were made by them. Each finds that fragmentation, misplaced attention, and an over-reliance on a single vision of the world, no matter how comprehensive, ultimately make for a weakened society, flawed scholarship, and limited theology. Similarly, Sarah Osborn, the eighteenth-century New England Calvinist to whom Catherine Brekus devotes her essay, was as deeply troubled by the social and ecclesial implications of what she knew of the Enlightenment as she was by its theology and anthropology, and as are many of the writers here. Her diaries and surviving manuscripts, on which Dr. Brekus bases her essay, show how even the most difficult and abstruse theological question carries with it practical, everyday implications. Life, she discovered without benefit of study in seminary, could not be lived well without reflection or theology, or without, as one might say today, getting right with God.

Generally said, the writers in this volume, like those who wrote the texts to which they attend, all examine ways in which actual human beings are imagined, constructed, and threatened in the world in which they find themselves. In doing so, they show how the disciplines of theological research, as well as the subject from which theology itself derives its name and inspiration, can enhance that imagination, improve the construction, and minimize or redeem what threatens. Their gifts are not just to the world of academic discourse, but to all who care deeply about lives of faith, hope, and inspiration as practiced now, and as refracted through the past.

The Henry Luce III Fellows in Theology program, inaugurated in 1994, is administered by the Association of Theological Schools in the United States and Canada. All full-time faculty members at ATS accredited and candidate institutions are eligible to apply. Fellows receive a yearlong sabbatical to concentrate on a major project in theological research. The fruits of that research are meant to be shared widely with the academy, communities of faith, and the broader public. For further information or to apply to the program, please contact the Association directly. We hope you enjoy the essays of the 1999-2000 class of Fellows.

Sarah Osborn's World: Popular Christianity in Eighteenth-Century America

Catherine A. Brekus
UNIVERSITY OF CHICAGO
CHICAGO, ILLINOIS

She could not remember when she had first decided to write her life story. Although she had often thought about writing a memoir, the grinding routine of her daily life always seemed to get in the way. There were always dirty clothes to wash, chamber pots to empty, fires to tend, pots of meat and vegetables to boil, floors to sweep, and accounts to settle. There were shirts to mend and linens to bleach and children to teach in her school. There was firewood to buy before the cold days of winter came. On good days there were pies to make for feasts of thanksgiving. On bad days there were loved ones to wash and dress for burial. Although she longed to sit down quietly by her hearth and reflect on what her life meant, there never seemed to be time for anything more than work and a few hours of prayer or Bible reading. Yearning for something more, she began keeping a diary, filling at least three volumes with her thoughts about her relationship to God, but the larger questions kept returning: Why had her life unfolded as it had? How had God ordered her experiences? What could her story tell her about herself and about God?[1]

It was not until 1743, when she was twenty-nine years old, that Sarah Haggar Wheaten Osborn finally sat down in front of a blank sheet of paper with a pen in her hand to compose her entire life story. Although the paper was small, much smaller than the stationery or notebook paper we use today, it looked large and empty to her. Wondering how to begin, she dipped her pen in a pot of ink, leaned forward, and wrote a breathless sentence that stretched all the way down the page. Near the bottom of the page, she explained why she felt so compelled to write: she wrote "for the incouragement of any who may providentialy lite on these Lines after my disease to trust in the Lord and never dispair of his mercy."[2] She *wanted* her words to be read. Hoping to glorify God and to encourage others not to despair, she spent days, perhaps weeks, composing the unforgettable story of her life.

After finishing her memoir, Sarah continued to write, reflecting on her life in hundreds of letters to friends, in a short theological tract that she published anonymously in 1755, and in an astonishing number of diaries, more than fifty volumes in all. Even though her formal education had been limited to a few months at a girls' boarding school at the age of only seven or eight years old, she was an eloquent writer who seemed to feel compelled to record her life on paper. As she explained in 1754, writing helped her "get near or wrestle with God." "I seem to Lie u[nder] necessity to improve my Pen if [I w]ill be at all Lively in religion," she wrote. All told, more than 1500 pages of her manuscripts survive in archives across New England. According to Samuel Hopkins, her minister in Newport, she left behind anywhere between five and fifteen thousand pages.[3]

Few people today have ever heard of Sarah Osborn, but by the end of her life in 1796, she had become one of the most respected female religious leaders of her time. Her life story, as she admitted in her memoir, was as dramatic as a novel. Raised by parents whom she later described as "severe," she seems to have had a difficult childhood. As a teenager (the dates are not clear, but she was probably 14 or 15) she struggled with temptations to commit suicide. The rest of her life was marked by recurring tragedy: she eloped at the age of seventeen with a sailor, Samuel Wheaten, who died two years later, leaving her with a one-year-old son to support; remarried a successful tailor, Henry Osborn, a widower with three children, who suffered a physical or mental breakdown that left him unable to work; and toiled long hours as a schoolteacher and a seamstress in order to pay her family's bills. Soon after her second marriage, she and her husband were forced to sell all their possessions in order to repay their creditors. Despite her constant battle to achieve economic security, she remained so indigent throughout her life that her name never appeared on Newport's tax lists. Her beloved son, her only child, died at the age of twelve. Through everything, she suffered chronic bouts of illness. (Although it is impossible to offer an accurate diagnosis based on her fragmentary descriptions, she may have suffered from either multiple sclerosis or rheumatoid arthritis.) She spent the last twenty years of her life almost entirely confined to her house, unable to walk and almost entirely blind. The woman who had spent almost her entire life writing finally had to put down her pen. Only a few scraps of her writings survive after 1776, including a letter that she dictated through a friend.[4]

Yet despite all these tragedies, Sarah was so charismatic that many people in Newport sought her spiritual counsel. Like the followers of medieval women saints, they seemed to interpret her afflictions as a mark of her sanctity, a symbol of her closeness to the suffering Christ. Reputed to be gifted in prayer, she became more popular than any of the ordained ministers in her town. During the winter of 1766-67, she emerged as the leader of a remarkable religious revival that brought as many as five hundred people—including more than one hundred slaves—to her house each week for prayer meetings. Although she remained poor, strangers from as far away as Canada and the West Indies sent money to help defray her expenses, eager to help a woman who had become virtually a Protestant saint.[5]

Sarah's rich manuscripts offer a fascinating window onto popular Christianity in eighteenth-century New England. Besides offering a glimpse of a devout Calvinist woman, her writings also shed light on the dramatic religious changes that took place during the decades before the American Revolution. As Sarah poured out her heart in prayer, she filled her diaries and letters with her thoughts about God, Satan, human nature, and the meaning of human existence. Because her life was filled with hardship and suffering, she also reflected on the meaning of affliction. Identifying with Job, she repeatedly asked God why he had "disappointed all my hopes and expectations."[6]

On the broadest level, Sarah's manuscripts reveal how a pious, intelligent woman responded to the changes that historians have described as the Enlightenment and the emergence of modernity. Although Sarah could only dimly sense the changes that were reshaping her world, she wrestled with the same pressing theological questions that Enlightenment thinkers raised in their work—questions about original sin, religious certainty, the hiddenness of God, and especially theodicy (the problem of why God allows the exist-

ence of evil). On one hand, Sarah never used the term "Enlightenment" in her writings (the term was not coined until the nineteenth
century), and she never mentioned such thinkers as John Locke.
Based on the books she mentioned in her diaries and letters, her
personal reading tastes ran more toward devotional writers like
Isaac Watts.[7] But on the other hand, Sarah also seems to have been
troubled by the new currents of thought that emerged during the
1700s. Between 1714, the year of her birth, and 1796, the year of
her death, Christianity was transformed by a growing faith in human goodness, human reason, divine benevolence, and free will.

Since few recent historians have shown much interest in these
theological changes, it may seem surprising to place Sarah's life
within the frame of the Enlightenment. (The last survey of the Enlightenment in America, written by Henry May, was published in
1976.)[8] Because they have tended to think of the Enlightenment as
a high-minded, intellectual movement that was limited to a small
circle of erudite men, most have chosen to focus on the enduring
power of Puritanism in shaping people's lives. Contrary to the great
historian Perry Miller, who argued that New England Puritanism
declined during the eighteenth century, recent scholars have insisted that it continued to influence everything from gender roles to
the coming of the American Revolution. Today Puritanism, not the
Enlightenment, is our main category for understanding religion in
eighteenth-century New England.[9]

Yet as Sarah's example illustrates, the "new learning" also had
a profound influence on how ordinary Americans thought about
themselves and God. Of course, there were many areas of rural New
England where Enlightenment ideas spread fairly slowly. But Sarah lived in Newport, a commercial port that was one of the largest
and most religiously diverse cities in eighteenth-century America,
and she was exposed to a wide variety of religious beliefs. (Today
we tend to think of Newport as a small resort town where wealthy
people vacation, but in the eighteenth century, only Boston, New
York, and Philadelphia had larger populations.) There were not only
Congregationalists in Newport (Congregationalists were the descendants of the Puritans), but Roman Catholics, Quakers, liberal Anglicans, several kinds of Baptists, and even a small group of Jews.[10]
Touro Synagogue, the oldest synagogue in the United States, was
built in Newport in 1762.

Besides being religiously diverse, Newport was also a cosmopolitan, wealthy city where the leading men prided themselves on their knowledge of the latest British ideas. The "Philosophical Society," a group of clergymen and merchants that included George Berkeley, the Dean of Derry, met regularly to discuss theological and philosophical works. They founded the Redwood Library, where members could borrow the latest books from England.[11]

In this environment, Sarah seems to have been particularly aware of the new, liberal religious ideas that threatened to undermine many of her most cherished beliefs. As a Calvinist, she believed in predestination, original sin, human helplessness, God's sovereignty, the reality of heaven and hell, and the salvation of the elect by God's grace alone, not good works. Yet many of the leading philosophers of her day had begun to undermine the Calvinist orthodoxy. To give just a few examples: John Locke questioned the doctrine of original sin; Samuel Clarke (a Deist) challenged the doctrine of eternal punishment; and John Taylor (a British Presbyterian) condemned the belief in infant damnation. As historian Henry May has argued, eighteenth-century Americans showed little interest in radical skeptics such as David Hume, but they were profoundly influenced by "moderates" such as Francis Hutcheson, Locke, and John Tillotson. In fact, historians who have studied estate inventories and library catalogues have argued that Tillotson, a liberal Anglican (or "Latitudinarian"), was one of the most popular authors in early America.[12]

While historians have lumped together many different thinkers under the category of "the Enlightenment," placing John Locke's belief in the "reasonableness of Christianity" next to David Hume's skepticism, there were three strands of Enlightenment thought that seem to have influenced Sarah the most: the growing faith in human reason, the questioning (or outright rejection) of the doctrine of original sin, and the emergence of humanitarianism. On one hand, Sarah incorporated Enlightenment categories into her thought, unconsciously echoing such key words as reason, nature, benevolence, sympathy, virtue, and compassion. For example, even though she insisted that human reason was naturally limited and corrupt, she also described her piety as "rational" and "experimental": it was not only based on her reading of scripture, but on her careful scrutiny of her life. Obsessively recording her religious experiences in thousands of pages of diary entries, she repeatedly examined them as "evidence" of God's providence. In 1763, twenty years after finishing her memoir, she wrote on its cover: "this Book I have reread again and again."[13] Whenever she was tempted to doubt either God's goodness or her own salvation, she re-read her memoir and her diaries in order to assure herself that her faith was grounded on "rational" evidence.[14]

Yet even though Sarah saw little inherent conflict between piety and reason, she rejected the growing faith in human goodness. Beginning in the late seventeenth and early eighteenth centuries, a small group of ministers (many of them British Anglicans) began to question the doctrine of original sin. For example, writing in 1710, Daniel Whitby complained that the entire idea of inherited sin was "exceeding cruel, and plainly inconsistent with the Justice, Wisdom, and goodness of our gracious God." In 1740, only a few years before Sarah wrote her memoir, John Taylor, a Presbyterian, condemned the doctrine of original sin as "one of the greatest Absurdities in all the System of *corrupt religion*." Taylor's book, entitled *The Scripture-Doctrine of Original Sin Proposed to Free and Candid Examination*, was published in three editions in only six years.[15]

Often the debates over original sin revolved around the nature of children. Hoping to provoke controversy (and succeeding), liberal ministers and philosophers repeatedly asked how a just God could hold children responsible for sins they had not personally committed. Decrying the Calvinist belief in infant damnation as cruel, they insisted that God would never condemn newborns to hell because of a sin committed by Adam and Eve. "Consider seriously what a God he must be," one minister asked, "who can be displeased with, and curse his innocent Creatures, even before they have a Being. *Is this thy God, O Christian?*" By 1757, the Reverend Samuel Niles, a Massachusetts Congregationalist, could claim that the doctrine of original sin was the one "most eagerly struck at, and virulently oppos'd by many, in the present Age."[16]

In contrast, Sarah clung to an older view of innate corruption. As she lamented in her memoir, all humans "have a fountain of corruption in them that is ever flowing." Gripped by an overwhelming sense of her sinfulness, she used particularly harsh language to describe herself: she was "unworthy as a dog," "vile," "unclean," "filthy and Poluted," and a "leper."[17] Disdaining the new, liberal faith in children's innocence, Sarah claimed that she had begun to sin as soon as she was capable of it. Looking back on her childhood, she remembered herself as "a monster in sin," a "lyar," and "the most ignorant and vile of all creatures." Her "bace ingratitude," her "deep-rooted enmity" against God, her "angry ungratefull temper," and her dreadful "corruptions" made her entirely unworthy of God's love. In her opinion, her childhood proved the dark wisdom of the Psalms: "The wicked are estranged from the womb: they go astray as soon as they are born, speaking lies."[18]

Sarah also claimed that she had needed to be "corrected"—in other words, spanked or beaten. "My corruptions prevailed dreadfully," she confessed. Despite her resentment when her mother punished her, she also insisted that it had been for her own good. In her words: "I remember [I] partook of an angry ungratefull temper stirring in me especially when corrected by my mother. But must acknowledge to the glory of god that he preserved such a tenderness of concience in me that if at any time my mother convinc'd me that she did it because it was her duty for my sin against god, I could bear it patiently and wilingly—yea, thankfully."[19] In contrast to John Locke, who argued that parents should not subject their children to "Beating . . . and all other Sorts of slavish and corporal Punishments," Sarah believed that sinful children needed to be disciplined.[20] In her work as a schoolteacher, Sarah repeated the lessons she had learned from her parents, beating the students who were the most "unruly." As she explained in her diaries, she loved the children in her school—they were her "little ones" and her "dear lambs"—but she also believed they needed to be "trained." Whenever she grew frustrated by "the darkness of their Minds, the blindness of their understandings, the stubbornness of their wills," she used force to "subdue" them.[21]

Sarah's dark vision of children's corruption was not unique. On one hand, growing numbers of Americans questioned the doctrine of original sin. According to Jonathan Edwards, the great Calvinist theologian, many New England parents mistakenly regarded their children as "innocent."[22] Yet on the other hand, conservative Calvinists were so troubled by the liberal faith in human goodness that they expressed their beliefs in increasingly harsh language. According to Edwards, for example, children were not only corrupt, but "young vipers, and. . .infinitely more hateful than vipers. . . ."[23] Other Calvinist ministers defended their beliefs in catechisms, sermons, and even children's songs. For example, Isaac Watts's popular hymnbook, *Divine and Moral Songs for the Use of Children*, which was published more than seventy-five times in eighteenth-century America, included the hymn "Heaven and Hell":

> There is beyond the sky
>   A heaven of joy and love;
> And holy children, when they die,
>   Go to that world above.

> There is a dreadful hell,
>   And everlasting pains:
> There sinners must with devils dwell
>   In darkness, fire, and chains.[24]

Although Sarah never recorded the names of the books she read as a child, she may have owned a copy of this book. As she remembered, she was delighted when a minister kindly gave her a "Little book of spiritual songs."[25]

Besides objecting to the liberal faith in human goodness and children's innocence, Sarah also protested against the strand of Enlightenment thought that historians have labeled "humanitarianism." On one hand, she was a compassionate woman who believed that Christians had a duty to help those who were suffering. Despite her battle to make ends meet, she gave away her hard-earned money to others in need. According to her minister, she gave more money to her church than "many wealthy persons of the same congregation." She also took several destitute or orphaned children into her home. In 1758, she prayed that God would enable her to take in a "Poor Child," perhaps her husband's grandson. "Is it not Hungry? is it not Naked ? is it not Neglected soul and body?" she asked. "Is it not a Proper object of charity as any the town Produces? does not charity begin at Home?" Remembering her struggles after her first husband's death, she resolved to be kind to the "widow" and the "fatherless."[26]

Yet even though Sarah believed in the virtue of charity, she could not sympathize with humanitarians who seemed to elevate God's *benevolence* over his sovereignty. Because they believed that a compassionate God had created the world in order to promote human happiness, they denied that God ever deliberately caused people to suffer. They especially objected to the belief in hell, which, in their opinion, made God appear cruel and vindictive.[27] In contrast, Sarah insisted that even though God *was* benevolent, he had created the world in order to demonstrate his glory, not to make humans happy. Although it might be difficult to accept, suffering and evil—even hell—were ultimately part of God's plan.

As Sarah explained in her diaries, suffering was never the result of accident or bad luck; it was always pregnant with divine meaning. For example, after her only child, Samuel, died at the age of twelve, she concluded that God had taken him away because she had loved him too much. Because she had sinfully worshipped him as an "idol," a jealous God had torn him away. "Lest my heart should be joined to idols," she lamented, "he will have an only son!"[28]

Sarah was especially distraught after Samuel's death because of her anxiety over whether or not he had been saved. Even though she sat next to his bed during the last few days of his life, begging him to accept Christ as his savior, he never seems to have experienced conversion. As she lamented, "I could discern no evidence of a work of grace wrought on his soul, for which I did plead from day to day. I did not so much as once, in all his sickness, pray for his life, but for some evidence that his soul might live. And for want of this, I sometimes seemed to be crushed down, having a sense of his doleful case, if not reconciled to God."[29] After his death, she seems to have been haunted by fears that his soul had gone to hell. "Crushed" by her grief and anxiety, she never mentioned Samuel again in any of her surviving manuscripts.

Yet despite her pain, Sarah insisted that Samuels' death had been for her own good. Remembering her sorrow during the first hours after his death, she wrote: "[God's] word, His *rod* comforted me. I saw no frown in it: No, but the kind chastisements of my indulgent Father. This portion of scripture was very sweet to me. . . whom the Lord loveth he chasteneth." (She was quoting from Hebrews 12:6.)[30]

Sarah interpreted her suffering within a Calvinist theological framework. Because of her belief that God had made a binding covenant with the faithful, or in Calvinist terminology, the "elect," she assumed that God had punished her in order to prepare her for salvation. Unlike the "wicked," who had every reason to expect eternal damnation, true believers knew that God afflicted them for their own good. As ministers explained, God usually afflicted people in retribution for their sins, but sometimes he was motivated by other purposes as well: to test their faith, to make them more humble or compassionate, to wean them from the world, to demonstrate his power, or to purify them. Their afflictions were like a potent, caustic medicine that brought intense pain, but also salvation.[31] Instead of seeing Samuel's death as a sign that God had abandoned her, Sarah insisted that he had "corrected" her in order to prepare her for eternal life in his kingdom.

Although eighteenth-century liberals were deeply troubled by this harsh explanation of suffering, Sarah found it immensely reassuring. No matter what happened to her, she clung to her faith in a transcendent God who controlled every detail of human life. Indeed, Sarah found it more alarming to imagine that God was *not* responsible for her afflictions. If there was no guiding intelligence behind the world, but only fate or luck, then human life was sheer chaos, a meaningless abyss that was even more frightening than hell. Either God controlled everything, including her suffering, or there was no God. Although it sometimes caused her anguish, she prayed that what her ministers told her every week in church was true: that her afflictions were not a sign of God's absence, but God's love. Echoing the words of the Psalms, she wrote, "I know, O Lord, thy judgments are right, and in very faithfulness thou hast afflicted me."[32] There could be no real tragedy in a world that was completely controlled by God.

Like many other eighteenth-century Calvinists, Sarah responded to the humanitarian critique of Christianity by expressing her devotion in increasingly extreme language. Angered by accusations that the Calvinist God was arbitrary and vindictive, she insisted that true Christians not only accepted their sufferings, but rejoiced in them. "Strike me, covenant faithful God, as thou Pleasest," she wrote. "Tis my Just deserts, tis the effect of sin, but Let me kiss the dear, dear Hand that strikes." Like Samuel Hopkins, Sarah's minister in Newport, who became famous for his theology of "disinterested benevolence," she claimed that true believers had to be willing to be damned for the glory of God.[33]

In one of the ironies of history, while the Enlightenment eventually undermined traditional Calvinist theology, in the short term it made it more severe. While historians have debated whether Puritanism declined in the eighteenth century or continued to shape American culture, Sarah's manuscripts suggest a different interpretation. Puritanism did not gradually fade away in the decades before the American Revolution, but exploded in a final burst of religious intensity. As we have seen in our own day, religious groups tend to state their beliefs in especially strong terms when they feel threatened.

Like Jonathan Edwards, Samuel Hopkins, and many of the other leading Calvinists of her time, Sarah was deeply ambivalent about Enlightenment "progress." Yet instead of writing learned theological treatises, she transformed the story of her life into a poignant defense of Calvinist orthodoxy. As she testified on virtually every page of her manuscripts, God had repeatedly rescued her from the brink of despair. Despite all of her suffering—her youthful temptations to commit suicide, her poverty, her loss of her first husband and her only child, her painful illnesses—she insisted that a sovereign, majestic God had never abandoned her. The truth of Calvinism was written on every page of her life. "Thou wise and wonderful God," she wrote in her diary, "thou...has said thou wilt never fail me nor forsake me, and thou never wilt." She refused to see her life as tragic, but as "a life of wonders."[34]

The people who knew Sarah regarded her as an icon of true holiness, a living example of God's grace and power. When she died in 1796 at the age of 83, her friends and acquaintances passed around her manuscripts as devotional literature, treasuring her words as evidence of Christian truth. They seem to have treated her diaries like printed books, inscribing their names on them as a sign of ownership. For example, Caleb Tenney, who succeeded Samuel Hopkins as the minister of Newport's First Church from 1804 to 1814, wrote his name in large letters on the first page of Sarah's memoir. "Miss Clara Allen," who listed her town as Northampton, Massachusetts, wrote her name in pencil on the inside cover of one of Sarah's diaries. (Since Tenney moved to Northampton in 1842, he may have given this diary to Allen as a gift.)[35]

Sarah's fame was heightened in the early nineteenth century when Samuel Hopkins published two collections of her writings: *Memoirs of the Life of Mrs. Sarah Osborn*, which included edited extracts from her memoir and diaries, and *Familiar Letters, Written by Mrs. Sarah Osborn and Miss Susanna Anthony*, which offered a small sampling of her correspondence with her closest friend. Besides offering Christians an inspiring example of faithfulness under affliction, Hopkins tried to use Sarah's story to bolster his theology of "disinterested benevolence." As he explained, "she had an affecting and strong abhorrence of every thing which she saw in herself, even all moral depravity; and which appeared in others, as having a tendency to dishonor God. This was a constant source of grief and trouble to her. By this she manifested a high degree of disinterested, benevolent love to God. . . ."[36] In his opinion, her life offered a model of Christian sacrifice and submission.

Yet in the decades after Sarah's death in 1796, growing numbers of Christians began to question Calvinist understandings of original sin, predestination, and free will. In the words of historian Elizabeth Clark, many Protestants "shifted their focus from the drama of God, the sovereign judge, sentencing the depraved human to an afterlife of unremitting suffering, to that of God, the benevolent father, working for his children's physical and spiritual well-being. The purpose of worship shifted from the glorification of God to the salvation and celebration of man."[37] Unlike earlier Christians, who had accepted suffering as a part of the divine plan, many now found it shocking—even obscene—to imagine that a compassionate, benevolent God would deliberately inflict physical or psychological pain. Even though many Christians seem to have been inspired by Sarah's devotion, they also denigrated parts of her theology as "morbid."[38] "It cannot be said that our ancestors failed to write diaries," wrote the literary historian Moses Coit Tyler in 1878:

> Unluckily, however, the diaries that they wrote . . . were generally records of events which took place only inside of them; psychological diaries, more or less mystical and unhealthy; chronicles of tender, scrupulous, introverted natures, misled into gratuitous self-torture; narratives of their own spiritual moods of fluctuating hour by hour, of

> visitations of Satan, of dullness or of ecstasy in
> prayer, of doubts or hopes respecting their share in
> the divine decrees; itineraries of daily religious
> progress, aggravated by overwork, indigestion, and
> a gospel of gloom.[39]

Influenced by Scottish Common Sense philosophy, nineteenth-century Americans embraced a more rationalistic, optimistic, and *modern* view of the universe. Just as Sarah had once feared, Calvinism had been profoundly transformed by its encounter with the Enlightenment.

Because we stand on the other side of the Enlightenment, it can be hard for us to understand Sarah's reflections on her life. Reading Sarah's memoir is like meeting someone from a different country who speaks our language, but who has a different understanding of the things we take most for granted. "The past is a foreign country," the English novelist L. P. Hartley wrote in 1953. "They do things differently there."[40] While the meaning of her words would have been transparent to other eighteenth-century Calvinists, modern Americans may find her language strange and bewildering, even disturbing. While we believe in human freedom, she assumed that people are powerless to do anything without God's will. While we believe in self-assertion and self-expression, she thought the self had to be tamed and disciplined. We see everyday life, especially family life, as the most meaningful part of existence, but she feared loving her child, her husband, and her friends too much. We believe in teaching children to be autonomous and independent, but she tried to "break the will." We urge people to resist illness and death with all of their power. "Do not go gentle into that good night," wrote Dylan Thomas. "Rage, rage against the dying of the light." But Sarah begged Christians to submit patiently to their afflictions. "Let us not murmur, but submit and kiss the dear, dear hand that Holds the rod," she counseled. "'Tis the hand of our God and Father."[41] And the list could go on.

But the past is not *completely* alien. Whether or not we agree with Sarah's theological assumptions, it is hard not to see ourselves as part of the same broad historical era, an era stretching all the way from 1700 to the present. Although we tend to describe ourselves as postmodern, our culture is still preoccupied with the questions that Enlightenment thinkers posed three hundred years ago—questions about the nature of God and humanity, the meaning of happiness, the limits of human freedom and responsibility, the definition of sin, and (as fundamentalists often remind us) the existence of objective truth. The Enlightenment transformed Protestantism in the eighteenth century. We are still feeling the reverberations today.

When Sarah died in 1796, she counted her manuscripts among her most cherished possessions. She had treasured them for years, carefully preserving them in the hopes that they would be read by future Christians. On the cover of her memoir, she left a small inscription: "Sept 4th 1763 this Book I Have reread again and again and now commit it to be disposd of as shall be most for. . ." Although her words trail off, erased by sunlight and time, it is clear how she would have finished her sentence. On the cover of every one of her diaries, she bequeathed her words "to the disposal of providence." Her greatest hope was that someday her manuscripts would be read by people who shared her hunger to communicate with a personal, majestic, sovereign God. Two centuries later, her written prayers can help transport us back to the world of eighteenth-century popular Christianity, a world that stood on the brink of modernity, a world that has much to say to our own.

Endnotes

1.   Since Sarah marked her memoir with the number "4," it is likely that she wrote three volumes of daily diaries before her life story. Unfortunately, however, none of these volumes survive today, and Samuel Hopkins did not include any material from them in his edited version of her diaries, *Memoirs of the Life of Mrs. Sarah Osborn: who died at Newport, Rhodeisland, on the second day of August, 1796. In the eighty third year of her age.* (Worcester, Mass.: Leonard Worcester, 1799).

2.   Sarah Osborn, *Memoir*, p. 1, Beinecke Rare Book and Manuscript Library, Yale University, New Haven, Connecticut. Sarah numbered the pages of her memoir. However, she did not always number the pages of her diaries. For the sake of clarity, I have identified each diary by the number she wrote on the cover, and I have also given both the dates and the page numbers of her diary entries wherever possible.

3.   Sarah Osborn, *Diary #15* (1754), undated entry at end of diary, p. 129, Connecticut Historical Society, Hartford, Connecticut. According to Hopkins, Osborn wrote more than 50 volumes of diaries, "the least containing near 100 pages, the bigger part above 200, and a number 300, and more, besides letters to her friends, and other occasional writing." See Samuel Hopkins, ed., *Memoirs of the Life of Mrs. Sarah Osborn* (Worcester, Mass.: Leonard Worcester, 1799), 358. Although the majority of Sarah's diaries and letters have been lost, more than 1500 pages have been preserved in the following collections: Sarah Osborn, *Diaries, 1753-1772*, Newport Historical Society, Newport, Rhode Island; Sarah Osborn, *Diaries and Memoir, 1757-*

1769, Beinecke Rare Book and Manuscript Library, Yale University, New Haven, Connecticut; Sarah Osborn, *Letters, 1743-1770*; *1779*, American Antiquarian Society, Worcester, Massachusetts; Sarah Osborn, *Diaries, 1754, 1760-1761*, Connecticut Historical Society, Hartford, Connecticut; *Letters from Sarah Osborn to Joseph Fish*, Simon Gratz Manuscript Collection, Historical Society of Pennsylvania, Philadelphia, Pennsylvania. See also Sarah Osborn, *The Nature, Certainty, and Evidence of True Christianity* (Boston, 1755), and Samuel Hopkins, ed., *Familiar Letters, Written by Mrs. Sarah Osborn and Miss Susanna Anthony, Late of Newport, Rhode Island* (Newport: Newport Mercury, 1807). Several of Hopkins's letters to Osborn are preserved in the *Samuel Hopkins Papers*, Andover Library, Andover Newton Theological School, Newton, Massachusetts.

4.   Scholarship on Osborn includes Charles E. Hambrick-Stowe, "The Spiritual Pilgrimage of Sarah Osborn (1714-1796)," *Church History* 61, no. 4 (December 1992): 408-421; Sheryl Anne Kujawa, "'A Precious Season at the Throne of Grace': Sarah Haggar Wheaten Osborn, 1714-1796" (Diss., Boston College, 1993); Sheryl Anne Kujawa, "Religion, Education, and Gender in Eighteenth Century Rhode Island: Sarah Haggar Wheaten Osborn, 1714-1796" (Diss., Columbia University Teacher's College, 1993); and Jacqueline Hornstein, "Sarah Osborn," *American Women Writers: A Critical Reference Guide from Colonial Times to the Present*, ed. Lina Mainiero (New York: Ungar, 1979-1994), Volume 3, 311. All of these works are based on Samuel Hopkins's edited, published version of Osborn's diaries and memoir. Although Kujawa lists Sarah's manuscripts in her bibliography, she rarely quotes from them, and given her description of Sarah's early life, it's clear that she never read the original memoir. For a transcription of one of Sarah's letters to Joseph Fish (from the collection at the American Antiquarian Society), see Mary Beth Norton, ed., "'My Resting Reaping Times': Sarah Osborn's Defense of Her 'Unfeminine Activities,'" *Signs* 2 (1976): 515-29.

5.   Sarah discusses her religious meetings in her diary for 1767 (which has no number), Newport Historical Society, as well as in several letters. See her letter to Joseph Fish, 12 June 1766, in the *Sarah Osborn Letters, 1747-1769*; *1779*, Folder 6, American Antiquarian Society; and also her undated letter to Fish in Folder 1. See also Hopkins, *Memoirs of the Life of Mrs. Sarah Osborn*, 76-77, 357.

6.   Osborn, diary entry for 14 November 1756, reprinted in Hopkins, *Memoirs*, 197.

7.   Sarah mentions Watts in her *Memoir*, 118, and in her letter to Joseph Fish, 12 June 1766, Folder 6, American Antiquarian Society.

8.   Henry F. May, *The Enlightenment in America* (New York: Oxford University Press, 1976). See also Donald H. Meyer, *The Democratic Enlightenment* (New York: G. P. Putnam's Sons, 1975). For a more recent study of the effect of the Enlightenment on American Christianity, see Leigh Eric Schmidt, *Hearing Things: Religion, Illusion, and the American Enlightenment* (Cambridge: Harvard University Press, 2000).

9.   The scholarship on Puritanism is enormous. For a sampling, see Perry Miller, *The New England Mind: The Seventeenth Century* (New York: The Macmillan Co., 1939); Perry Miller, *The New England Mind: From Colony to Province* (Cambridge: Harvard University Press, 1953); Harry S. Stout, *The New England Soul: Preaching and Religious Culture in Colonial New England* (New York: Oxford University Press, 1986); Sacvan Bercovitch, *The American Jeremiad* (Madison: University of Wisconsin Press, 1978); *Worlds of Wonder, Days of Judgment: Popular Religious Belief in Early New England* (New York: Knopf, 1989); and Laurel Thatcher Ulrich, *Good Wives: Image and Reality in the Lives of Women in Northern New England 1650-1750* (New York: Oxford University Press, 1980).

10.   For statistics on church membership in Newport, see Elaine Forman Crane, "Uneasy Coexistence: Religious Tensions in Eighteenth-Century Newport," *Newport*

History 53, no. 5 (Summer 1980): 101-111. For overviews of life in eighteenth-century Newport, see Elaine Forman Crane, *A Dependent People: Newport, Rhode Island in the Revolutionary Era* (New York: Fordham University Press, 1985), Lynne Withey, *Urban Growth in Colonial Rhode Island: Newport and Providence in the Eighteenth Century* (Albany: State University of New York Press, 1984), Richard Henry Rudolph, "The Merchants of Newport, Rhode Island 1763-1786" (Diss., University of Connecticut, 1975), Sheila Skemp, "A Social and Cultural History of Newport, Rhode Island 1720-1765" (Diss., University of Iowa, 1974), and George Champlin Mason, *Reminiscences of Newport* (Newport: Charles E. Hammett, Jr., 1884).

11.   George Champlin Mason, *Annals of the Redwood Library and Athenaeum, Newport Rhode Island* (Newport, R.I. : Redwood Library, 1891).

12.   On Enlightenment challenges to Puritanism, see Peter Dan Jauhiainen, "An Enlightenment Calvinist: Samuel Hopkins and the Pursuit of Benevolence (Diss., University of Iowa, 1997), especially Chapter One; Clyde A. Holbrook, "Original Sin and the Enlightenment," in *The Heritage of Christian Thought: Essays in Honor of Robert Lowry Calhoun*, ed. Robert E. Cushman and Egil Grislis (New York: Harper and Row, 1965); Norman Fiering, "The First American Enlightenment: Tillotson, Leverett, and Philosophical Anglicanism," *New England Quarterly* 54 (September 1981): 307-344; Norman Fiering, "Irresistible Compassion: An Aspect of Eighteenth-Century Sympathy and Humanitarianism," *Journal of the History of Ideas* 37 (April-June 1976): 195-218; Norman Fiering, *Jonathan Edwards's Moral Thought and Its British Context* (Chapel Hill: University of North Carolina Press, 1981); Kerry S. Walters, *Rational Infidels: The American Deists* (Durango, Colorado: Longwood Academic, 1992); James Turner, *Without God, Without Creed: The Origins of Unbelief in America* (Baltimore: The Johns Hopkins University Press, 1985), 35-72; Conrad Wright, *The Beginnings of Unitarianism in America* (Boston: Starr King Press, 1955), and Joseph Haroutunian, *Piety versus Moralism: The Passing of the New England Theology* (New York: Henry Holt and Co., 1932). On the "moderate Enlightenment," see May, *The Enlightenment in America*, 3-101. On Tillotson's popularity, see the charts in David Lundberg and Henry F. May, "The Enlightened Reader in America," *American Quarterly* 28, no. 2 (Summer 1976): 272-293.

13.   Osborn, Memoir, cover.

14.   For one example of her use of the word "rational," see Sarah Osborn, *Diary #27*, 11 November 1760, p. 132, Connecticut Historical Society. "I believe thou wilt deal kindly with me," she wrote to God. "I would only act the rational Part and Leave all my cares with thee."

15.   Daniel Whitby, *A Discourse Concerning the True Import of the Words Election and Reprobation* (London, 1710), quoted in H. Shelton Smith, *Changing Conceptions of Original Sin: A Study in American Theology Since 1750* (New York: Charles Scribner's Sons, 1955), 12-13; and John Taylor, *The Scripture-Doctrine of Original Sin Proposed to Free and Candid Examination* (London, 1740). Taylor's book was first published in either 1738 or 1740. On the controversy over dating, see Jonathan Edwards, *The Great Doctrine of Original Sin Defended*, ed. Clyde A. Holbrook, Volume 3 of *The Works of Jonathan Edwards* (New Haven: Yale University Press, 1970), 2, n. 5.

16.   Taylor, *The Scripture-Doctrine of Original Sin*, 151. Samuel Niles, *The True Scripture-Doctrine of Original Sin Stated and Defended* (Boston, 1757). For other ministers who questioned whether God would sentence infants to hell, see Jonathan Mayhew, *Two Sermons on the Nature, Extent, and Perfection of the Divine Goodness* (Boston, 1763), 62-63, and Samuel Webster, *A Winter Evening's Conversation Upon the Doctrine of Original Sin* (New Haven, 1757), 5. On changes in ideas about children and childrearing in England, see J. H. Plumb, "The New World of Children in Eighteenth-Century England," *Past and Present* 67 (May 1975): 64-95.

17. Osborn, *Memoir*, 18-19, 43; Sarah Osborn, *Diary #14*, 1 September 1753, p. 47, Newport Historical Society; Sarah Osborn, *Diary #20*, entries for 2 May 1757, p. 153; 22 April 1757, p. 147; and 1 February 1757, p. 40, Newport Historical Society.

18. Osborn, *Memoir*, 1-3, 17. She was quoting from Psalm 58:3.

19. Osborn, *Memoir*, 3-4.

20. "Beating then, and all other Sorts of slavish and corporal Punishments, are not the Discipline fit to be used in the Education of those we would have wise, good, and ingenuous Men; and therefore very rarely to be applied, and that only in great Occasions, and Cases of Extremity." See John Locke, *Some Thoughts Concerning Education*, reprinted in *The Educational Writings of John Locke*, ed. James L. Axtell (Cambridge: Cambridge University Press, 1968), 150.

21. Sarah Osborn, *Diary*, no number on cover (March 1759-April 1760), entries for 5 April, 1760, p. 246; 19 April 1760, p. 261; 24 April 1760, p. 275; and 25 April 1760, p. 278, Newport Historical Society. Osborn, *Diary #27*, entries for 23 June 1760, p. 5; and 10 August 1760, pp. 37-38, Connecticut Historical Society. Osborn, *Diary #14*, 16 November 1753, p. 89. Sarah Osborn, *Diary # 30*, 26 March 1762, p. 59, Beinecke Library.

22. Jonathan Edwards, *Some Thoughts Concerning the Present Revival* (1742), in *The Works of Jonathan Edwards*, Volume 4: *The Great Awakening*, ed. C. C. Goen (New Haven: Yale University Press, 1972), 394.

23. Edwards, *Some Thoughts Concerning the Present Revival*, ibid., 394.

24. Isaac Watts, *Divine and Moral Songs for the Use of Children* (London: J. van Voorst, 1848), 27. The statistic on its publication comes from C. John Somerville, *The Rise and Fall of Childhood* (Beverly Hills: Sage Publications, 1982), 142.

25. Osborn, *Memoir*, 8.

26. Hopkins, *Memoirs*, 370. Sarah Osborn, *Diary*, no number on cover (19 February 1758 – 2 April 1758), 3 March 1758, p. 155, Newport Historical Society; and Sarah Osborn, Diary #29, 12 November 1761, p. 165, Beinecke Library.

27. See D. P. Walker, *The Decline of Hell: Seventeenth-Century Discussions of Eternal Torment* (London: Routledge and Kegan Paul, 1964); and Fiering, *Jonathan Edwards's Moral Thought*, 200-260.

28. Hopkins, *Familiar Letters*, 50.

29. Hopkins, *Memoirs*, 67.

30. Hopkins, *Memoirs*, 69.

31. For a few examples of Calvinist interpretations of suffering, see Cotton Mather, *The Nightingale: An Essay on the Songs Among Thorns. Or the Supports and Comforts of the Afflicted Believer* (Boston: B. Green, 1724); Benjamin Wadsworth, *Hearty Submission and Resignation to the Will of God, Under Afflictions, Pressed Upon Christians; as a Very Necessary and Important Duty* (Boston: B. Green, 1716); Samuel Shaw, *The Voice of One Crying in the Wilderness* (1665; rpt., Boston: Rogers and Fowle, 1744); and Joseph Emerson, *A Word to those that are afflicted very much* (Boston: J. Draper, 1738).

32. Hopkins, *Memoirs*, 69. Osborn was quoting Psalm 119:75.

33. Osborn, *Diary #21*, 20 May 1757, p. 15, Beinecke Library. On Hopkins's theology, see Jauhiainen, "An Enlightenment Calvinist"; Hugh Heath Knapp, "Samuel Hopkins and the New Divinity" (Diss., University of Wisconsin, 1971); and William Breitenbach, "Unregenerate Doings: Selflessness and Selfishness in New Divinity Theology," *American Quarterly* 34, no. 5 (Winter 1982): 479-502.

34. Osborn, *Diary #20*, 20 April 1757, p. 143; Osborn, *Memoir*, back cover.

35. See the cover of Osborn, *Memoir*, and the inside cover of Osborn, *Diary #21*, Beinecke Library. On Caleb Jewett Tenney, see William B. Sprague, *Annals of the American Pulpit* (New York: Robert Carter and Brothers, 1857-69; rpt. New York: Arno Press, 1969), Vol. II, 472-475.

36. Hopkins, *Memoirs*, 364.

37. Elizabeth B. Clark, "The Sacred Rights of the Weak: Pain, Sympathy, and the Culture of Individual Rights in Antebellum America," *Journal of American History* 82, no. 2 (September 1995): 471. See also Ava Chamberlain, "The Theology of Cruelty: A New Look at the Rise of Arminianism in Eighteenth-Century New England," *Harvard Theological Review* 85:3 (1992): 335-56.

38. Charles E. Hammett, Jr., "A Sketch of the History of the Congregational Churches of Newport, R.I.," (1891), 107. Typescript at the Newport Historical Society.

39. Moses Coit Tyler, *A History of American Literature 1607-1783*, abridged and edited by Archie H. Jones (1878; rpt., Chicago: The University of Chicago Press, 1967), 84.

40. Leslie Poles Hartley, *The Go-Between* (1953), prologue.

41. Dylan Thomas, "Do Not Go Gentle into that Good Night," in *The Norton Anthology of English Literature*, ed. M. H. Abrams (New York: W.W. Norton and Company, 1979), Fourth Edition, Vol. II, 2416. Osborn, *Diary #21*, 12 July 1757, p. 69.

Early Christian Sexual Politics and Roman Imperial Family Values: Rereading Christ and Culture

Mary Rose D'Angelo
UNIVERSITY OF NOTRE DAME DEPARTMENT OF THEOLOGY
NOTRE DAME, INDIANA[1]

Recent American political campaigns have illustrated the way that public life has become an arena for competing appeals to "family values," often accompanied by explicit or implied claims to biblical or Christian warrants. Indeed, "the family" and "family values" are often seen as the province of biblical ethics—despite the fact that modern constructions of family are so alien to the biblical worlds that no close equivalent to the modern word "family" can be found in any of their languages.[2] Contemporary pleas for "family values" have a long historical underside: Roman imperial politics of the first two centuries made lavish use of similar appeals to "family values," which in turn exerted considerable pressure on early Jewish and Christian communities' formulation of their own sexual and familial mores. My project seeks to expose and explore two related facets of the problem of culture and the interpretation of Bible and tradition: the hermeneutical question of the role of culture in the formation of the tradition and the problem of the reconstruction of context.[3] Both aspects of the problem have become more acute in the recent political recourse to "family values." Christian "family values" have been both the product and the producer of sexual politics in ways that are rarely considered on either side of the culture wars.[4] This essay attempts to bring to the surface and address problematic practices in the interpretation of Christian origins as reflected by the facets of tradition formation and cultural context.

Two Problems

At the larger hermeneutical level, I wish to call into question the way in which the relationship of culture to revelation has functioned in the use of scriptural warrants. More sophisticated Christian circles, including many feminists, have essentially treated biblical discussions of family in much the same ways as fundamentalist interpreters: biblical dicta on family either proceed from divine commands and therefore must be preserved at all costs, or derive from cultural influences, and so may (or must) be discounted. Appeals to cultural context tend to take the form of "debunking" and are often perceived as an attack on sacred texts. On the other hand, using freedom from "cultural influence" or the "countercultural" character of claims as warrants for revelatory status resorts to an implicit theological reductionism that produces a brittle and unstable ground on which to build contemporary theological thinking. While Elisabeth Schüssler Fiorenza's early work had already decried this treatment of culture as a container from which the kernel of timeless truth can be dislodged, the interpretive pattern has changed little at the practical level, even among feminists.[5] Those feminists whose work demonstrates a sophisticated appreciation of cultural context often evade, refuse or postpone questions about the normative character of the text. Ross Kraemer, for instance, explicitly asserts the non-theological character of her work.[6] Elizabeth Castelli positions her own use of texts as strategic tools in the process of "thinking about theory, power, solidarity, and resistance around the crucially reorienting categories of gender, ethnicity, race, and class which dominate cultural thinking today" over against that of feminists who seek to redeem the text.[7] My own interpretive stance has varied from hers largely in being more explicitly concerned with theological categories and less explicit about my refusal to "redeem" the texts.

The problem of the role of culture in the formation of tradition and the discernment of revelation is compounded by a second defect at the more concrete level of the reconstruction (or construction) of cultural context. Nineteenth- and twentieth-century biblical scholarship largely dichotomized the context of Christian origins into Judaism and Hellenism—or Judaism versus Hellenism. The question about context thus emerges as whether any specific aspect of an early Christian text is an outgrowth of Jewish tradition or a product of Hellenistic influence. Framed this way, question has often been heavily loaded with theological apologetic. Proving that something is truly Jewish has either guaranteed its religious character or discredited it as legalistic, while "Hellenization" can be seen as either a positive, universalizing force or a negative, corrupting influence. The formative pressures of Roman imperial politics have been obscured by this long-term practice of assigning problematic aspects of Christian origins to either "Jewish background" or "Hellenistic influence." While "background" and "influence" can be and are used interchangeably in these discussions, there is a real sense in which what is "Jewish" is seen as "background," while what is "Hellenistic" is generally treated as "influence." Judaism is thus relegated to the past of Christian origins, and treated as a source either of patriarchal prescriptions and attitudes beyond which Christian faith ought to have progressed, or of true prophetic messages which must be preserved from secular taint. Hellenism, on the other, is generally positioned as "influence"—an external force that can be understood either as having corrupted the originally pure prophetic (or egalitarian, or non-patriarchal) teaching of Jesus, or as having introduced a universalizing intellectualism into the narrowly particularistic concerns of Jewish thought. In large degree, Rome enters this picture only occasionally, through the neutral matrix of the *pax Romana*, which allowed Hellenism scope to contend with Judaism over the rather inert matter of a reified Christian message.

This description does not do justice to the sophistication and delicacy of much of the fine recent scholarship on early Judaism and Christianity. In particular, it bypasses the increasing attention scholarly circles have given to the literary remains of the Greek-speaking Jews of antiquity, and a small but significant body of material concerned with the interaction of the earliest Christians with Roman politics. But the dichotomy I described above accurately represents the way context enters into many discussions of the relevance of biblical text to communal and political practice.

The elision of Roman politics in the reconstruction of context has been exacerbated in the last twenty years by the turn toward anthropological theories and categories among one group of scholars of Christian origins. While there is considerable variety in the ways these interpreters use anthropology and in the conclusions they draw, a number of problematic aspects are common to much anthropological interpretation of Christian origins. One problem is more or less endemic to the enterprise of turning anthropology onto antiquity: whereas most social anthropologists perceive themselves as using interviewing, observation, and related techniques to collect data from which to generate theory, scholars of antiquity are faced with a dearth of the information anthropologists rely on. They must use theories developed from outside scholarship on antiquity not only to organize but also to generate information. This practice is sometimes masked by the widespread assumption of the "cultural unity of the Mediterranean," an assumption which frequently allows the interpreter to draw upon material from locales and periods quite distant from the early Christian texts.[8] Other problems intervene when cultural differences are taken to be absolute and cultures are treated as closed and completely consistent systems, so that values and experiences from one cannot be transmitted to another system of an alien type. This claim of the internal coherence of culture "naturalizes" social arrangements and constructs reflected in texts, masking their political commitments and protecting them from critical evaluation.[9] At the same time, the closed character of the system distances the text from the world of the interpreter: no analogies with the text can raise critical questions about current power relations. The anthropological reading thus impinges not only on the reconstruction of context, but also upon the hermeneutical question, sealing the texts irretrievably in the past, so that interpretation is limited to demonstrating their cultural distance from and irrelevance to contemporary mores.

Approaches to the Texts:
Different Rules for Jesus and the Letters

Amid the interaction of problematic and dichotomized reconstructions of the context of Christian origins with views of culture as a container, texts that are understood to touch upon "family values" receive very different treatment depending on whether they are to be found in the letters or in Gospel traditions attributed to Jesus. In the first instance, prescriptions about women and family in the letters of the New Testament are frequently seen as time and culture-bound. This is the case with the so-called "household codes" found in Colossians, Ephesians, 1 Peter, 1 Timothy, and Titus (as well as *1 Clement* 21 and Ignatius *To Polycarp* 4-6 and Polycarp *To the Philippians* 4-6) in which women, children, and slaves are exhorted to show proper piety toward their husband/ father/ master (and sometimes vice-versa). The codes are widely understood as the product of a Hellenistic philosophical position deriving from Aristotle;[10] in general, some or all aspects of these prescriptions are understood as time-bound and culturally determined. Recent Christian interpreters frequently point to these texts as evidence of the increasing patriarchalization of the early communities, sometimes as a backlash aimed at attempts to challenge the boundaries of patriarchy within the communities.[11] The correctness of these prescriptions for antiquity is not always questioned, but even in more conservative circles, at least the prescriptions for slaves are usually understood as having no contemporary relevance. Sometimes the prescriptions for slavery are quite explicitly separated from the rest of the household code. For instance, the Roman lectionary for 1970 excised the prescriptions for slaves from the readings of Col 3:28-4:1 and Eph 5:21-6:9, but continued to require that the demands for submission from women and obedience from children be read in the eucharistic liturgy.[12] Clarice Martin has also pointed to a similar inconsistency in interpretations of these passages by African American men.[13] Even where the household codes themselves are rejected, the continuity between these codes and the theological perspectives of the texts in which they appear gets little attention, especially in those more pastoral and homiletic settings in which they do the most harm.[14]

In the undisputed letters of Paul, passages like the strange justification for the veiling of women (1 Cor 11:2-16) and his concerns with meat offered to idols are often relegated to his Jewish background (1 Cor 8:1-11:1); some interpretations attempt to draw some sort of lesson from such passages while recognizing that the circumstances that occasioned them no longer hold. In all these cases, the cultural context is understood as a container for the message, one that may bring with it unfortunate appendages but that can and should be, with varying degrees of difficulty, detached from the text's message.

On the second instance, material in the Gospels is frequently isolated as the "teaching of Jesus" and detached from or opposed to its cultural context. One particularly widespread and problematic example is the assertion that the title "father" for the deity is the unique teaching of Jesus. On this view, based largely on the studies of Joachim Jeremias, Jesus is deemed to have used the Aramaic word *'abba* to address God; this address supposedly demonstrated the peerless intimacy and tenderness of Jesus' relationship with the deity and would have been impossible for or offensive to other Jews of his day.[15] To address God as father is thus understood to constitute a special revelation for Christianity, and to be uniquely non- or extra-cultural and therefore immune from the claim that this language reflects past cultural practice (and reinforces the patriarchal organization of society and the churches in the present). The "criterion of dissimilarity" operated in Jeremias's argument in ways that illustrate particularly well the argument's historically dubious and ethically problematic character. By stringently restricting the already limited evidence for the use of this title in ancient Judaism, Jeremias misrepresented the range of Jewish imagery for God in order to create a uniquely superior content for the teaching of Jesus.[16]

Some Jewish and Christian scholars tried to reverse Jeremias's claims by arguing (with considerable justice) that the title *'abba* and its concomitant portrayal of God as a tender and intimate father could only have come to Jesus from his own Judaism.[17] This argument did not have the attraction of claiming uniqueness for Jesus, and was less than successful, but recently the expansion of the evidence from the discoveries at Qumran has garnered more attention, and the Jewish context of "Father" as address to the deity is more widely recognized.[18]

As feminism began to cast a critical eye on theological language, the claim of "unparalleled intimacy" became a means of asserting the "non-patriarchal" character of the title and providing a bulwark against the feminist critique.[19] But the linguistic basis of Jeremias's argument proved problematic.[20] The explicit or implied assumption that patriarchal family structures meant an absence of familial affection and intimacy is even more problematic. Excluding intimacy and tenderness from the construction of the patriarchal family not only misrepresents the evidence from Roman, Jewish, and Greek antiquity, but also disguises the realities of patriarchal relations in the present: it is precisely from the bonds of intimacy, affection, and tenderness that patriarchal and even abusive family relations get their power.[21]

Another problematic reading of Jesus depicts him as the liberator from culture-bound institutions, using the controversy stories and miracle narratives from the Gospels as demonstrations of his opposition to "religious authorities," "temple elite," and "purity systems."[22] These abstractions avoid the words "Jews," "Pharisees," "Jewish leaders," and "Jewish Law" in an attempt to evade the charge of anti-Judaism by generalizing the structures named in the Gospel accounts. Sometimes the generalizations are further sanitized by being given the status of anthropological categories which supposedly held throughout the ancient Mediterranean. But because these phrases disguise the apologetic character of the texts, they are little more than euphemisms that salve scholarly consciences. At the pastoral level, such terms as "temple elite" and "religious authorities" have become instantly popular with many Catholic feminists who can find ready analogues for the conflicts reflected in the Gospel controversy stories in the appalling disregard of the Roman Catholic hierarchy for Roman Catholic women and indeed for most Roman Catholics. But the implicit apologetic remains the same: these are the "bad" aspects of first-century Judaism from which Jesus liberated Christians. And it is precisely in the pastoral settings in which the texts are most effective that the substitutions are most dangerous: every Christian congregation knows whose temple, "religious authorities" and purity codes are at issue in the Gospels. In addition, evasions of this sort are noxious to scholarship. They foster unacknowledged misrepresentations of early Judaism and obscure the cultural complexities of the context of Christian origins.

Approaches to the Gospels that mine them for a uniquely revelatory message of Jesus, one that offers a level of religious teaching that would have been impossible without him and that manifests itself as an extra-cultural challenge to his own context, expose the rifts within dogmatic Christology when it is put to the task of imagining Jesus. Searches for the uniqueness of Jesus tend to substitute a heroic humanity for the incarnation—Jesus must produce a message, often a social message, that shows him to be the perfect and far-sighted leader who can see beyond his own culture. But at the same time, they infringe on the humanity of Jesus by disqualifying him from sharing the limited horizons of his cultural context. In the terms of classical Christology, they confuse rather than join the human and divine natures, diminishing both.

The Tasks: Rereading the Context

The Roman context of earliest Christianity in general has been obscured by both scholarly approaches and present-day political realities. Discussion of context has often been narrowed to attempts to prove influence in the same way that literary dependence is established. At another level, the disappearance of the Roman imperial interest from the context of the New Testament is the product of a collaboration between the ancient texts and their nineteenth- and twentieth-century interpreters. For the earliest Christian texts and many of the texts of the Roman period Judaism, the Roman order, as the largest political reality in their world, was frequently either too obvious or too threatening to invite mention. The nineteenth- and twentieth-century imperial cultures in which classical and biblical studies have been done (Germany, England, France, the United States) were deeply and explicitly identified either with the Roman empire itself (Germany, England, France), or the imperial republic (France and the United States). Scholars of classical and biblical literature have been inclined to see the empire as either beneficent (as the scholars tended to see the governments they served) or neutral (as they saw themselves). In recent years, liberation and political theology and academic critiques of scholars' ideology in literature and social sciences have called into question both the veracity and the ethical propriety of claims of scholarly neutrality; the disasters left in the wake of colonial empires' dissolution or withdrawal have fostered skepticism of historical empires as well.

Thus the stage is set for rethinking the cultural identity of our material so as to recognize that all early Jews and Christians whom scholars can study functioned at present within the largely Greek-speaking Roman imperial world. The potential for such rethinking has been enhanced by recent studies of the early Christian texts in light of Roman period rhetoric, whose political base is hard to ignore. Driven in part by the "family values" impulse, Classics, Judaica, and New Testament studies have all produced some work on the family in antiquity.[23] In addition, Classics has put forward a number of excellent studies on first- and second-century propaganda, especially the political uses of moral claims.[24] These have as yet had limited effect on NT studies.[25]

That Jesus died as a revolutionary against Rome is widely recognized and it is now more frequently acknowledged that the preaching of God's reign must inevitably have been heard politically by the Romans. There is less scholarly agreement that it was so understood by Jesus and his companions.[26] Even where these views are fully developed, it has proven singularly difficult to replace the picture of the Pharisees as the opponents of Jesus with a reconstruction that depicts the Roman imperial interest as the true opposition to Jesus.[27] When attention has been paid to Roman realities in matters of gender and family, Roman social mores and the supposed liberation of women in the first century have too often been treated as the positive alternative to Judaism.[28] My aim is not to move from "blaming the Jews for patriarchy" to "blaming the Romans."[29] Rather, I wish to stress that Roman imperial politics must be taken into account in reckoning the development of both early Christian and Jewish sexual politics.

Family language and the regulation of sexual and social mores played a major role in the political struggles attendant upon the creation of the Roman empire. The assumption of the title *pater patriae* was a major step in the emergence and solidification of the new world order Augustus constructed as the basis of his rule. The title *parens patriae* was awarded to Julius Caesar late in his life, possibly at the urging of Cicero; it functioned to establish a relation of *pietas* between Caesar and the Roman people.[30] Augustus officially acquired the title *pater patriae* in 2 BCE, but *pater* and *pater patriae* were already in use for him, as *parens patriae* had been used of Julius Caesar.[31] *Pater* reflects an understanding of the empire as a great *familia* in which the emperor functions as a *paterfamilias*, whose *auctoritas* is based on his ability to regard the whole Roman people as his clients.[32] After 2 BCE, the title *pater patriae* formalized the emperor's status as the *paterfamilias* of the Roman people and the empire.

Augustus's consolidation of his imperial power was accompanied by legal measures to strengthen the patriarchal family (*Lex Iulia de maritandis ordinibus, Lex Iulia de adulteriis coercendis,* both ca.18 BCE; *Lex Papia Poppaea* 9 CE). Most scholars continue to view these laws as irrelevant to early Christianity in general and to the Gospels in particular. As has frequently been noted, the Augustan legislation applied only to citizens, and is generally thought to have been unsuccessful. But these genuine limitations do not adequately represent the intent, effect, and context of the Augustan marriage legislation. For one thing, "unsuccessful" is a relative term. If the Augustan laws did not succeed in repopulating the army with citizens or in stopping adultery and *stuprum*, they did achieve a kind of success in two areas: they produced a significant degree of social insecurity and even some criminal accusations for political ends and they generated a truly astonishing number of billable hours for jurists whose advice was enlisted on ways to evade the inheritance penalties or to institute, defend from, or insure against charges of adultery.[33] Indeed, these laws ultimately "attracted more comment from the Roman jurists than did any other laws."[34]

More importantly, these laws functioned on the level of propaganda. In the words of Catherine Edwards, "The *lex Iulia de adulteriis* was the last word in rhetorical invective."[35] The marriage laws, together with sumptuary regulations and careful regulation of social rank, played a major role in a sort of "family values" campaign on the part of Augustus as a buttress to his claim to have liberated and restored the republic. In *Res Gestae* 2.8, Augustus described the social legislation in rather oxymoronic terms: "By passing new laws I restored many *exempla* of the ancients that had fallen into desuetude."[36] Innovations in law could not but clash with the mores of antiquity, and indeed the laws were contradictory not only in articulation but also in effect. While claiming to support and protect the authority of the *paterfamilias* against the wife's adulterous desire or refusal to bear children, the laws undermined *patria potestas* by introducing the state into the regulation of the household. While some have argued that these laws undermined the authority of husbands and fathers to the advantage of women, the evidence makes clear that this was neither their intention nor their effect.[37] In fact, the marriage laws constituted a sort of politics of distraction: they focused both compliance and resistance on a problem presented not by Augustus's progressive reorganization of the Roman "constitution" but by the supposed deviance of women, children and slaves of the household, the neglect of the gods and the dis-order of society—the loss or blurring of distinctions among the orders. These anxieties were by no means invented by Augustus; they had provided grist for the competition for control of the aristocratic republic throughout the first century and had generated the imagery that Augustus marshaled for the massive building projects that he used to demonstrate his *pietas*.[38]

Augustus's legal measures were preceded and followed by a resurgence of nostalgia for the *mos maiorum* in regard to women, children, and the lower social orders. Arius Didymus's epitome of the Aristotelian theories to which Balch traced the household codes may well have been an aspect of Didymus's service as household philosopher to Augustus.[39] Livy's debate between Cato and Valerius over the Oppian law and Valerius Maximus's tales of ancient severity that kept women in line should probably be read as mythic in the fullest sense: that is, their historicity was of less significance than their ability to embody explanations and ideals that made sense of the social world of their tellers.[40] Writing during the reign of Augustus, between the *Leges Iuliae* and the modifications put forward by the *Lex Papia Poppaea*, Dionysius of Halicarnassus lionized Romulus as the greatest of lawgivers because of his recognition that the ordered state depends upon properly ordered households. Dionysius devoted particular attention to the indissolubility of ancient Roman (confarreate) marriage as a means to the control of women and the stringency of *patria potestas* in regard to unemancipated sons (*Ant* 2.24-25).[41] In doing so he hinted at the degeneration that had necessitated Augustus's reforms and implicitly flattered Augustus's wisdom in seeing the necessity of the legislation on marriage.

Throughout the formative years of earliest Christianity (from Tiberius through Hadrian) Augustus's successors invoked his mantle, reasserting his claim to have restored the republic. The emperors demonstrated their own *pietas* in building projects offered to the people and dedicated to the deities. They insisted on sexual and familial morality, revising or reasserting the laws on marriage, social distinctions, and conspicuous consumption. They displayed the imperial family in coinage and monuments. The title *pater patriae* became an increasingly important and eventually automatic marker of the emperors' *auctoritas*.

The marriage laws thus belonged to a much broader context of political discourse that might, in later terms, be called a "family values" campaign. Their impact is thus best understood in terms of their ability to reflect and consolidate public opinion. In this regard, there is no difference between citizen and non-citizen. Indeed foreigners, freedpersons, and slaves are, if anything, even more vulnerable to such propaganda. In the absence of assets like ancestry, citizenship or property, a display of family piety enabled them to stake out a ground claimed as particularly Roman, a ground from which they could offer themselves as "more Roman than thou," proclaiming to the guardians of the empire, "we practice the Roman family values you only preach about." With the emergence of formal apology in early Christianity, this claim becomes explicit. Justin assures the emperor that the Christians are his best allies in achieving order in the empire (1 *Apology* 12-17). Tertullian indulges in satiric vignettes deriding the inconsistencies proceeding from a rescript of Trajan that penalized the name Christian even without crime (*Apologeticum* 2-3). These are closely followed by a detailed denunciation of Roman abandonment of the *mos maiorum*. He details a laundry list of violations of the sorts of prescriptions included in the household codes of 1 Peter and 1 Timothy (*Apologeticum* 6).

Because of their disconnect with Roman social reality, such Roman texts as the marriage laws, the *Res Gestae*, the letters of Seneca or the satires of Juvenal are sometimes seen as irrelevant to early Christian moral prescriptions and social sanctions.[42] On one very real level, this complaint is entirely justified. Neither the tirades of Juvenal and Tertullian nor the pieties of Plutarch and 1 Timothy should be seen as an accurate reflection of real Roman (or Christian) practice. But accurate depiction of practice is not the issue. The interpretation of early Christian texts like the household codes took an important hermeneutical step forward with the recognition that such texts do not describe but prescribe: they put forward a state of affairs the author wishes to bring about. As

Tertullian shows, the opportunity for apology lay in that disjuncture between the *mos maiorum* urged upon the conduct of private life by imperial propaganda and the realities of the Roman social world. The intersection of apologetic with propaganda does not draw its power from social reality.

Apologetics was an activity, to some extent an initiative, of the early Christian (and Jewish) communities. This is not to say that it did not respond to real and even mortal threats. But the kind of response these threats evoked could differ very substantially. Ancient Jews and Christians who were attempting to live with the empire were negotiating a massive power imbalance, and they did so through varying degrees of resistance and accommodation.

Jews in the Roman empire, including Jesus and his companions in the reign-of-God movement, as well the earliest Christian communities, were sometimes invited and sometimes coerced to develop and deploy their own sexual politics. Familial language and moral demands could serve as a basis for either an appeal from or resistance to Roman claims. Indeed resistance to Rome and apologetic appeal to its values were by no means mutually exclusive. They could be combined, and often were.

One particularly interesting illustration of this can be seen in the differing ways that 1 Timothy and 4 Maccabees appropriate the imperial virtue that best approximates "family values" combined with religious observance—*eusebeia*, the Greek version of *pietas*. Both texts give *eusebeia* a central role, and both are explicitly concerned with the threat of persecution. Both texts have frequently been assigned to the first half of the second century. 4 Maccabees announces *eusebeia* or *eusebes logismos* (pious reason) as the theme of its discourse: "whether *eusebes logismos* is the ruler of the passions" (1:1). The first few verses locate *eusebeia* as the primary of the cardinal virtues, replacing prudence (*phronesis*) as the source of the other three (justice, fortitude, and temperance). This odd substitution has attracted considerable comment, and is usually explained as the result of the author's Judaism.[43] While Jewish adaptations of philosophy surely played a role, another factor deserves attention in explaining the shift from *phronesis* to *eusebeia*. *Pietas* had already supplanted one of the four (probably *phronesis*) in the fourfold virtue list that celebrated Augustus in such honorary propaganda as the "shield of virtues."[44] In 4 Maccabees, *eusebeia* is demonstrated in the bloody but pious defiance and deaths of the seven sons and their mother, which attest the power of *eusebeia* to conquer the passions. At the same time, their piety is underscored in their family relationship, their loyalty and love for each other and for their mother and hers for them. The final (actually posthumous) speech of the mother credits her sons' nobility to the instruction of their dead father, the husband for whom she "guarded the built rib" (18:13). In 1 Timothy, on the other hand, *eusebeia* (without a philosophical context) is demonstrated specifically in communal practices that reflect the good order of the ideal household: the assembly is the household of God, and within it and its individual households proper relations of domination and submission must be observed: the subordination of women, children, unemancipated sons, slaves, and the lower orders to the authority of the (male) head of the household. The threat of persecution is clear: prayers are to be offered for emperors and governors that "we may have a quiet and tranquil life" (1 Tim 2:1).

In neither case am I arguing that the accommodation is total; while 1 Timothy avoids any suggestion of defiance, the many exhortations to martyrdom in 2 Timothy makes clear that the point of ultimate resistance was expected. Nor, however, do I wish to argue that the authors of either the Jewish or Christian texts were merely forced to accommodation for survival. On the contrary, both clearly believe what Tertullian believed: that their true piety enabled them to practice what the unenlightened Romans could not but respect. And both deploy the proper control of women as evidence for their piety—though in very different ways.

Thus both authors should be seen as deeply engaged with "cultural constructions" in that they encounter real political pressures and respond to them politically; in doing so they quite consciously accept and adapt some aspects of their opponents' assumptions and arguments. But these adaptations are not limited to a few prescriptions in which they can match or outdo the household propriety of their masters. Rather, they are perfused through the central proposition of the virtue of *eusebeia*. Texts and authors are producers as well as products of culture.

Some scholars and practitioners may be willing to dispense with texts as near (or beyond) the canonical margins as 1 Timothy and 4

Maccabees; in fact, the comfort with which many Christians accept a critical reading of the post-Pauline and even the Pauline texts reflects a willingness to award lower status to some parts of the canon. But what about the case of the Gospels, and the questions about Jesus? Focusing on Jesus is often a way of divorcing early Christianity from problematic aspects of its context, and it is by no means unusual for interpreters to contrast the "liberating practice" of Jesus with the patriarchal texts from the Pauline tradition. But without a deeper regard for the continuity of Jesus with his context, the practices of "blaming the Jews. . ." for Christian patriarchal arrangements will continue.

Some years ago, I published two articles presenting a fairly comprehensive critical assessment of the claims made about 'abba and "father" as a divine title attributable to the teaching of Jesus, and offering an alternate suggestion for the possible (but by no means certain) function of that title in the preaching of God's reign.[45] Here I wish to rearticulate two aspects of that suggestion. First, readings that extract Jesus' teaching—or attempt to extract it—from the Gospel texts should look not for language and ideas that were a new and unique revelation but for those that would have been deeply and readily comprehensible and communicative to his Jewish audience. And here, it should be said, "father" as a title for and address to God qualifies. Secondly, readings of Jesus should seek to locate "the teaching of Jesus" in the context of his death at the hands of the Romans. Here, too, the use of the title "father" rings true: as the reign is God's and not the emperor's, so "our father" is not the Romans' imperial father, but the deity who for the moment suffers Caesar's rule in the world "he" has created. If indeed Jesus proclaimed and prayed for God's reign in this way, he spoke from within the same dialectic of resistance and accommodation as 4 Maccabees and 1 Timothy. When he spoke of and to God as father, the address was formed not only by his own Jewish tradition and by the expectations and practice of his companions, but also by the terms of his opponents.

The Tasks: Rethinking Christ and Culture

What then of the hermeneutical problem, the question of Christ and culture? In addressing the concrete problem of the reconstruc-

tion of context, I have inevitably modified the more common hermeneutical approaches both to Jesus and the Gospels and to the letters and discourses of early Christianity.

The most difficult task is what might be called the inculturation
of Jesus, the attempt to conceive the uniqueness of Jesus as a real
historical uniqueness, a qualitatively human uniqueness. This enterprise both enables and requires reading the texts with a
Christology that is neither heroic nor monophysite. The prerequi-
site is locating Jesus within Judaism. Its difficulty springs in part
from the long history of scholarship that has been shaped by the
"criterion of dissimilarity," that is, the claim that "authentic" teaching of Jesus can be detected in material that is dissimilar to, dis-
continuous with or distinctive from the teaching of the early church
and the Judaism of Jesus' day. The use of the criterion of dissimilarity has contributed to the creation of a monolithic "Judaism of Jesus'
day" against which sayings and sometimes narratives could be
judged: All too often the question of how the material had been
formed by early Christian experience fell by the wayside. Aside from
the many problems surrounding the retrieval of first-century
Judaism(s), constructing a Jesus dissimilar from them all is bound
to produce an a-historical freak.[46] This criterion should be renounced
in favor of seeking to delineate ways in which the tradition of Jesus'
sayings shows continuity with what can be known about the diverse concerns of first-century Judaisms and attempting to locate
the sayings within this diversity.

In addition to locating Jesus within Judaism, it is essential to
remove Jesus from the heroic isolation which the Gospels and the
tradition of Christian piety have awarded him, and locate him instead within a movement. This relocation has been begun by scholars who speak of the Jesus movement. But the shift remains a surface adjustment until the movement is defined not by Jesus' per-
sona, but by the focus of the preaching: God's reign.[47] Seeing the
movement as evoked by and centered on the preaching of God's reign
rather than on the personal authority of Jesus makes it possible to
award it the degree of exchange and negotiation that is essential to
the way movements work, and so to envisage Jesus as engaged in
that exchange and negotiation, in trial and error, in learning as
well as teaching.

If returning Jesus to his context is one exigency, then allowing
the early Christians to emerge from theirs is another. This means
refusing to ascribe the more problematic aspects of early Christian
texts to "influence" and "background,"and choosing instead to describe the ways that early Christians took the initiative in their
interactions with their imperial milieu as diverse cultural actors. A
number of accounts of gender in the Pauline corpus make a start on
this task by depicting the gender prescriptions of the Pauline and
post-Pauline letters as dispatches from contested ground. Among
the reconstructions that have proven deeply engaging in both academic and pastoral settings is Elisabeth Schüssler Fiorenza's de-
lineation of the early Christian mission as characterized by contests between an emerging hierarchical leadership and the "*ekklesia*
of women."[48] Antoinette Clark Wire's analysis of 1 Corinthians as
reflecting struggles between Paul and the women prophets of the
community has also been influential.[49] Studies that attend to the
diversity of early Christianity by examining gender in works outside the canon likewise play an important role in generating less
monolithic understandings of the function; Dennis Ronald
MacDonald's opposition of the *Acts of [Paul and] Thecla,* and the
widespread reading of the *Gospel of Mary* and *Hypostasis of the
Archons* as the product of gender disputes in antiquity, deserve attention here.[50]

The energy generated by reading the early Christian texts as
the product of human conflicts is dissipated rather than enhanced
when interpreters decide to choose a site of revelation. MacDonald's
decision for the Paul of the "genuine" (undisputed) letters seems to
undo his work. Schüssler Fiorenza's choice of the movements behind the texts over the texts was likewise ineffective, and has been
superseded by her later, more complex approaches.[51] Is it really
necessary to choose a site of revelation within and among the diverse voices of the texts? Another approach would be to use the
texts to "think with," to consider "theory, power, solidarity, and resistance" in the disputes in which these texts are invoked. Delineating the politics of early Christian initiatives, both on the more
immediate level of the community and on the larger level of its interaction with the empire not only stresses agency on the part of
the community but also offers a prophylactic against veiling political concerns in the present.

This observation leads to an issue on which I have been less explicit thus far. Reading Christ and culture in antiquity means being more alert to the political uses of culture and of Christianity in the present. The current politics of *eusebeia*—public piety and "family values"—illustrates some of the many complexities of the issue. On the one hand, the politics of distraction plays a very clear role in the focus on "family values" in the current electoral campaigns, displacing attention from the increasing corporate reorganization of resources and wealth and refocusing it on the deviance of women and children, especially African American women and children, as well as on African American men. On the other hand, "thinking with" the texts is complicated by the differences between the situations of the early Christian and contemporary communities. If the texts manifest that in antiquity Christian culture(s) cannot be fully disengaged from secular culture, electoral campaigns are making clear the ways in which cultural Christianity is embedded into American social discourse.

While contemporary Christianities do not face the massive power imbalance that early Judaism and Christianity had to negotiate, they do face, and all too often do not address, the problem of their own diversity. Kathryn Tanner has argued that Christian culture is too vague a term to be used in opposition to secular culture, or even as one pole in critical correlation.[52] My own experience is that Christianity is not so much too vague, as it is far, far too specific to be defined this way—too diverse and too complex, even at the earliest period. Especially in the twenty-first century, "Christianity" falls on both sides of too many questions. The claim of a Christian counterculture too frequently has less to do with transforming outsiders to such a culture than with bringing one's own into line. One example of this is the current papal campaign to define a "culture of death" (largely American) as a way to recontextualize the anti-abortion campaign by removing it from its rather obvious context among prohibitions of contraception, divorce, sexual contact outside of marriage, vilification of homosexuals, and rejection of women from ordination and positions of authority in church structures, and to realign it with a different set of issues: opposition to capital punishment, nuclear weapons, poverty, and other genuine political problems much less vociferously condemned by the Vatican.

Conclusion

In such a complex situation, no single set of hermeneutical or exegetical tools can offer itself as a panacea. But some requirements emerge. First, an incarnational Christology that allows for a Jesus learning and unlearning among and from his companions might encourage later Christian churches to believe in their ability and obligation to loose as well as to bind. Second, a more circumspect approach to Christian origins that recognizes the diversity and creativity of the early communities should evoke a similar level of creativity on the part of continuing Christian communities, while acknowledging and affirming the diversity that exists within and among them. Third, both must be accompanied by unflagging attention to the dynamics of accommodation and resistance in the ways that contemporary apologetic addresses contemporary politics. The apologetic of the early Christian communities passed a sediment of imperial family values into the sexual and social politics that proved the occasion of sin for many centuries— in Christian endorsements of slavery, the subjugation of women and the abusive "discipline" of children. A rush to the defense of "the family" in response to the contemporary conservative deployment of sexual politics may well be equally injurious to the long-term moral health of Christianity.

A certain amount of "debunking" remains essential of ethically responsible readings of the scripture, debunking that consists not only in recontextualizing the texts, but also in catechizing the power relations that surround both their origins and their current deployment. Recognizing that the politics of distraction that formed the early Christian texts is central to and must be accompanied by the recognition, for example, that the political cult of "fatherhood" propagated recently in the Unites States arose as a late twentieth-century exercise in a politics of distraction.[53] The massive destruction of African American and other poor and minority men is blamed not on for-profit imprisonment and devastating abuses of labor, but on "personal choices" like feminism and other forms of female licence.[54] Recently, the churches have been invited to facilitate a more comprehensive refusal of collective responsibility for the children, the impoverished and the vulnerable of the United States through increasing conservative endorsement of volunteerism and "faith based initiatives." In the face of this set of exigencies, theology must devote the most meticulous and searching attention to its apologetic, forgoing the temptation to prove Christianity's truth and worth by offering itself as defender of "family values." Instead, the apologetic dimension of theology must mobilize the courage to speak truth to and about itself to and about power. This means, for instance, not only acknowledging that the long implication of the "Christian family values" of the household codes in sustaining the structures of slavery and its successors constituted a central violation of divine and human justice, but also addressing the role of the "prison-industrial complex" and its profiteers in devaluing the lives and families of the poor, especially of the African Americans who are so disproportionately represented in that system.[55]

In considering the demands of biblical interpretation in this context, I think with some envy of Margaret Mitchell's retrieval of Chrysostom's hermeneutic of love.[56] Can there be engagement with text and tradition as passionate as Chrysostom's affair with Paul that does not forgo an ethical and discerning criticism? This query receives a partial answer in an analogy that I have long found helpful in defining the function of the canonical scriptures in contemporary Christianity, the analogy of family memories. Most (extended, intergenerational) families have a collection of "official" memories, i.e., narratives and exhortations that get rehearsed at family gatherings and attached to family slide shows. Some of these are understood to be humorous or inspirational affirmations of family history; some are communally recognized as traumatic. Other memories are never mentioned and are censored as threatening or perhaps simply passed over, because they are not seen to have meaning. For some members of the family most of the time, these narratives and their official "readings" are the ones that best explain who they are and how they are related to others. But for some other member, the funny story told about him is a tale of deep and abiding humiliation; for another still, the reminder of her past heroic generosity is far too costly. For yet a third member, the others' memory of a tragic loss signals liberation from a destructive relationship. For still others, the silenced or unshared memories are the most relevant. Over time, the positions and interpretations of these narratives change. Some recede, and some are added from the pool of stories that do not get told. Others come to be seen in a new light: this one had deeply racist implications, that narrative about a wayward aunt becomes a paradigm of autonomy and ingenuity.

In Christianity, the Bible holds a place analogous to those official family memories: it occupies the central and official memories shared and contested by several families of communities. But the canon is not the whole story, and its narratives and exhortations likewise sound differently in differing ears. In recent years, a surprising number of "lost" memories have surfaced from the sands of Egypt, the caves of the Judean desert, monastic libraries, or from the oblivion of time and repetition, and have been juxtaposed to official narratives, providing sometimes seismic contextual shifts. Hallowed readings have been challenged as abusive by post-holocaust, Black, feminist, and liberation hermeneutics. For some members, the abuse is too great—only rejection can heal the damage and then sometimes only partially. But for those who do not or cannot let go, engaging the family memories remains a work of the most painful and passionate love.

Endnotes

1.   In addition to The Association of Theological Schools, I owe a considerable debt of gratitude to a number of colleagues for their readings of and responses to this paper. My particular thanks go to Margaret Farley (Yale University Divinity School), Francine Cardman (Weston Jesuit School of Theology), Kathleen Cannon (University of Notre Dame), and Ellen M. Leonard (University of St. Michael's College/Toronto School of Theology).

2.   So also Halvor Moxnes, "What Is Family?" in *Constructing Early Christian Families: Family as Social Reality and Metaphor,* ed. Halvor Moxnes (London and New York: Routledge, 1997), 20-21; the closest Greek and Hebrew equivalents mean household or tribe. Miriam Peskowitz accepts the translation of *mispahah* (tribe, clan, lineage) as *family*, while making clear the complexities involved in reconstructing the families of ancient Judaism see " 'Family/ies'in Antiquity: evidence from Tannaitic Literature and Roman Galilean Architecture" in *The Jewish Family in Antiquity*; ed. Shaye J.D. Cohen, Brown Judaic Studies No. 289 (Atlanta: Scholars Press, 1993), 9-36, discussion of *mispahah* 21-24. For a comprehensive review of *familia* and *domus* see Richard P. Saller, "*Familia, Domus* and the Roman Concept of Family," *Phoenix 38 (1984)*: 336-358. Jane F. Gardner remarks the difference between the words *familia* and family, while noting that families as we understand them did exist; see *Family and Familia in Roman Law and Life* (Oxford: Clarendon Press, 1998), 1-5. For a contemporary approach to the questions see also Jane Collier, Michelle Z. Rosaldo, and Sylvia Yanagisako, "Is There a Family? New Anthropological Perspec-

tives," *The Sex/Gender Reader: Culture, History, Political Economy*; ed. Roger N. Lancaster and Micaela di Leonardo (New York: Routledge, 1997), 71-81.

3.   In a sense, I have been addressing the function of culture in interpretation, usually implicitly or tangentially, for over twenty-five years. The first article I published was entitled "Women and the Earliest Church: Reflecting on the Problématique of Christ and Culture," in *Women Priests: A Catholic Commentary on the Vatican Declaration*; ed. Leonard Swidler and Arlene Swidler (New York: Paulist Press, 1977), 191-201.

4.   For a recent exploration of the ambiguities of the role of Christianity in the forming of family structures, see Rosemary Radford Ruether, *Christianity and the Making of the Modern Family* (Boston Beacon Press, 2000).

5.   Elisabeth Schüssler Fiorenza, *In Memory of Her: A Feminist Theological Reconstruction of Christian Origins.* (New York: Crossroad, 1983), 14-21; her categorization of the positions she analyses here as a "neo-orthodox" model of feminist hermeneutics is problematic.

6.   Ross Shepard Kraemer, *Her Share of the Blessings: Women's Religions Among Pagans, Jews, and Christians in Greco-Roman World* (New York and Oxford; Oxford University Press, 1992), vii-ix.

7.   "Romans," in *Searching the Scriptures 2: A Feminist Commentary*, ed. Elisabeth Schüssler Fiorenza (New York: Crossroad, 1994), 296.

8.   See, for instance, Keith R. Bradley's critical assessment of attempts to explain the Roman family through the "Mediterranean family" in *Marriage, Divorce, and Children in Ancient Rome,* ed. Beryl Rawson (Canberra: Humanities Research Center; Oxford: Clarendon Press, 1991), 94-97. Halvor Moxnes's treatment of honor and shame carefully acknowledges the rise of caution about the claim of a unified Mediterranean among anthropologists, while continuing to argue for a common gendering of these categories; see "Honor and Shame," *The Social Sciences and New Testament Interpretation,* ed. Richard L. Rohrbaugh (Peabody, MA: Hendrickson Publishers, 1996) 19-40, esp. 31-33.

9.   Thus Moxnes cites Balch's study of household codes, but explains the codes not with the political philosophy and apologetic concerns which Balch offers as their context, but by the concept of shame derived by Lila Abu-Lughod from her studies of Bedouin women; see Moxnes, "What Is Family?" 33.

10.   The basic research was done by David L. Balch in *Let Wives be Submissive: The Domestic Code in 1 Peter* (Chico, CA: Scholars Press, 1981). It was widely disseminated through Elisabeth Schüssler Fiorenza's adaptations in *Memory*, 254-270 and *Bread, Not Stone: The Challenge of Feminist Biblical Interpretation* (Boston: Beacon Press, 1985), 65-92.

11.   For the basic argument, see Schüssler Fiorenza, *Memory,* 254-70.

12.   Col 3:12-21 was assigned to the Sunday within the octave of Christmas (the celebration of the "Holy Family.") This is a particularly deceptive selection; it interrupts the formal unit of the household code by cutting off the counsels to slaves and master, while incorporating a larger theological context to justify the prescriptions. Eph 5:21-33 was offered as one of ten options for the nuptial mass. See also the second reading for the twenty-first Sunday of the year, which requires Eph 5:21-32; the weekday lectionary presents 5:21-33 on Tuesday of the 30th week and 6:1-9 on Wednesday.

13.   Clarice J. Martin, "The *Haustafeln* (Household Codes) in African American Biblical Interpretation: 'Free Slaves' and 'Subordinate Women,'" in *Stony the Road We Trod: African American Biblical Interpretation*, ed. Cain Hope Felder (Minneapolis: Fortress Press, 1991), 206-231.

14.   See on Ephesians, Schüssler Fiorenza, *Memory,* 265-270; on Colossians, D'Angelo, "Colossians," in *Searching the Scriptures 2: A Feminist-Ecumenical Commentary*, ed. Elisabeth Schüssler Fiorenza (New York: Crossroad, 1994), 313-324.

15.   The case was made by Joachim Jeremias, *Abba: Studien zur neutestamentlichen Theologie und Zeitgeschichte* (Göttingen: Vandenhoeck und Ruprecht, 1966), 15-67; 'Abba,' *The Prayers of Jesus*, trans. John Bowden (London: SCM.1967), 11-65.

16.   See on this D'Angelo, "Abba and 'Father': Imperial Theology and the Traditions about Jesus," *Journal of Biblical Literature* 111 (1992): 611-630.

17.   See the essays in Jakob J. Petuchowski and Michael Brocke (eds.), *The Lord's Prayer and Jewish Liturgy* (New York: Seabury Press, 1978).

18.   D'Angelo, "Abba and 'Father,'" 617-622; Eileen Schuller, "4Q372 1: A Text about Joseph," *Revue de Qumran* 14 (1990):343-70; "The Psalm of Joseph (4Q372 1) Within the Context of Second Temple Prayer," *Catholic Biblical Quarterly* 54 (1992):67-79; Angelika Strotmann, *"Mein Vater Bist Du!" (Sir 51,10): zur Bedeutung der Vaterschaft Gottes in kanonischen und nichtkanonishcen fruhjudischen Schriften* (Frankfurt am Main: Verlag J. Knecht, 1991).

19.   Robert Hamerton-Kelly, *God the Father: Theology and Patriarchy in the Teaching of Jesus* (Overture to Biblical Theology 4; Philadelphia: Fortress, 1979); "God the Father in the Bible," *God as Father?* ed. Johannes-Baptist Metz and Edward Schillebeeckx; English language editor Marcus Lefébure; *Concilium: Religion in the Eighties* 143: Dogma (Edinburgh: T&T Clark; New York: Seabury Press, 1981), 95-102 .

20.   See also the linguistic critique of these terms in James Barr, "'Abba' Isn't Daddy," *Journal of Theological Studies* n. s. 39 (1988):28-47; "'Abba' and the Familiarity of Jesus' Speech," Theology 91(1988):173-79.

21.   Among other accounts of the ambiguities surrounding patriarchal authority and intensity of feeling around the Roman family, see Suzanne Dixon, *The Roman Family* (Baltimore: Johns Hopkins University Press, 1992), 28-35; on patriarchy and tenderness, see Mary Daly, *Beyond God the Father: Toward a Philosophy of Women's Liberation* (Boston: Beacon Press 1973), 16; on the cycle of abuse and affection in battering see Lenore E. Walker, *The Battered Woman* (New York: Harper & Row, 1979), esp. 55-70.

22.   For analyses of the problem with regard to a specific text, see D'Angelo, "Gender and Power in the Gospel of Mark: The Daughter of Jairus and the Woman with the Flow of Blood," in *Miracles in Jewish and Christian Antiquity: Imagining Truth*, ed. John C. Cavadini (Notre Dame: University of Notre Dame Press, 1999), 83-109, and Amy-Jill Levine, "Discharging Responsibility: Matthean Jesus, Biblical Law and Hemorrhaging Woman," in *Treasures New And Old: Recent Contributions to Matthean Studies* (ed. Mark Allan Powell and David R. Bauer; Atlanta: Scholars Press, 1996), 379-397.

23.   Keith R. Bradley, *Discovering the Roman Family: Studies in Roman Social History* (New York: Oxford University Press, 1991); Suzanne Dixon, *The Roman Family*; Jane F. Gardner, *Family and Familia;* Jane F. Gardner and Thomas Wiedemann, *The Roman Household: A Sourcebook* (London and New York: Routledge, 1991); Beryl Rawson (ed.), *The Family in Ancient Rome: New Perspectives* (Ithaca: Cornell University Press, 1986); Rawson (ed.), *Marriage, Divorce, and Children in Ancient Rome* (Canberra: Humanities Research Center; Oxford: Clarendon Press, 1991); Rawson and Paul Weaver (eds.), *The Roman Family in Italy: Status, Sentiment, Space* (Oxford: Oxford University Press, 1997); Sarah Pomeroy, *Families in Classical and Hellenistic Greece: Representations and Realities* (Oxford: Clarendon Press, 1997); Shaye J.D. Cohen (ed.), *The Jewish Family in Antiquity* (Atlanta: Scholars Press, 1993); Halvor Moxnes (ed.), *Constructing Early Christian Families: Family as Social Real-*

ity and Metaphor (New York: Routledge, 1994); Carolyn Osiek and David L. Balch, *Families in the New Testament World: Households and House Churches, The Family, Religion and Culture* (Louisville: Westminster John Knox Press, 1997).

24. Of particular note are Catherine Edwards, *The Politics of Immorality in Ancient Rome* (Cambridge: Cambridge University Press, 1993); Jane DeRose Evans, *The Art of Persuasion: Political Propaganda from Aeneas to Brutus* (Ann Arbor: University of Michigan Press, 1992); Denis Feeney, *Literature and Religion at Rome: Cultures, Context and Beliefs* (Cambridge: Cambridge University Press, 1998); D.S. Potter and D.J. Mattingly *Life, Death and Entertainment in the Roman Empire* (Ann Arbor: University of Michigan Press, 1999); Anton Powell (ed.), *Roman Poetry and Propaganda in the Age of Augustus* (London: Bristol Classical Press, 1992); S. R. F. Price, *Rituals and Power: The Roman Imperial Cult in Asia Minor* (Cambridge: Cambridge University Press, 1984); Edwin S. Ramage, *The Nature and Purpose of Augustus' "Res Gestae." Historia: Einzelschriften* 54 (Stuttgart: Franz Steiner Verlag Wiesbaden, 1987); Kurt Rauflaub and Mark Toher (eds.), *Between Republic and Empire: Interpretations of Augustus and His Principate* (Berkeley: University of California Press, 1990); Andrew Wallace-Haddrill, *Augustan Rome*; Classical World Series (London: Bristol Classical Press, 1993); Wallace-Haddrill, "The Golden Age and Sin in Augustan Ideology," *Past and Present* 95(1982):19-36; Paul Zanker, *The Power of Images in the Age of Augustus;* Jerome Lectures 16; tr. Alan Shapiro (Ann Arbor: University of Michigan Press, 1988).

25. Among works that do raise these issues in regard to early Judaism and Christianity are Loveday Alexander (ed.), *Images of Empire*, Journal for the Study of the Old Testament 122 (Sheffield: Sheffield Academic Press, 1991); Douglas R. Edwards, *Religion and Power: Pagans, Jews, and Christians in the Greek East* (New York: Oxford University Press, 1996); Richard A. Horsley (ed), *Paul and Empire: Religion and Power in Roman Imperial Society* (Harrisburg: Trinity Press International, 1997), Larry J. Kreitzer *Striking New Images: Roman Imperial Coinage and the New Testament World,* Journal for the Study of New Testament 134 (Sheffield: Sheffield Academic Press, 1996).

26. For a Christological reading that does argue that it was, see Elisabeth Schüssler Fiorenza's assessment of the issue in *Jesus, Miriam's Child, Sophia's Prophet: Feminist Christology* (New York: Continuum, 1994), 67-128.

27. Schüssler Fiorenza called for this shift in *In Memory of Her,* but herself constructed a contrast between Jesus' understanding of God's reign ("wholeness") and "dominant ethos" of "holy nation" represented in particular by the Pharisees and the sectarian Qumran texts (110-114, 118-140). See also my attempts in "Re-membering Jesus: Women, Prophecy and Resistance in the Memory of the Early Churches," *Horizons: Journal of the College Theology Society* 19 (1992), 199-218; D'Angelo, "Gender in the Origins of Christianity: Jewish Hopes and Imperial Exigencies" in *Equal at the Creation: Sexism, Society and the Christian Tradition*; ed. Joseph Martos and Pierre Hégy (Toronto: University of Toronto Press, 1998), 25-48.

28. The idea of a liberation of Roman women in the first century is heavily based on a naive reading of certain highly rhetorical texts from about 100 BCE to about 125 CE, such as Juvenal's 6th satire.

29. See Sara Tanzer's objections to this practice in "Ephesians" *Searching the Scriptures 2*, 330.

30. See Stefan Weinstock, "The Father," *Divus Julius* (Oxford: Clarendon Press, 1971), 200-207.

31. See Suetonius, *Augustus* 58; Cassius Dio, *Roman History* 55.10.10. The title had Republican origins; for survey of the function of the title, see Andreas Alföldi, *Der Vater des Vaterlandes in Römischen Denken* (Darmstadt: Wissenschaftliche Buchgesellschaft, 1971); Lily Ross Taylor, *The Divinity of the Roman Emperor* (APA

Monograph Series 1; Middletown: Scholars Press, 1931; reprinted, no date), 47-49, 67, 93; on the association with divinity, 200-201, 217-218.

32. Niels Hannestad, *Roman Art and Imperial Policy* (Aarhus: Aarhus University Press, 1988), 29, 44, 55. On the emperor as *paterfamilias*, see W. K. Lacey, "Patria Potestas" in *The Family in Ancient Rome*, 121-144, esp. 139, also Geza Alföldi, *The Social History of Rome*, trans. David Braund and Frank Pollock (Baltimore: Johns Hopkins University Press, 1988), 101.

33. On the content and effect of the laws, see Susan Tregiarri, *Roman Marriage: Iusti Coniuges From the Time of Cicero to the Time of Ulpian* (Oxford: Clarendon Press, 1991), 277-298, 453-458.

34. Karl Galinsky *Augustan Culture: An Interpetive Introduction* (Princeton: Princeton University Press, 1996), 128.

35. Edwards, *The Politics of Immorality in Ancient Rome*, 62.

36. *legibus novis latis complura exempla maiorum exolescentia iam ex nostro usu revocavi*. The Latin is partially reconstructed from the Greek version: Εισαγαγὼν καινοὺς νόμους πολλὰ ἤδη τῶν ἀρχαίων ἐθῶν καταλυόμενα διωρθωσάμην; see Frederick W. Shipley (ed. and trans.), *Velleius Paterculus, Compendium of Roman History and Res Gestae Divi Augusti*, Loeb Classical Library 152 (Cambridge: Harvard University Press, 1924), 358. [Ed.: The Symbol Greek II font used in this endnote is available from Linguist's Software, Inc., www.linguistsoftware.com.]

37. See for example, Tregiarri, *Iusti Coniuges* 277-298, 453-458, esp. 294 where she speculates, "The law must have made it considerably more difficult than before for a woman to divorce a husband unilaterally and to form a successful new marriage, especially if there was an emotional motive or even a previous acquaintance with the husband." See also Tregiarri, Divorce Roman Style: How Easy and Frequent Was It?" in Beryl Rawson, ed., *Marriage, Divorce, and Children*, 31-46, esp. 41-44.

38. Jane DeRose Evans, *The Art of Persuasion: Political Propaganda from Aeneas to Brutus* (Ann Arbor: University of Michigan Press, 1992); Paul Zanker, *The Power of Images in the Age of Augustus*, trans. Alan Shapiro (Ann Arbor: University of Michigan Press, 1988), 1-31.

39. Balch, *Let Wives be Submissive*, 41-43, 117.

40. Livy, *Ab urbe condita* 34.1-8; Valerius Maximus *De Dictis et Factis Memorabilibus* 6:9.

41. Dionysius of Halicarnassus, *Antiquitates Romanae* 2.24-25, cited in Dio Cocceianus, *Roman History. Book 53-55.9:The Augustan Settlement*, ed. and trans. J.W. Rich (Warminster, UK: Aris & Phillips, 1990); on Augustus to the senate, 54.16.4-5.

42. Sara Tanzer, "Ephesians," *Searching the Scriptures 2*, 330-332 and the literature cited there; she rightly points to the inappropriateness of monolithic depictions of the lives of Roman women.

43. See Jan WillemVan Henten, *The Maccabean Martyrs as Saviours of the Jewish People: A Study of 2 and 4 Maccabees* (Leiden: Brill, 1997), 281-282.

44. *Res Gestae* 34: *virtutis, clementiaeque et iustitiae, et pietatis caussa*; equivalents from the Greek version: *areten kai epieikeian kai dikaiosunen kai eusebeian*. On the *clupeus virtutum* see Zanker, *Power of Images in the Age of Augustus*, 95-96.

45. Much of the critical portion of the articles has been either accepted or addressed in a recent work on the divine title in the New Testament. But the suggestion has largely been passed by; see Marianne Meye Thompson, *The Promise of the Father: Jesus and God in the New Testament* (Louisville: Westminster John Knox Press, 2000), 56-63 and a brief reference in n. 28, p.109. Mary C. Boys recognizes the degree

to which the study is concerned with avoiding Christian anti-Judaism; see *Has God Only One Blessing? Judaism as a Source of Christian Self-Understanding* (New York: Paulist Press, 2000), 135-136.

46. For one recent summary of the critical issues around this criterion, see John P. Meier, *A Marginal Jew: Rethinking the Historical Jesus I: The Roots of the Problem and the Person* (New York: Doubleday 1991), 171-174. My conclusions differ.

47. See D'Angelo, "Gender in the Origins of Christianity: Jewish Hopes and Imperial Exigencies" in *Equal at the Creation: Sexism, Society, and the Christian Tradition*, ed. Joseph Martos and Pierre Hégy. (Toronto: University of Toronto, 1998), 25-48; D'Angelo, "Remembering Jesus: Women, Prophecy, and Resistance in the Memory of the Early Churches," *Horizons: Journal of the College Theology Society* 19 (1992), 199-218.

48. Schüssler Fiorenza, *In Memory of Her,* 204-315.

49. Antoinette Clark Wire, *Corinthian Women Prophets: A Reconstruction Through Paul's Rhetoric* (Minneapolis: Fortress Press, 1990); differently, D'Angelo, "Veils, Virgins and the Tongues of Men and Angels: Women's Heads as Sexual Members in Ancient Christianity," in *Off with Her Head! The Denial of Women's Identity in Myth, Religion, and Culture* ed. Howard Eilberg-Schwarz and Wendy Doniger.(Berkeley: University of California Press, 1995), 131-164.

50. Dennis R. MacDonald, *The Legend and the Apostle: The Battle for Paul in Story and Canon* (Philadelphia: Westminster, 1983); Anne McGuire, "Virginity and Subversion: Norea Against the Powers in *Hypostasis of the Archons,*" *Images of the Feminine in Gnosticism*, ed. Karen L. King, Studies in Antiquity and Christianity 4 (Philadelphia: Fortress Press, 1988), 239-258; King "The Book of Norea, the Daughter of Eve," and "The Gospel of Mary Magdalene," in *Searching the Scriptures 2* 66-85, 601-634; D'Angelo, "Reconstructing Real Women from Gospel Literature: the Case of Mary Magdalene," *Women in Christian Origins*, 105-128.

51. McDonald, *Legend* 102; Schüssler Fiorenza, *Memory*, 29; see also her treatments of the "Jesus movement" and the early Christian mission (i.e., the context of the letters of Paul), 99-203. For her recent hermeneutical work, see *Rhetoric and Ethic: the Politics of Biblical Studies* (Minneapolis: Fortress Press, 1999).

52. Kathryn Tanner, *Theories of Culture: A New Agenda for Theology,* Guides to Theological Inquiry (Minneapolis: Fortress Press, 1997).

53. See David Blankenhorn, *Fatherless America: Confronting Our Most Urgent Social Problem* (New York: Basic Books, 1995); Wade F. Horn, David Blankenhorn, Mitchell B. Pearlstein, eds., *The Fatherhood Movement: A Call to Action* (Lanham: Lexington Books 1999).

54. Judith Stacey, "The Neo-Family Values Campaign" in *The Sex / Gender Reader* 452-70; see also Stacy, *Brave New Families: Stories of Domestic Upheaval in Late Twentieth Century America* (New York: Basic Books, 1990) and Stacy, *In the Name of the Family: Rethinking Family Values in the Postmodern Age* (Boston: Beacon Press, 1996).

55. For the phrase "prison-industrial complex," see David Barsamian, "Angela Davis: Interview," *The Progressive* 65/2 (February 2001) 33-38.

56. Margaret M. Mitchell, *The Heavenly Trumpet: John Chrysostom and the Art of Pauline Interpretation* (Tübingen: Mohr Siebeck, 2000), Margaret M. Mitchell, "His Most Devoted Interpreter: John Chrysostom and the Art of Pauline Interpretation" in *The Papers of the Henry Luce III Fellows in Theology*, Vol. 5, ed. Christopher I. Wikins (Pittsburgh: The Association of Theological Schools in the United States and Canada, 2002).

The Social Imago:
The Image of God and
the Postmodern (Loss of) Self

Stanley J. Grenz
CAREY THEOLOGICAL COLLEGE AND REGENT COLLEGE
VANCOUVER, BRITISH COLUMBIA

In the mid-1990s, airwaves and CD players across North America were monopolized by Canadian pop diva Alanis Morissette's "All I Really Want." The lyrics of this nearly unsingable tune ramble through a hodgepodge of seemingly disconnected preferences and competing desires that the singer finds present within and around her. Although Morissette bemoans life in a world populated by superficial people, she cannot simply opt-out of her communal context, for she desperately yearns for a soulmate, a kindred spirit, someone who truly understands.

Sixteen-year-old Aminah McKinnie of Madison, Mississippi, may be too young to have been enthralled with Morissette's particular expression of confusion. Yet she shares similar feelings of isolation mixed with longings to be "connected." Like many others of her generation, she spends much of her non-school waking hours on the Internet—shopping, looking for a job, doing homework, and talking to her friends. Moreover, she lives in a strangely paradoxical realm in which the opinions of peers and relationships are crucial, and yet where social groups are fluid, friendships change over a period of months or even weeks, and the possibility of lifelong "best friends" is not even on the radar screen.[1]

The fluidity characteristic of the contemporary ethos is epitomized by the Internet chat room. Here participants are able to be whomever they want, to try on new identities with ease, even to the point of becoming a different person with each foray into cyberspace.

Do the resources of the Christian anthropology, understood as the reflection on humans as God's creation, have anything to offer in the contemporary, postmodern realm described by Alanis Morissette or inhabited by Internet devotees and chat-room dwellers? The search for an answer to this question requires a theological conversation involving scripture, read within a particular hermeneutical context, and the intellectual-cultural trajectory that forms the conceptual underpinnings of the postmodern condition.

The Cultural Context:
The Rise and Demise of the Self

No concept has been more important for the understanding of the human person in Western intellectual history than the self. The term *self*, together with the idea that every human being is a self, belongs to the standard vocabulary of Western society. Writing in the *Oxford Companion to Philosophy*, E. J. Lowe pinpoints the modern understanding. He declares that a self is "a subject of consciousness, a being capable of thought and experience and able to engage in deliberative action. More crucially, a self must have a capacity for *self*-consciousness . . .a self is a being that is able to entertain first-person thoughts."[2]

From Interiority to Psychotherapy:
An Archeology of the Self

Rather than being given "in the beginning," the "self" as delineated by philosophers such as Lowe is a modern invention, albeit one that emerged as the product of a long process. The trajectory that gave rise to the modern self begins with Augustine.[3]

The soul's journey to God. Building from the Greek dictum, "know thyself," Augustine transposed the focus of the search for self to the realm within. Indeed, he was convinced that the inward journey marks the pathway to God.[4]

The Augustinian turn inward elevated the cognitive aspect of the soul, i.e., the mind. In this manner, the church father opened the door to what Charles Taylor calls "the stance of radical reflexivity or adopting the first-person standpoint."[5] That is, Augustine inaugurated the turn toward one's own act of being aware, which for him became the foundation of the search for truth. In addition to the cognitive, however, Augustine's inward turn also involves a strong affective dimension: the desire for the good, which Augustine, as a Christian, interpreted as the desire for, or love for, God.

Augustine's inward journey was at least in part motivated by the desire to overcome the fragmentation that he sensed in his own life and that characterized the times in which he was living.[6] He was convinced that without God providing its unity, the self could only remain scattered. Therefore, Augustine viewed the inward call as none other than God's own voice inviting him to cling to the divine unity and thereby to find the unity of his own life restored in God.[7]

The world-mastering / self-mastering rational self. Augustine's inward turn launched the process that led to the concept of the self as the stable, abiding reality that constitutes the individual human being. The modern self that stands at the end of this trajectory assumes several forms. Yet the mode of the self that has predominated in the Western philosophical tradition since the Enlightenment focuses on mastery. The "mastering self" takes charge of the world it inhabits in both the outer and the inner dimensions of that world. The self seeks mastery so as to constitute itself and determine its identity.

The Enlightenment linked the human person to the power of reason. This was not a new idea. What was new in the Age of Reason was a particular understanding of the rationality that comprised the self. Rather than understanding reason as the ability to see the presence of the eternal within the material, which typified the outlook of ancient philosophy, the thinkers of the Age of Reason equated reason with proper method. By hitching this human power to a mechanistic view of the world, they came to view reason as the means to objectify the world in the cause of gaining mastery and exercising instrumental control over it. Moreover, rather than being the static, contemplative soul of the medieval ideal, the Enlightenment philosophers conceived of the human person as a restless, discontented transformer of the world.[8] The active agent in the task of world-mastery was assumed to be the rational self that establishes itself through the exercise of instrumental reason.

To this process, Rene Descartes contributed the self as a rational subject. Locke added the idea of the self as a "conscious thinking thing,"[9] thereby linking personal identity to self-consciousness.[10] But the turn toward the knowing subject was not complete until Immanuel Kant postulated the active mind as the definitive agent both in the knowing process and in the life of duty. This, in turn, gave birth to what Robert Solomon calls the "transcendental pretence" of modernity.[11] In reflecting on itself, Kant's self did not merely know itself, but it supposed that it knew all selves, as well as the structure of every possible self.

The rise and spread of the new instrumental science in the Enlightenment found its religious parallel in the Puritan and Pietist movements, together with the eighteenth century evangelical awakenings they spawned. The new religious consciousness abetted the fledgling instrumental stance toward the world by providing it with a spiritual purpose.[12] Yet even more significant was its elevation of the self as the agent in the task of self-mastery, which at least initially was viewed as a religious vocation. In shifting the focus in this manner, the religious stream from the Puritans to the revivalists developed the other side of mastery endemic to the Enlightenment, namely, the attempt not only to manipulate nature but also to gain control over the self.[13]

The self-sufficient self. The impulse toward the self-mastering self that lay at the heart of evangelical piety opened the door to the self-sufficient, self-constructing, "therapeutic self"[14] authored by modern psychology. One important voice in this process was Erich Fromm, who declared that the goal of therapy is not adjustment but the optimal development of a person's potentialities and individuality. Even more important than Fromm's pop-psychology, however, was Abraham Maslow's scientific psychological approach. In a manner somewhat similar to Fromm, Maslow spoke of the human ideal as "self-actualization" or "full-humanness,"[15] and he characterized his proposal as "a growth and self-actualization psychology,"[16] at the heart of which was his widely-known "hierarchy of needs."[17] Maslow was convinced that he had uncovered a morally neutral, essential human nature, the actualization of which led to health, and the thwarting of which was pathological.

The ascendancy of modern psychology marks what Philip Rieff aptly characterizes as "the triumph of the therapeutic." In this emergent kingdom of the self, the individual self is looked to as providing the "center" that is able to hold together even as the surrounding world disintegrates.[18] Moreover, the individual self assumes the role of being the arbiter and focal point of meaning, values, and even existence itself. The highest value that this self can posit is freedom, which, when understood as the flip side of self-consciousness or self-awareness, involves the capacity either to mold[19] or to actualize oneself.

From Autobiography to Preference:
The Undermining of the Self

The modern self emerged as the product of a 1500-year intellectual journey that stretched from Augustine to Maslow. This pilgrimage netted a self-assured, self-sufficient, centered self that was believed to constitute a stable identity in the midst of a chaotic world. Yet the reign of the modern self was short-lived. The centered self of the modern era has become one of the casualties of the postmodern dethroning of all ruling monarchs. The postmodern condition entails the undermining of another approach to the centered self as well.

The self-focused self. Although the Cartesian rational self imbued with a Kantian transcendental pretense became the dominant mode for understanding the modern self, the forays of other thinkers into the inner sanctum netted a particular rather than a universal self, a self-focused rather than an essence-focused self. In their estimation, the self does not emerge so much through self-mastery as through self-expression, that is, through the expression of the self's own uniqueness.

Self-construction through self-expression requires self-exploration as a first step. Indeed, self-expression presupposes an awareness of one's unique self, which in turn arises by means of observing and cataloguing one's personal thoughts and feelings. The self that emerges from this process of looking inward to find one's unique individuality might well be called the "autobiographical self." This self was invented by the sixteenth century French civil servant, Michel de Montaigne, who used the literary form of autobiography to discover the unique self within. Jean-Jacques Rousseau, in turn, engaged in writing autobiography to discover the particular nature that constituted him as a unique self, which, however, he believed was at the same time the soul of humanity. In the process, Rousseau pronounced the self intrinsically good.[20]

The autobiographical self is not yet the complete self, however. Self-construction demands not only self-discovery but also self-expression. The development of the self-expressive self was the work of the heirs of Montaigne and Rousseau whose writings coalesced in what is often designated the Romantic movement. The Romantic vision was driven by the belief that ultimate reality, viewed as the cosmic self, is intricately connected with the individual self and that the world is in some profound sense the creation of the self.[21] The attendant Romantic belief that the self is the expression of the infinite led to the self-reliant self that the American Romantic, Ralph Waldo Emerson, championed.

The demise of the centered self. But what happens when the concept of the infinite within the finite, upon which the self-expressive self depends for its sense of stability and for its ability to overcome its own particularity, proves to be an unstable center? The destabilizing of this Romantic self came on the heels of explorations into the world-constructing self, especially the self as will, charted by the nineteenth century German idealists. The result was an intellectual crisis precipitated by the conclusion that the universal will was irrational and impersonal (Schopenhauer) and that human values were undergirded merely by the will to power (Nietzsche).

This crisis was especially felt by the turn-of-the-twentieth-century Vienna "modernists"[22] (including Freud), who sensed that an unhappy and unstable "psychological man" was emerging out of "the dissolution of the classical liberal view of man," to cite Carl Schorske's apt description.[23] By displacing interest in questions regarding the unity of personal identity-development in favor of an emphasis on the mechanism of the process, Freud effectively undercut the older concept of the unitary self characterized by permanence, continuity and cohesion. Only a short step led from Freudian psychoanalysis to the sense of a free-floating self without any semblance of a fixed identity, that is, to the sense that the self is—as Jacques Le Rider states—merely "an endless, unpredictable interplay of conscious and unconscious identities" and that the supposed "opposition between reality and fantasy is meaningless in any attempts to understand a personality."[24]

The modernists nevertheless continued the quest to discover an inner "depth," even if this required that they cast aside the dream of the centered self. Yet the die was cast. What Irving Howe observes as the "demotion, even dispossession" of the self[25] soon followed. The conceptual tools for this final demolition of the self were provided by Ferdinand de Saussure's structural linguistics[26] and the structuralism of such anthropologists as Claude Levi-Strauss, that dissolved the self into the structures of the social realm without and the brain within.

The death and (re)birth of the self. Yet structuralism was itself the last gasp of modernism. The postmodern turn was finally completed when Michel Foucault admonished his scholarly colleagues to leave behind all pretense of neutrality and accept what he saw as their legitimate task, namely, to bring to light the authorless, subjectless, anonymous system of thought present within the language of an epoch. In so doing, Foucault declared that subjectivity is the product of the unconscious internalization of a host of social factors[27] that govern how people think, live and speak.[28] In short, Foucault extended Nietzsche's metaphor of the death of God to encompass the death of the self as well.

The postmodern ethos is characterized not only by the loss of the self but by the *embrace* of its demise. As Louis Sass observes, postmodern thinkers "seem to take an inordinate delight in dancing round [the self's] burning image."[29] Yet the postmodern turn away from the self does not mark the inauguration of pure selflessness. The postmodern condition retains a semblance of a "self" or, perhaps better stated, a trace of the now absent self. Consequently, the language of the self remains, although this residual, postmodern "self" differs radically from its modern predecessor.

Rather than being the agent of subjectivity, the postmodern "self" is a self-referential system. This understanding leads to a highly social conception of the self that views a person as a being who has learned a theory in terms of which his or her experience is ordered.[30] Moreover, insofar as this experience-ordering "theory" is a narrative, the socially-constructed postmodern "self" is a narrative self[31] whose organizing "plot" arises from one's social group (or community of reference).[32] Postmodern thinkers routinely picture this socially-constructed "self" as a position in a vast web, a nexus, a point of intersection,[33] a crossroad within a "web of interlocution."[34] The postmodern self, therefore, looks to relationships for identity.[35] In a fast-changing world, this readily results in a highly unstable, impermanent self, that is little more than a bundle of fluctuating relationships and momentary preferences.

The instability of the "self" is exacerbated by the postmodern elevation of difference at the expense of universality and the attendant celebration of the plurality or multiplicity of options. The advent of the centerless postmodern universe means that no single proposed view of the world, or limited number of such world views, can provide a map of the "self." Rather, Foucault's "heterotopia"[36] consists of a market place in which a variety of maps can be readily obtained and freely exchanged. Moreover, the postmodern condition marks the loss of assurance that any particular map of the external world can somehow express or manifest the realm of the internal self.[37] Hence, the postmodern "self" becomes both the final extension of and the contradiction to the central assumption of the Romantic movement, namely, the coherence between the inner self and the external world mediated by the presence of the infinite within the finite.

The instability inaugurated by the metamorphosis of the modern ideal of the self, characterized as it was by unity, stability, and constancy through time, into the decentered, fleeting "self" constructed in each moment of existence readily translates into "psychic fragmentation," to cite Fredric Jameson's designation.[38] That is, it leads to the splintering of the self into multiple subjectivities. This fragmentation, in turn, gives birth to what Johann Roten calls the "chaotic self,"[39] which "attempts to absorb 'alterity' in all its forms to overcome separation and isolation, only to find itself in the end in a state of spiritual chaos."[40]

The spiritual chaos endemic to the postmodern condition may lead to the celebration of the death of the self. But it may also occasion a new quest for some semblance of meaning[41] in the face of the terrifying emptiness introduced by, or the search for some measure of stability in the midst of the vertigo endemic to, the postmodern condition.

The Theological Resource: The Concept of the *Imago Dei*

Throughout much of Christian history, theologians responded to the challenge posed by the search for an identity-producing self by appealing to the biblical concept of the *imago dei*. To a culture enamored with the inward turn, they declared with confidence that each human is created in the divine image. But does the language of the *imago dei* continue to speak after the demise of the self? What insight does it offer to a situation in which the self has dissipated into a constantly shifting bundle of relationships? The quest for a culturally relevant understanding of the image of God leads inevitably to the biblical texts, albeit only after a glance has been directed toward theological history.

The Imago Dei *in Theological History*

Although the *imago dei* has played a crucial role in the construction of Christian anthropology throughout the history of the church, exegetes and theologians have not been in agreement as to what the concept entails. The most commonly-held recounting of theological history finds two basic approaches to the image of God within the tradition.[42] The substantial or structural view that has predominated throughout the history of the church understands the *imago dei* as consisting of certain attributes or capabilities lodged within the person, and consequently it characterizes humans as being shaped in the image of God after the manner of a sculpture or painting. The relational view, in contrast, sees the divine image as referring to a fundamental relationship between the human creature and the Creator, and hence it speaks of humans as reflecting the divine reality somewhat like a mirror.[43]

Sometimes overlooked in sketches of the history of theological anthropology is the presence of overtones of a third understanding. This view sees the image as the divinely-given goal or destiny[44] that awaits humankind in the eschatological future and toward which humans are directed from the beginning. The impetus for such an approach dates to the work of Irenaeus, who pictured Adam as a childlike being destined by God to grow into the divine likeness through the exercise of his will. Theologians in the West abandoned Irenaeus's eschatologically-focused, developmental view in favor of the idea that pre-fallen Adam was created perfect, complete and mature, and was endowed at creation with "original righteousness." Nevertheless, the tradition retained an impetus toward a developmental perspective, insofar as theologians maintained a Christocentric dimension in their understanding of the *imago dei* as well as an anticipation of a future, eschatological completion of the process of restoring the lost image, which renovation is begun, but not completed, in this life.

The developmental understanding of the *imago dei* reemerged in a strand of German theology that has its genesis in the work of the late eighteenth-century thinker, Johann Gottfried Herder. Herder set forth what Wolfhart Pannenberg characterizes as an "evolving image of God," in contrast to the concept of a static image present in humans before the fall, generally shared by Catholic and Protestant theologians alike.[45] Herder's developmental understanding of the human person as directed toward a future destiny may be summed up in his dictum, "we are not yet human beings, but are daily *becoming* so."[46] In this manner, Herder opened the way for a reformulation in the context of modern thought of the tentative interpretations of the human being as a history found in patristic theology.[47] This challenge has motivated theologians who follow in Herder's wake. The American Lutheran theologian Philip Hefner, for example, picks up the idea when he declares, "The image of God (*imago dei*) presents a fundamental image of human being as being-with-a-destiny."[48]

From Humankind to the True Human:
The Imago Dei *and Biblical Christo-Anthropology*

The concept of the *imago dei* as destiny forms one aspect of a constellation of themes that focuses on a communal understanding of relationality that emerges as a product of the contemporary renewal of Trinitarian theology. The pathway to such a conception, however, leads through the biblical texts that narrate the human journey into the divine image.

Humankind and the imago dei. Claus Westermann notes that the "most striking statement" of the biblical creation narrative, "over and above God being the creator, preserver and sustainer of creation, is that God created human beings in his image."[49] Despite its importance to biblical and Christian anthropology it was most likely not invented by the ancient Hebrews.[50] Rather, the background for the idea lies in the kingship ideology of ancient Near Eastern cultures. The Genesis creation narratives surfaced as a "counter myth" to, or polemic against, the teachings of the surrounding cultures, in the context of which Israelite theology, cosmology, and anthropology were sharpened.[51]

The term "image of God" may well have evoked a range of ideas and impressions among the ancient Hebrews. Nevertheless, at the heart of the concept likely lay the idea of representation, leading to the conclusion that humankind is to function as "God's vice-regent on earth."[52] In the ancient Near East, images were viewed as representatives of the entity they designated. This was the case with the physical images that monarchs often erected in conquered territories to represent their occupation of the land. The representational motif was especially strong, however, when an image was designed to depict a deity. According to ancient Near Eastern understandings, the god's spirit or immaterial fluid actually indwelt the image (or idol), for it was able to permeate the physical substance of which the image was made.[53] This effected a close connection between the god and its image.[54] Thus, Clines claims that an image was "the most perfect type of representative" known to the ancient peoples, in that "it is the only representative that is actually in spiritual union with the one it represents."[55]

Images were often thought to represent—and even mediate—the presence of one who is physically absent, whether this absent reality be the conquering king whose throne is in a distant city or a deity whose abode is on the remote mountain of the gods. The concept of the *imago dei*, therefore, indicates that humans are somehow to mediate within creation the immanence of the transcendent Creator. Viewed from this perspective, Gen. 1:26-27 stands at the pinnacle of the biblical creation narrative that, unlike the myths of other ancient peoples, posits a God who creates an external world and then places humankind within that creation as a creaturely representation of the transcendent deity.[56]

These considerations suggest that the story of the creation of humankind as the *imago dei* was included in the Genesis narrative for the purpose of undermining the exclusivity of the royal ideology out of which the biblical concept emerged. By extending the divine image to humankind, the first creation narrative—in a manner akin to Psalm 8—declared that humankind, and not merely the king, is the representation of and witness to God on earth. At the same time, neither the *Wortbericht* nor the *Tatbericht* in Gen. 1:26-27 refers to individuals as individuals. Rather, both have in view humankind (as is evident by the use of the corporate term *adam*[57]) or perhaps humans-in-relationship (suggested by the reference to male and female in Gen. 1:27). Rather than embodying a "democratization" of the royal ideology, therefore, the first creation narrative effects a "universalizing" of the divine image.

Although the use of the two descriptive nouns, "image" and "likeness," suggests that as the divine image humans are to resemble their Creator, Gen. 1:26-27 only hints at the nature of this resemblance. The search for the full meaning of the *imago dei*, that is, the quest to understand how humans are to fulfill the role of being the divine image, leads to the full sweep of the biblical narrative. Because this wider narrative centers on Jesus as the Messiah of Israel, the open-ended character of Gen. 1:26-27 clears the way for a move from a creatio-centric to a Christocentric anthropology.

The imago dei *and the True Human.* The Old Testament concern to link the *imago dei* with humankind is not lost in the New. Nevertheless, the predominant interest of the New Testament texts that speak about the divine image is not to uphold its universal presence in humankind and thereby set forth a creation anthropology, but to elevate Jesus Christ as the image of God. This is implicit in the glory-Christology developed throughout the New Testament, which has its basis in the kind of Christological interpretation of Psalm 8 evident in Heb. 2:6-9. But it comes to explicit expression in the texts that speak of Jesus Christ as the *eikon* of God, a Greek term that is stronger than its Hebrew counterpart, for it implies an archetype or prototype of which it is a copy and from which it is derived, thereby positing a clear resemblance between the image and what it depicts.[58]

The first text, 2 Cor. 4:4-6, occurs in the midst of Paul's lengthy vindication of his ministry against those in the Corinthian church that were questioning his apostolic authority. In his response, Paul links Christ as the *imago dei* with the glory-Christology evident throughout the New Testament. The apostle declares that his message centers on Christ's glory as the image of God (v. 4). For Paul, being the *imago dei* means that Christ radiates the very glory of God (v. 6) and hence "is the place where God himself, the invisible, is known," to cite C. K. Barrett's words.[59]

Rather than offering some abstract, philosophical assertion about the ontological nature of Christ, however, Paul's statement evidences a narrative focus. It embodies an implicit allusion to the creation of humankind in the divine image narrated in Gen. 1:26-27 as understood through the lens of Jesus Christ as the Second Adam.[60] The narrative tone is evident as well in Paul's linking of the efficacy of his gospel with the causative power of God, which he connects to the metaphorical concept of light. To this end, the apostle forges a link to the divine act of calling light out of darkness narrated in Gen. 1:3, albeit perhaps under the influence of Psa. 112:4 as well. Thereby, Paul identifies the Creator of light with the one who illumines believers' hearts.[61] Paul's linking of God's glory and the divine image to Jesus Christ produces the strongest Christological statement possible, yet one that remains focused on salvation history rather than speculation about the nature of the divine reality.

The centrality of narrative is even more pronounced in Col. 1:15-20. What the author senses is at stake here is not merely apostolic authority but the entire Christian faith, which is being undermined by an attractive alternative religious system. In the face of this challenge, Paul[62] incorporates what appears to be an edited version of a previously formed hymn (Col. 1:15-20),[63] that not only emphasizes Christ's preeminence over all things but extols his centrality in the narrative of creation and redemption.

The hymn presents Christ's preeminence in a series of affirmations in two[64] strophes that form a "cosmology of creation" and a "cosmology of redemption."[65] Crucial for understanding the nature of the *imago dei* in the Colossian hymn is the twofold assertion that Christ is the "firstborn" (*prototokos*), which brings together the themes of the two strophes. The hymn declares that the one who is the *eikon theou* is the "firstborn of all creation" (v. 15 NRSV) and, reiterating a theme found elsewhere in the New Testament (Rev. 1:5; cf. Rom. 8:29), the "firstborn from the dead" (v. 18 NRSV). In this manner, the repetition of the term links the "beginning" (primordial creation) with the "new beginning" (eschatological resurrection), and it draws the entire creation/salvation-historical narrative into its central focus, Jesus Christ, who as the center of God's actions is the preeminent one and the *imago dei*.

Like other Christological assertions in the New Testament, Paul's statement articulates his conclusion regarding the significance of the narrative of Jesus that evoked it and which it, in turn, calls to mind. Similar to the great Johannine declaration of the incarnation, "the Word became flesh and lived among us" (John 1:14 NRSV), Paul draws together into a single whole the entire life of Jesus as it centers on his resurrection as the prolepsis of the eschaton (v. 18) and on his death as God's great act in reconciling all creation (v. 20). The apostle's intent is to declare that this historical life is the dwelling place of the fullness of deity, understood in accordance with the wisdom tradition and as the fulfillment of the creation story. Or stated in the opposite manner, the point of this Christological assertion—as well as the hymn as a whole—is to declare that the entire narrative of the invisible God making God's own self known by means of the divine wisdom, together with the Genesis story of humankind being created in the divine image, can only be rightly understood when viewed in the light of the narrative of Jesus, who as the preeminent Christ is the *eikon* of God.

The book of Hebrews was written to encourage a group of Hebrew Christians who are being drawn away from the Christian faith by a Jewish-oriented rival.[66] The opening four verses of the epistle, which comprise one sentence in the Greek, sound the theme of the entire book, namely the superiority of Jesus Christ.

Having denoted Jesus as the one who has the rank of Son as is confirmed by his status as the divinely-appointed "heir of all things" (cf. Psa. 2:8) and by his role as the one through whom God created "the worlds" (v. 2 NRSV), the author fuses glory and image language (Heb. 1:3), even though no explicit reference to the *eikon theou* occurs in the text. Instead, by declaring that Jesus is the reflection of God's glory and the imprint of God's being, the verse expresses by illustration what it means to say that as the one who is "Son," Jesus Christ is the *imago dei*.[67] Jesus manifests who God is, but not by being a passive reflector of the divine reality, similar to a mirror that can only reflect the light issuing from another source. Rather, Jesus *is* this light. Or stating the point using another metaphor, he is the pattern according to whom those who are stamped with the divine image are conformed. He is the active impress of God, the agent through whom God engages in the work of imprinting the divine image wherever it is to be found in creation.

The high point toward which the author moves comes with the declaration of Jesus' historical work of making "purification for sins," for only when this had been accomplished, did he sit down "at the right hand of the Majesty on high" (v. 3). Rather than merely ascribing to Christ the role in creation the wisdom tradition had reserved for the divine wisdom, the introduction to Hebrews finds the wisdom of God displayed preeminently in the passion and death of the crucified Jesus on behalf of sinful humankind. In elevating the passion to the place at the center of the wisdom-story, the text echoes Paul's declaration that the proclamation of "Christ crucified" is the very wisdom of God (1 Cor. 1:23-24). The point of Heb. 1:1-3, therefore, is to declare that Jesus Christ, who as the Son is the visible manifestation of the divine reality, ultimately fulfills this role and therefore only comes to possess this accolade through his historical work in salvation history. In short, the point of this text— indeed the point of New Testament Christology in general—is that Jesus Christ fully reveals God, and thereby is the *imago dei* in fulfillment of the Genesis creation story, as he fully redeems humankind.

From Eschatological Hope to Ongoing Task: The Imago Dei *and the New Humanity*

Genesis 1:26-27 sets forth the idea that humankind is created in the image of God, but then leaves the task of defining the nature of the *imago dei* to the broader biblical narrative. According to the New Testament writers, the Genesis narrative points to Jesus, Israel's Messiah, who as the embodiment of the saving nature and the revelation of the glory of God is the image of God. The biblical narrative does not end here, however. Not only is Jesus the divine image, he is also the head of a new humanity destined to be formed according to that image, in fulfillment of God's intent for humankind from the beginning.

The image of God as eschatological goal. Two verses explicitly articulate this eschatological dimension of the *imago dei*. In the first, Rom. 8:29, Paul states the point in Christocentric language reminiscent of Gen. 1:26-27. According to the apostle, God's intention is that those who are in Christ participate in his destiny and thereby replicate his glorious image.

Despite the protracted theological battles Paul's use of the terms "foreknew" and "predestined" have generated, the apostle is not concerned to speculate about the mystery of personal faith, but to remind his readers that the only basis for an assurance that the divine purpose will be attained lies in God. God's set disposition toward those who participate in the life of the Spirit entails an unalterable decision guaranteeing that the divinely intended goal for them will be reached. Moreover, at the heart of God's eternal purpose is that this community of believers be conformed to Christ and thereby share in the *imago dei*.

Despite the attempts of some exegetes to see it as a reference to earthly existence,[68] the text bears an eschatological orientation. As Brendan Byrne helpfully notes, "Paul is spelling out here the *goal* of the divine *prothesis*—the end God has in view for us."[69] This conclusion is confirmed by the prefix *syn-* in the word *symmorphos*, which carries overtones of a central theme of Paul's theology, namely, the idea of being "in Christ."[70] In Romans 8:29, therefore, Paul declares that his readers will be caught up on the Christ event and become copies of God's Son.[71] Above all, however, the eschatological focus is evident in the crucial phrase, the "image of his Son" with its overtones of the Son-Christology found repeatedly in the pages of the New Testament. By declaring that they are destined for conformity to the *eikon tou huiou autou*, Paul is reminding his readers of God's purpose to imprint them with the very qualities of Christ, who as the image of God is the divine Son.[72]

The climax of the verse comes in the subordinate clause that follows, "that he might be the firstborn," which expresses the Christological intent of God's foreordination,[73] namely, the preeminence of Christ[74] among those who participate in the eschatological resurrection. The designation of these as Christ's *adelphoi* reveals the communal interest of the text. Here Paul is adding his voice to the chorus of New Testament writers who are convinced that Christ's preeminence among many *adelphoi* is nothing short of God's intent from the beginning (cf. John 17:24). This eschatological purpose is the goal that was already in view in the creation of humankind in the divine image. In this sense, Rom. 8:29 delineates the final exegesis of Gen. 1:26-27. In his risen glory, Jesus Christ now radiates the fullness of humanness that constitutes God's design for humankind from the beginning. Yet God's purpose has never been limited to this. God's goal is that as the Son, Jesus Christ be preeminent within a new humanity stamped with the divine image. Consequently, the humankind created in the divine image is none other than the new humanity conformed to the *imago Christi*, and the *telos* toward which the Old Testament creation narrative points is the eschatological community of glorified saints. In this manner, the narrative of the emergence of the new humanity provides the climax to the entire salvation-historical story and becomes the ultimate defining moment for the Genesis account of the creation of humankind in the *imago dei*.

But in what does conformity to Christ consist? This question leads beyond Rom. 8:29 to its "essential commentary,"[75] 1 Cor. 15:49. Here Paul connects the *imago Christi* with the resurrected new humanity by means of an Adam-Christ typology with its correlate last-Adam Christology. Earlier in the chapter (vv. 20-28), Paul sets forth an Adam-Christ typology to present Christ's resurrection as the guarantee of the eschatological resurrection. In so doing, he depicts the resurrection of believers, which marks the final victory over death, as the climactic scene in the salvation-historical drama, that centers on the dominion of Christ as the true human, in fulfillment of Psa. 8:6 and, by extension, of Gen. 1:26-27.[76]

Paul's second use of the Adam-Christ typology occurs in his discussion of the nature of the resurrection body that the new humanity will share by being "in Christ" (vv.35-49). Here an eschatologically orientated, Christologically determined anthropology[77] comes more explicitly to the fore. Paul sets forth Jesus' resurrected body as the paradigm for all who will bear his image. To delineate further what this resurrection body is, Paul introduces an antithesis between the *psychikon soma* and the *pneumatikon soma*, and then draws a contrast between Adam and Christ as the exemplars (and, in the case of Christ, the source) of these two differing kinds of body or as representations of these two corporate realities.[78] Involved here is a type of "midrashic" reflection on Gen. 2:7 in the light of the apostle's own experience of having seen the risen Jesus.[79] Paul's Christological reading of this Old Testament text yields the conclusion that the advent of the spiritual body was in view at the creation,[80] yet not as an aspect that was inherent within human nature from the beginning but as the eschatological destiny of the new humanity in Christ. Paul's Adam-Christ typology, therefore, indicates that the creation of Adam did not mark the fulfillment of God's intention for humankind as the *imago dei*. Instead, this divinely given destiny is eschatological. It comes only with the advent of the new humanity. Members of this new humanity participate in the *pneumakon soma* by means of their connection to the last Adam, Christ, who through his resurrection became a "life-giving spirit"[81] and thereby is not only the pattern of the resurrected body that they will one day share but also comprises the spiritual vitality who will bring about their glorious transformation.

Paul concludes the chapter by delineating the force of his entire Adam-Christ typology: the anthropological narrative moves from "Adam" to "Christ," from inherited participation in the "earthly" to anticipated participation in the "heavenly," and hence from "humanity" to "new humanity." In language that calls to mind the Genesis *imago* texts, the apostle declares that those who belong to the new humanity inaugurated by the last, heavenly Adam are as destined to be stamped by his glorious characteristics as they now find themselves stamped by the earthy characteristics of the first Adam. In this manner, Paul paints Christ as the true image of God imparting his spiritual (or supernatural) characteristics to his spiritual progeny, similar to Adam passing on his natural traits to his physical offspring.

The image of God as a present reality. The biblical narrative of the *imago dei* that climaxes with the glorified new humanity sharing in the divine image contains a present component as well. Members of the new humanity already share in the divine image through their participation "in Christ."

The idea that the *imago dei* is a present reality is explicitly stated in 2 Cor. 3:18, which comes as the climax to Paul's midrash on Exo. 34:29-35.[82] In this verse, Paul brings together the key elements found in the previous verses to provide a statement of his understanding of the essence of the Christian life as unity with Christ.[83] The entire text brims with exegetical difficulties. Yet perhaps the best interpretation sees in it a contrast between believers who now see the Lord's glory, albeit indirectly, and Israelites who in Moses's day could not look upon God's splendor[84] and who in Paul's day remained veiled.[85] Reading the text in the light of 2 Cor. 4:6 suggests that the apostle here asserts that believers see the reflected glory of God through Christ who is the image of God,[86] yet who is likewise the divine glory seen as in a mirror. As in 2 Cor. 4:6, Paul no doubt has in view here the historic person of Jesus as the one in whom the invisible God becomes visible.[87]

The central assertion of the verse is that participants in the new humanity are being transformed into that image. Paul does not simply equate the new humanity with the divine image, however, but declares that those who behold the divine glory are participants in a process of transformation into that image that is gradual and progressive.[88]

Margaret Thrall rightly notes that this "assimilation to Christ as the image of God produces a visibly Christ-like character, so that the divine image becomes visible in the believer's manner of life."[89] Moreover, this building of character occurs through the new narrative that is inaugurated at conversion and culminates at the eschatological resurrection. Yet Paul envisions no mere private beholding leading to an individualistic "me-and-Jesus" understanding of transformation. Rather, the metamorphosis he has in view involves the reformation of relationships and the creation of a new community of those who share together in the transforming presence of the Spirit. A. M. Ramsey rightly perceives the great sweep of salvation history evoked in this verse. In his estimation, Paul is declaring that in Christ humankind is allowed to see not only the radiance of God's glory but also the true human image into which Christ's people are now being transformed, and in virtue of this transformation into the new human "they are realizing the meaning of their original status as creatures in God's image."[90]

In Colossians and Ephesians, the apostolic author takes the matter a step further. Those who are destined to be the new humanity and therefore are already in the process of being transformed into the divine image carry the ethical responsibility to live out that reality in the present.

The first of these two texts, Col. 3:9-11, presents the indicative as the source of the imperative. Sandwiched between admonitions to "put off" a variety of inappropriate behaviors and character traits (Col. 3:5-9a) and to "put on" appropriate qualities and conduct (Col.

3:12-17) is a declaration that through conversion/baptism into Christ, the Colossians have put off the "old human" and have put on the "new." This declaration evidences an underlying Adam-Christ typology.[91] For Paul, being "in Adam" and being "in Christ" designate two orders of existence as well as the way of living that characterizes each. In this text, the apostle uses the imagery of changing garments to signify an exchange of identities. The old and new human designate two frames of reference from which participants in each realm gain their identity, and out of which, on the basis of which, or in keeping with which they readily conduct their lives.

Furthermore, the old and new human bring into view two distinct narratives. The former looks to the story of creation and fall, as well as the entire narrative of sinful humankind. The latter, in contrast, draws into focus the narrative of God's gracious saving actions on behalf of humankind, the center of which is the story of Jesus of Nazareth and the ongoing story of Christ's presence in the church through the Holy Spirit. In believers, these two narratives coalesce into a composite story, namely, the ongoing narrative of being transferred from the sin-story into the grace-story.

At the heart of the Colossians text is the assertion that the way of living that belongs to the realm in Christ is communal; it entails what is appropriate to life in the new community. As Markus Barth and Helmut Blanke explain, "The 'old self' is the Adam as representative of the old order . . . and the 'new self' is Christ as representative of the new, redeemed order of humanity. To put on Christ and to take off (the old) Adam means then to allow the redeemed humanity to become visible in the deeds of the community (cf. Gal 3:27b/29), whose representative is Christ."[92] The social nature involved in "putting on Christ" and the corporate character of the new humanity renewed after the divine image are evident in Paul's declaration that the new humanity not only does not emerge from the distinctions that separate humans into competing communities but that the new humanity has no place whatsoever for such peculiarities,[93] and this because "Christ is all and in all."

Furthermore, the new status inaugurated in conversion/baptism entails the continual renewal of the "new human,"[94] "according to the image of its creator" (Col. 10 NRSV). By introducing the allusion to Gen. 1:26 in this context, Paul is once again linking creation and redemption (as in Col. 1:15-20). Rather than a "first-Adam" anthropology, this phrase denotes a second-Adam, Christologically determined anthropology, for the *eikon* of the Creator of the new human is Christ. Moreover, the apostle is suggesting a Trinitarian conception of renewal: The Spirit renews believers,[95] who as those who have put on the new human are "in Christ," in accordance with the image of God made explicit in Christ.

Colossians 3:9-11 finds an echo in Eph. 4:17-24, which draws heavily from it.[96] Here the apostle reminds the Ephesians that through baptism they have been linked to Jesus Christ, so that the narrative of his life, death, and resurrection is of central significance for the forming of their new identity. Furthermore, their union with Jesus and his narrative is to give shape to the ongoing story of their lives. According to the author, this identity-forming Jesus-narrative consists in putting off the old life and putting on the new.[97]

According to the Ephesians text the imperative is bound up with the indicative. To this end, the author presents a series of three infinitives—"to put away," "to be renewed," and "to clothe." Taken together the two infinitives that sandwich the third portray the powerful imagery of changing garments,[98] so as to remind the readers that the indicative entailed in conversion/baptism implies that "the old life must be put away . . . and the new life, life in the body of Christ, must be put on."[99]

The *imago dei*, which is not explicitly mentioned anywhere in the text, comes to the fore in the final infinitive of the series, namely, the apostle's declaration that believers put on the "new human" (Eph. 4:24). In Eph. 2:15, the writer declares that Christ has created in himself "one new human" out of the formerly warring groups of Jew and Gentile. In Eph. 4:24, this corporate focus emerges again. Rather than referring to the new self in an individual sense, the term designates the new form of human life that results from redemption,[100] namely, "life patterned after God's"[101] or life in the imitation of God (cf. Eph. 5:1). This new realm is characterized by righteousness and holiness, because these qualities reflect the pattern of God's own character as revealed through the biblical narrative in its entirety.

The Application: Toward an Understanding of the *Imago Dei* in a Postmodern Context

Reading the biblical texts in the light of the developmental, eschatological, *telos*-oriented understanding of the *imago dei* that begins with Ireneaus and comes into its own in certain strands of modern theological anthropology leads back to the (loss of) self that characterizes the postmodern condition. Rather than providing the basis for an inward-focused, individually orientated self that in turn comprises the image of God, this reading unearths within the texts a social *imago*. This social *imago*, in turn, can come to voice in the postmodern context.

As the study of the biblical texts indicates, the phrase "image of God" is short-hand language for the biblical narrative viewed from one particular metaphorical perspective. The opening scene of this dramatic narrative recounts the creative act of God "in the beginning" that destines humankind to be the representation of the divine reality on earth. At the center of the entire drama of the divinely purposed destiny is Jesus whose appearance on the stage of the salvation-historical theater is anticipated by Act One. The narrative only comes to completion, however, in the third act, as God's intentions for humankind are realized in a community through whom the divine character, revealed in Jesus Christ, truly shines forth.

But why is this final act necessary? The answer emerges from another crucial recent theological development, the renewal of Trinitarian theology. Following a trajectory that begins with Hegel but has moved well beyond his speculative depiction of the self-actualization of the Absolute Spirit, modern theology has traded the outmoded and unhelpful idea of God as the single divine Subject and hence the transcendent Self for a more appropriate social conception that takes seriously the threeness within the one God, that is, the relationality of the three persons of the Trinity. Insofar as this emergent Trinitarianism elevates the *perichoretic* life of the three persons as comprising the one God, the renewal of Trinitarian theology entails a more profound understanding of God, namely, that the God of the biblical narrative is inherently relational and dynamic. The relational impulse has led, in turn, to a new ontology of communion that proponents find at work in a trajectory that existed alongside the Augustinian inward turn. John Zizioulas, to cite one important voice, declares that the Cappadocian fathers concluded that Being means communion and, by extension, that humans could only speak about God through the relational language of communion.[102]

According to this Trinitarian communal ontology, the three members of the Trinity are "person," precisely because they are persons-in-relationship; that is, they each derive their personhood from their reciprocal relations to the other two. The resulting Trinitarian ontology of personhood, which views being person as being person-in-relationship, offers a promising orientation point for the development of a postmodern understanding of human personhood and identity as well. The crucial link between the conception of the three Trinitarian persons as persons-in-relationship and human personhood lies in the *imago dei*. Stating the matter succinctly, the divine intent that humankind be the representation of the divine reality means that the goal of human existence is to be persons-in-relationship after the pattern of the perichoretic divine life that has been disclosed in Jesus Christ.

Zizioulas points out that a communal ontology is closely linked with "ecclesial being." The concept of ecclesial being undermines the idea that personal identity emerges as the product of an inward turn. Instead of finding its focus in a static, inward self, personhood is bound up with relationality. Moreover, the fulness of relationality lies ultimately in relationship to the triune God.

The one who creates this relational fulness is the Spirit, who places humans "in Christ" and thereby into relationship with the one whom Jesus called "Father" (John 14:16-23). In this manner, the Spirit effects human participation in the dynamic of the divine life.

Viewed from the human perspective, being "in Christ" entails participating in the narrative of Jesus, with its focus on the cross and the resurrection (cf. Rom. 6:1-14). It involves retelling one's own narrative in accordance with the plot of the Jesus-narrative and thereby speaking the biblical language of the "old" and the "new." The paradigmatic narrative in accordance with which those who are in Christ find their identity, however, is a shared story—a communal narrative. Consequently, being-in-relationship with the triune God not only inherently includes, but is even comprised by being-in-relationship with those who participate together in the Jesus-narrative and thereby are the ecclesial new humanity.

Forging a people-in-relationship is likewise the Spirit's doing. In creating the community of those united with Christ, the Spirit fashions in the present the foretaste of the new humanity. To this end, the Spirit engages in the work of transforming this ecclesial people-in-relationship so that they together reflect God's own character and thus shine as the *imago dei*. Understood rightly, John Fawcett's old hymn expresses well the essence of this communal participation through the Spirit:

> Blest be the tie that binds our hearts in Christian love;
> The fellowship of kindred minds is like to that above.[103]

As the hymn suggests, the indwelling Spirit shapes the fellowship of Christ's followers after the pattern of the love that pre-exists in the triune life. Stated from the theological perspective, the Spirit proleptically comprises the new humanity as the *imago dei* after the pattern of the *perichoretic* life of the triune God. In so doing, the Spirit constitutes continually the "self" of those who are in Christ and therefore are participants in Christ's ecclesial community. In comprising the eschatological new humanity after the pattern of Christ who is the divine image, the Spirit is in the process of constituting the "self" of all humankind in fulfillment of Gen. 1:26-27, and by extension the being of the entire cosmos. This Spirit-created, relational "self," whose identity and longevity emerges from its centeredness in Christ in whom all things find their interconnectedness, offers hope in the face of the loss of self articulated in Alanis Morissette's poignant song and experienced by sixteen-year-old Internet devotees such as Aminah McKinnie.

Endnotes

1.   For this report on the millennial generation, see Sharon Begley, "A World of Their Own," *Newsweek*, May 8, 2000, 54-55.

2.   E. Jonathan Lowe, "self," in the *Oxford Companion to Philosophy*, ed. Ted Honderich (New York: Oxford University Press, 1995), 817.

3.   See, for example, Charles Taylor, *Sources of the Self: The Making of the Modern Identity* (Cambridge,: Harvard University Press, 1989), 121. Christopher Kaiser as-

serts, "The inter-personal models used by the earlier fathers, which culminated in Basil's distinction of the divine hypostases, led Augustine to postulate internal relations within the godhead, but the complete dissociation of these eternal intra-Trinitarian relations from ordinary human relations forced him into a rather static concept of the deity, on the one hand, and an individualistic concept of humanity, on the other." Christopher B. Kaiser, *The Doctrine of God: An Historical Survey* (London: Marshall, Morgan and Scott, 1982), 81. Colin Gunton goes so far as to claim that the development of the individualistic concept of person which emerged out of Augustine's approach "has had . . . disastrous effects on modern Western thought." Colin E. Gunton, *The Promise of Trinitarian Theology* (Edinburgh: T. & T. Clark, 1991), 95.

4. Saint Augustine, Bishop of Hippo, *The Happy Life* 2.11, in the Fathers of the Church Series, V. 5, trans. Ludwig Schopp (New York: Cima Publishing Company, 1948), 5:58-59.

5. Taylor, *Sources of the Self*, 130.

6. Sandra Lee Dixon, *Augustine: The Scattered and Gathered Self* (St. Louis: Chalice Press, 1999), 37.

7. Dixon, *Augustine*, 199.

8. Giorgio de Santillana, *The Age of Adventure: The Renaissance Philosophers* (New York: The New American Library, 1956), 46.

9. John Locke, *An Essay Concerning Human Understanding* (1690), ed. P.H. Nidditeh (Oxford: Clarendon Press, 1975). II.27.17 (p.341).

10. Taylor, *Sources of the Self*, 49.

11. Robert C. Solomon, *Continental Philosophy since 1750: The Rise and Fall of the Self* (Oxford: Oxford University Press, 1988), 40.

12. Taylor, *Sources of the Self*, 231.

13. For this view of the Enlightenment, see Louis K. Dupré, *Transcendent Selfhood: The Loss and Rediscovery of the Inner Life* (New York: Seabury Press, 1976), 4.

14. Robert N. Bellah, et. al., *Habits of the Heart: Individualism and Commitment in American Life*, Perennial Library edition (New York: Harper & Row, 1986), 127.

15. Abraham H. Maslow, *Toward a Psychology of Being*, second edition (New York: D. Van Norstrand, 1968), vi-vii.

16. Maslow, *Toward a Psychology of Being*, 189-90.

17. Abraham H. Maslow, *Motivation and Personality* (New York: Harper and Row, 1954), 80-92.

18. Philip Rieff, *The Triumph of the Therapeutic: Uses of Faith after Freud* (New York: Harper & Row, 1966), 5.

19. See, for example, Rollo May, *Man's Search for Himself*, Delta book edition (New York: Norton,1953; Reprint edition New York: Dell, 1973), 160.

20. Solomon, *Continental Philosophy since 1750*, 1.

21. For a similar summary, see Solomon, *Continental Philosophy since 1750*, 75.

22. For this designation, see Jacques Le Rider, *Modernity and Crises of Identity: Culture and Society in Fin-de-Siècle Vienna*, trans. Rosemary Morris (New York: Continuum, 1993), 11. See also, Taylor, *Sources of the Self*, 456-66.

23. Carl E. Schorske, *Fin-de-Siècle Vienna: Politics and Culture*, Vintage Books edition (New York: Vintage Books, 1981), 22.

24. Le Rider, *Modernity and the Crises of Identity*, 43.

25. Irving Howe, "The Self in Literature," in *Constructions of the Self*, ed. George Levine (New Brunswick: Rudgers University Press, 1992), 264.

26. On this, see Émile Benveniste, *Problems in General Linguistics*, trans. Mary Elizabeth Meek (Coral Gables: University of Miami Press, 1971), 5, 8. Because language is "a system that has its own arrangement," Saussure excludes "external linguistics." Ferdinand de Saussure, *Course in General Linguistics*, eds. Charles Bally and Albert Riedlinger, trans. Wade Baskin (New York: Philosophical Library, 1959), 20-23.

27. David Couzens Hoy, "Foucault: Modern or Postmodern?" in *After Foucault: Humanist Knowledge, Postmodern Challenges*, ed. Jonathan Arac (New Brunswick: Rutgers University Press, 1988), 27.

28. Edward W. Said, "Michel Foucault, 1926-1984," reprinted in *After Foucault*, 10.

29. Louis A. Sass, "The Self and Its Vicissitudes in the Psychoanalytic Avant-Garde," reprinted in *Constructions of the Self*, ed. George Levine (New Brunswick: Rudgers University Press, 1992), 17.

30. Rom Harre, *Personal Being: A Theory for Individual Psychology* (Cambridge: Harvard University Press, 1984), 20.

31. Harre, *Personal Being*, 20.

32. See, for example, Alasdair C. MacIntyre, *After Virtue:A Study in Moral Theory*, second edition (Notre Dame: University of Notre Dame Press, 1984), 221.

33. Jean-François Lyotard, *The Postmodern Condition: A Report on Knowledge*, trans. Geoff Bennington and Brian Massumi (Minneapolis: University of Minnesota Press, 1984), 15.

34. Taylor, *Sources of the Self*, 36.

35. See, for example, George Herbert Mead, *Mind, Self, and Society: From the Standpoint of a Social Behavorist*, ed. Charles W. Morris (Chicago: University of Chicago Press, 1934, 1974), 138-58.

36. Michel Foucault, *The Order of Things: An Archaeology of the Human Sciences*, no translator named (New York: Pantheon Books, 1971), xviii.

37. Agnes Heller, "Death of the Subject?" reprinted in *Constructions of the Self*, 281.

38. Fredric Jameson, *Postmodernism, or the Cultural Logic of Late Capitalism* (Durham: Duke University Press, 1995), 90.

39. Johann G. Roten, "The Marian Counterpoint of Postmodern Spirituality," in *Divine Representations: Postmodernism and Spirituality*, ed. Ann W. Astell (New York: Paulist Press, 1994), 113-14.

40. Roten, "The Marian Counterpoint of Postmodern Spirituality," 114.

41. MacIntyre, *After Virtue*, 203-204

42. For an example of this taxonomy, see Philip J. Hefner, "The Creation," in *Christian Dogmatics*, ed. Carl E. Braaten and Robert W. Jenson, 2 vols. (Philadelphia: Fortress Press, 1984), 1:331.

43. Paul Ramsey, *Basic Christian Ethics* (New York: Scribner, 1950), 254.

44. Where a third option is mentioned, it is often not the goal-oriented view noted here. For example, Erickson offers an alternative three-item taxonomy consisting of the substantive, relational, and functional views. Millard J. Erickson, *Christian Theology*, 3 vols. (Grand Rapids: Baker Book House, 1984), 2:498-510. Two-item taxonomies either subsume Erickson's third category (which focuses on dominion) under the substantive view or see it as an outworking or consequence of the *imago dei* (e.g., François Turretin, *Institutio Theologiae Elencticae* (Geneva, 1679-1685) translated as *Institutes of Elenctic Theology*, trans. George Musgrave Giger, ed. James T. Dennison, Jr., 3 vols. [Phillipsburg, NJ: P & R Publishing, 1992], 1:466). Moreover,

as Charles Hodge points out, the post-Reformation theologians who elevated the idea of dominion nevertheless viewed this dominion as being "founded on man's rational nature." Charles Hodge, *Systematic Theology*, 3 vols. (New York: Scribner, 1872), 2:97.

45. Wolfhart Pannenberg, *Anthropology in Theological Perspective*, trans. Matthew J. O'Connell (Philadelphia: Westminster Press, 1985), 50.

46. Johann Gottfried Herder, *Outlines of a Philosophy of the History of Man* 4.6-7, trans. T. Churchill (New York: Bergman Publishers, 1800), 9.1. For this translation, see Johann Gottfried Herder, *Against Pure Reason: Writings on Religion, Language, and History*, trans. Marcia Bunge (Minneapolis: Fortress Press, 1993), 53. The quotation is on page 229 of the Churchill translation.

47. Pannenberg, *Anthropology in Theological Perspective*, 501.

48. Hefner, "Creation," 330.

49. Claus Westermann, *Genesis: An Introduction*, trans. John J. Scullion (Minneapolis: Fortress Press, 1992), 111.

50. Westermann, however, expresses some caution, suggesting that although the royal ideology lies behind Psalm 8, it may not be the sole explanation for Gen. 1:26. Westermann, *Genesis: An Introduction*, 38.

51. Phyllis A. Bird, "'Male and Female He Created Them': Genesis 1:27b in the Context of the Priestly Account of Creation," *Harvard Theological Review* 74 (1981): 143, 143 nt 36.

52. For this characterization, see Gordon J. Wenham, *Genesis 1-15*, Word Biblical Commentary, volume one, ed. David A. Hubbard, Glenn W. Barker, and John D. W. Watts (Waco: Word Books, 1987), 31-32.

53. Karl-Heinz Bernhardt, *Gott und Bild: ein Beitrag zur Begründung und Deutung des Bilderverbotes im Alten Testament* (Berlin: Evangelische Verlagsanstalt, 1956), 17.

54. Wenham, *Genesis 1-15*, 30-31.

55. D. J. A. Clines, "The Image of God in Man," *Tyndale Bulletin* 19 (1968), 93.

56. Clines, "Image of God in Man," 87-88.

57. Bird, "Male and Female He Created Them," 159.

58. Joseph B. Lightfoot, *Saint Paul's Epistles to the Colossians and to Philemon*, revised ed. (1879; Grand Rapids: Zondervan, n.d.), 145.

59. Charles K. Barrett, *The Second Epistle to the Corinthians*, in Harper's New Testament Commentaries, ed. Henry Chadwick (New York: Harper & Row, 1973), 135.

60. For an explication and defense of this connection, see Herman N. Ridderbos *Paul: An Outline of His Theology*, trans. John Richard de Witt (Grand Rapids: W.B. Eerdmans Publishing Company, 1975), 70-76.

61. Ezra P. Gould, "*Commentary on the Epistles to the Corinthians*," in *An American Commentary on the New Testament Series*, ed. Alvah Hovey (Philadelphia: American Baptist Publication Society, 1887), 5:170.

62. The use of "Paul" in this context is not intended to take a position on the contentious issue of the authorship of Colossians. For a helpful discussion of this matter, see James D. G. Dunn, *The Epistles to the Colossians and to Philemon: A Commentary on the Greek Text*, in the New International Greek Testament Commentary, (Grand Rapids: William B. Eerdmans Publishing, 1996), 35-39.

63. Patzia declares, "Scholars are virtually unanimous in their opinion that verses 15-20 constitute a hymn. Arthur G. Patzia, *Colossians, Philemon, Ephesians*, in the

Good News Commentary, ed. W. Ward Gasque (San Francisco: Harper & Row, 1984), 13. For a citation of the relevant critical literature, see Dunn, *Colossians and Philemon*, 83.

64. For a division of the hymn into three strophes, see Patzia, *Colossians, Philemon, Ephesians*, 13-14.

65. Dunn, *Colossians and Philemon*, 97.

66. For a similar perspective, see Thomas Hewitt, "The Epistle to the Hebrews: An Introduction and Commentary," in the *Tyndale New Testament Commentaries*, V. 15, ed. R. V. G. Tasker (Grand Rapids: Eerdmans, 1960), 39-41.

67. For a somewhat similar judgment, see Frederick F. Bruce, *The Epistle to the Hebrews: The English Text with Introduction, Exposition, and Notes*, in the New International Commentary on the New Testament, (Grand Rapids: W.B. Eerdmans Publishing Company, 1964), 6.

68. Ernst Käsemann, *Commentary on Romans*, trans. Geoffrey W. Bromiley (Grand Rapids: Eerdmans, 1980), 244.

69. Brendan Byrne, *Romans*, *Sacra Pagina* Series, vol. 6, ed. Daniel J. Harrington (Collegeville: Liturgical Press, 1996), 273.

70. Douglas J. Moo, *The Epistle to the Romans*, in the New International Commentary on the New Testament Series, (Grand Rapids: W.B. Eerdmans Publishing Company, 1996), 534.

71. Walter Grundmann, "Sun-Meta ," in the *Theological Dictionary of the New Testament*, trans. Geoffrey W. Bromiley, ed. Gerhard Kittel and Gerhard Friedrich (Grand Rapids: W.B. Eerdmans, 1971), 7:788.

72. Moo, *Romans*, 534, n. 151.

73. Byrne, *Romans*, 268.

74. John Murray, "The Epistle to the Romans: The English Text with Introduction, Exposition, and Notes," in the *New International Commentary on the New Testament Series*, two volumes (Grand Rapids: Eerdmans, 1959-1965), 1:319.

75. Byrne, *Romans*, 268.

76. For a statement of this widely acknowledged theme, see Nicholas T. Wright, *The Climax of the Covenant: Christ and the Law in Pauline Theology*, paperback edition (Minneapolis: Fortress, 1993), 29.

77. For the suggestion that anthropology is in view here, see Robin Scroggs, *The Last Adam: A Study in Pauline Anthropology* (Philadelphia: Fortress Press, 1966), 87. See also Wright, *Climax of the Covenant*, 30.

78. Bernardin Schneider, "The Corporate Meaning and Background of 1 Cor 15,45b— 'O Eschatols Adam Eis Pneuma Zoiopoioun," *Catholic Biblical Quarterly* 29 (1967): 456.

79. John S. Ruef, *Paul's First Letter to Corinth*, in the *Westminster Pelican Commentaries* (Philadelphia: Westminster Press, 1977), 174; Gordon D. Fee, *The First Epistle to the Corinthians*, in the *New International Commentary on the New Testament Series*, (Grand Rapids: W.B. Eerdmans Publishing Company, 1987), 788. Some recent commentators argue that the Damascus road experience shaped Paul's entire Christology, which was fundamentally an image-Christology. Hence, Seyoon Kim, *The Origin of Paul's Gospel* (Grand Rapids: W.B. Eerdmans Publishing Company, 1982), 260-68.

80. Geerhardus Vos, *The Pauline Eschatology* (Grand Rapids: W.B. Eerdmans Publishing Company, 1972), 169 n. 19.

81. Hans Conzelmann, *1 Corinthians: A Commentary on the First Epistle to the Corinthians*, trans. James W. Leitch et al. (Philadelphia: Fortress Press, 1975), 286-87; Fee, 789.

82. For a succinct summary of the scholarly discussion of this interpretation, see Paul W. Barnett, *The Second Epistle to the Corinthians*, the *New International Commentary on the New Testament Series*, (Grand Rapids: W.B. Eerdmans Publishing, 1997), 178 nt 3.

83. Jan Lambrecht, "Transformation in 2 Cor 3,18," *Biblica* 64 (1983): 254.

84. Victor Paul Furnish, *II Corinthians*, V. 32a of the *Anchor Bible*, (Garden City: Doubleday, 1984), 214.

85. Jacob Kremer, "*katoptrizomai*," in the *Exegetical Dictionary of the New Testament*, ed. Horst Balz and Gerhard Schneider, three volumes (Grand Rapids: W.B. Eerdmans Publishing, 1990), 2:275.

86. For a similar proposal, see Margaret E. Thrall, *A Critical and Exegetical Commentary on the Second Epistle to the Corinthians*, the International Critical Commentary on the Holy Scriptures of the Old and New Testaments, V. 2 (Edinburgh: T. & T. Clark, 1996), 2:284.

87. Charles K. Barrett, *A Commentary on the Second Epistle to the Corinthians*, Harper's New Testament Commentaries, ed. Henry Chadwick (New York: Harper & Row, 1973), 125.

88. Richard C. H. Lenski, *The Interpretation of St. Paul's First and Second Epistle to the Corinthians* (Columbus: Wartburg Press, 1937), 950; James Reid, "Exposition of II Corinthians," in the *Interpreter's Bible*, ed. George Arthur Buttrick, et al., twelve volumes (Nashville: Abingdon Cokesbury Press, 1953), 314.

89. Thrall, *II Corinthians*, 2:285.

90. Michael Ramsey, *The Glory of God and the Transfiguration of Christ* (London: Longmans, Green, and Co., 1949), 151.

91. See, for example, Charles F. D. Moule, *The Epistles of Paul the Apostle to the Colossians and to Philemon: An Introduction and Commentary*, the *Cambridge Greek Testament Commentary*, ed. C. F. D. Moule (Cambridge: Cambridge University Press, 1957), 119.

92. Markus Barth and Helmut Blanke, *Colossians: A New Translation with Introduction and Commentary*, vol. 62 of the *Anchor Bible*, trans. Astrid B. Beck, ed. William Foxwell Albright and David Noel Freedman (New York: Doubleday, 1994), 412.

93. Dunn, *Colossians and Philemon*, 223.

94. Dunn, *Colossians and Philemon*, 221.

95. Gordon D. Fee, *God's Empowering Presence: The Holy Spirit in the Letters of Paul* (Peabody, MA: Hendrickson Publishers, 1994), 647.

96. For a discussion, see Andrew T. Lincoln, *Ephesians*, V. 42 of the *Word Biblical Commentary*, (Dallas: Word Books, 1990), 272-74.

97. For a similar idea, see Ralph P. Martin, *Ephesians, Colossians, and Philemon*, *Interpretation: A Bible Commentary for Teaching and Preaching*, (Atlanta: John Knox Press, 1991), 59.

98. Markus Barth, *Ephesians*, Anchor Bible vol. 34A, two volumes (Garden City: Doubleday, 1974), 2:541.

99. Lewis R. Donelson, *Colossians, Ephesians, First and Second Timothy, and Titus*, *The Westminster Bible Companion*, (Louisville: Westminster John Knox Press, 1996), 90.

100. S. D. F. Salmond, "The Epistle of Paul to the Ephesians," in the *Expositor's Greek Testament*, ed. W. Robertson Nicoll, 5 vols. (Grand Rapids: W.B. Eerdmans Publishing, 1961), 3:344.

101. Lincoln, *Ephesians*, 287.

102. John D. Zizioulas, *Being as Communion: Studies in Personhood and the Church*, Contemporary Greek Theologians No. 4 (Crestwood: St. Vladimir's Seminary Press, 1985), 16-17.

103. John Fawcett, "Blest Be the Tie that Binds," v.1 (1782).

Introducing the
New Testament Theologically

Carl R. Holladay
CANDLER SCHOOL OF THEOLOGY OF EMORY UNIVERSITY
ATLANTA, GEORGIA

At a time of renewed interest in theology among biblical scholars and greater awareness of the pedagogical challenges fac-
ing those who teach introductory courses on biblical writings, there
is an urgent need to reexamine some of the basic assumptions of
the discipline of New Testament (NT) introduction. One side of the
challenge is the need to be attentive to the explicitly theological
dimensions of the NT writings, and, in doing so, to be responsive to
those interpreters, biblical scholars and theologians, who have continuously recognized the deeply profound theological implications
of biblical study. The other side of the challenge is to do so in a way
that is both intelligible and meaningful to those who are encounter-
ing these writings at some elementary level, especially those persons preparing for Christian ministry and those already engaged in
various forms of Christian ministry. Yet another challenge in attempting to write a theological introduction to the New Testament
is the inherent risk involved in blending into a single work perspectives and insights normally assigned to two well-established, quite
distinct genres: NT introduction, a scholarly discipline typically
preoccupied with historical and literary questions, and NT theology whose aim is either to present the theology contained in the NT
or a theological synthesis based on the New Testament.[1]

New Testament Introduction: A Review

To call for a rethinking of what it means to introduce the NT
theologically is not to ignore the explicit theological agendas that
have fueled the writing of NT introductions, whether one traces the
origin of the discipline to Richard Simon, whom Theodor Zahn called
the "founder of the science of New Testament introduction,"[2] or much
earlier to the second-century controversy sparked by Marcion, whose

radical opposition to the God of the Jewish Scriptures prompted him to devise a NT canon that suited his own theological outlook, and the subsequent efforts of those who, like Irenaeus, Origen, and Eusebius, assiduously investigated the Scriptures while clearly understanding the implications of their critical work for ecclesial thought and practice.[3] Even as the literary genre of NT introduction began to acquire its familiar form in the eighteenth century with J. D. Michaelis's *Introduction to the Divine Scriptures of the New Covenant*, first published in 1750 but whose fourth edition in 1788 treated comprehensively the individual writings, thereby "(inaugurating) the science of New Testament introduction,"[4] the theological implications of investigating the textual tradition of NT writings, their literary features, as well as the circumstances of their composition were all too clear. They were certainly not lost on J. S. Semler who in his *Treatise on the Free Investigation of the Canon* (1771-75) introduced the distinction between the Word of God and Holy Scripture as a way of explaining why certain writings could be included in the canon even though they represented a benighted outlook. For Semler, whether a particular writing in Scripture genuinely revealed the Word of God had to be decided on an individual basis, which meant, of course, that historical investigation of such questions as authorship helped determine whether a writing was actually an apostolic, inspired writing and thus authoritative for Christian belief and practice.[5]

That much was at stake theologically in these pioneering efforts of Simon, Michaelis, and Semler can be seen in the massive resistance their work encountered not only by church officials but by other biblical scholars, such as Zahn, who felt compelled to write NT introductions countering their radical claims.[6] By subjecting the canonical writings to rigorous historical and literary investigation, "the science of New Testament studies," W. G. Kümmel contends, "from its very beginning was brought up against a problem that it did not at first recognize, viz., how the pressing and unavoidable historical task was to be reconciled with the theological object of that task, namely, the New Testament."[7] In Helmut Köster's view, the discipline of NT introduction, as it developed in the late nineteenth and twentieth centuries, experienced a failure of nerve in responding to the dilemma noted by Kümmel. On the one hand, by its consistent failure to link historical investigation with an investigation of theological issues raised by the NT writings, or, more precisely, to use theological analysis in the service of historical reconstruction, as F. C. Baur had done in an exemplary fashion, NT introduction, Köster argues, tended to become an ancillary discipline preoccupied with archival interests. In a word, it ceased to be driven by theological interests. By its disclaimers and increasingly narrow focus, it insured its growing irrelevance to the larger theological enterprise. Apart from its escape into "theological innocence,"[8] the discipline of NT introduction also erred on the side of history, exhibiting a staunch unwillingness to take into account fully the sea change in our understanding of the complex, dynamic set of religious movements and impulses that were in play in the Mediterranean world of the first century. Rather than seeing early Christianity as a vital part of the stream of Mediterranean religions, as a movement that itself introduced revolutionary and revitalizing forces into the larger culture in ways that both challenged the larger culture even while seriously engaging and being radically shaped by it, NT introductions tended to work with conventional categories, such as Jewish and Graeco-Roman "backgrounds," and treated the NT writings, and thus the Christian beliefs and practices reflected in those writings, in isolation from their surrounding culture. Concluding his review of the origin and development of the discipline of NT introduction, Köster laments:

> Thus, New Testament "Introduction," having preserved its purity and austerity as a discipline, among liberals and conservatives alike, in spite of its great erudition has never managed to become an enterprise which is central for the vital interests of religious, theological and historical understanding. At best, it has been useful as an ancillary discipline, helping to secure genuine source-materials for scholars who wanted to base their discussions on reliable information; or aiding theologians who wanted to affirm the authenticity of canonical writings on which they based their doctrines and dogmas.[9]

We should take seriously Köster's call for conceiving NT introduction in a manner that is thoroughly sensitive to the theological issues raised by the NT writings while at the same time correlating our analysis and assessment of those issues with informed, imaginative historical reconstruction and interpretation of early Christianity. Following in the tradition of F. C. Baur, Köster rightly insists on a thoroughgoing theological assessment of the NT writings, not only identifying their theological slant (*Tendenz*) but also evaluating critically their theological claims, and doing so in order to develop a comprehensive picture of the complexities of early Christian belief and practice. Nor is Köster interested in making NT introduction a purely descriptive enterprise. Instead he insists that the fruits of such constructive work have far-reaching implications for contemporary Christian belief and practice, and by extension for theologians who seek to define and interpret Christian faith for a modern audience. "New Testament Introduction," he argues, "as a theological discipline should not be afraid to disturb the complacent religious and cultural assumptions of the world in which Christians live and of its inherited prejudices."[10] As a discipline, in other words, NT introduction has a prophetic, critical function. The results of critical, constructive work in this field, as it does in other sub-disciplines of NT study, should have some discernible effect on what Christians believe, preach, teach, and practice.

Köster's strategy for accomplishing what is clearly an admirable goal is fully in keeping with Baur's tradition of comprehensive historical reconstruction. For Köster, the essential task of NT introduction is "the reconstruction of the history of the origins of early Christian literature . . . a comprehensive task that must include all relevant writings of the period."[11] For all the historical work that must be done, this reconstruction, he insists, must be thoroughly theological: "(it) must also include an engagement of the theological perspectives, a critical discussion of the theological issues which determined the origin and tradition of such literature."[12] As he indicates in the preface to the second volume of his monumental *Introduction to the New Testament*, this takes "the form of a history of early Christianity in its contemporary setting."[13] "My primary concern," he writes, "is to present the history of the early Christian churches, since . . . the student of the New Testament must learn from the outset to understand the writings of the earliest period within their proper historical context."[14]

Even critics of Köster's NT introduction acknowledge the massive achievement represented by his richly textured and finely nuanced synthesis, yet it must be recognized for what it is: a history of early Christianity until around 200 CE. Admittedly, this is one strategy for getting at theological issues raised by NT writings, but it is by no means the only one. As early as 1964 Willi Marxsen, whose pioneering work as a redaction critic had given him special appreciation for NT writers as theological interpreters, asked specifically what was entailed in a theological approach to the NT. In Marxsen's view, whether one's approach to the NT was genuinely theological depended on what one saw as its essential subject matter. If the NT's "subject matter (is) theologically defined—i.e., the 'Word of God' or the 'Canon'—then the historical question never catches sight of the real theological element at all."[15] Yet if the NT writings reflect early Christian belief, or as Baur put it, are the records of early Christian dogma, "they are of course 'theological' documents" in the sense that they are "actualizations of the unique revelation that preceded them."[16] Preferring to think of the NT writings as representing different theological traditions within early Christianity, Marxsen sees the disciplines of NT introduction and NT theology as inseparable. Whereas "(NT) Introduction is primarily concerned with the *material* in which the authors have embedded the message, . . . (NT) theology unfolds the *message* by interpreting the material. Introduction is therefore 'the other aspect of theology'— and vice versa."[17]

Although not billed as a theological introduction to the NT, Luke Johnson's *The Writings of the New Testament*, first published in 1986 and published in a revised, expanded form in 1999, charted new territory.[18] Drawing on historical, sociological, and anthropological approaches, Johnson especially focused on the religious dimensions of the NT writings, thereby gaining access to their theological claims as well. Quite emphatically eschewing the "history of early Christianity model," or even a construal of the NT writings that is dominated or ordered by the historical principle, Johnson opted for an "experience-reflection" model that utilized the sociological construct "symbolic world" as both an analytic tool and organizing device for interpreting and presenting the NT writings. What commends this book, among other things, is its comprehensive attention to the historical, social, and religious worlds on which early Christianity drew in constructing its own symbolic universe, as well as its close, sympathetic attention to the literary dimensions of the NT writings.

Reflecting a sophisticated understanding of the complexities through which early Christian belief and practice were born and shaped, Johnson's introduction moved the discipline well beyond its traditional conceptual boundaries.

On a much smaller scale, Eduard Schweizer's *A Theological Introduction to the New Testament*, first published in German in 1989 and translated into English in 1991, departed from the traditional comprehensive format of earlier NT introductions. Like Marxsen, Schweizer saw his work as drawing on, and in one sense combining, the two genres of NT introduction and NT theology:

> . . . the following treatment differs from the usual introduction in that the historical issues serve only as a foundation for perceiving as well as possible the theologically important assertions of the New Testament Scriptures. It differs from the usual theology of the New Testament in that it is not oriented toward concepts, such as sin and grace, but toward individual writings. It is thus also more definitely the presentation of a historical process and to that extent a much more modest undertaking.[19]

Marxsen, Johnson, and Schweizer are by no means the only examples of NT introductions that have sought over the last three decades to move the discipline in a decidedly theological direction. They are mentioned here primarily as alternative approaches to Köster's "history of early Christianity" model, as well as to illustrate the way different scholars have sought to conceive the discipline of NT introduction as an essentially theological enterprise. They also pose in different ways a challenge to more decidedly historical conceptions of the discipline, represented, for example, by Kümmel, who insisted that "the science of (NT) introduction is a strictly historical discipline which, by illuminating the historical circumstances of the origin of individual writings, provides for exegesis the necessary presuppositions for understanding the writings in their historical uniqueness."[20] More recently, this essentially historical conception of the enterprise has been embodied in Bart Ehrman's *The New Testament: A Historical Introduction to the Early Christian Writings*, a work specifically dealing with "questions that pertain to the history of early Christianity and to the early Christian writings both as they reflect that history and as they helped to shape it."[21] But unlike Köster who sees his historical reconstruction as inextricably tied to theological analysis, Ehrman sees himself as an historian dealing "with past events that are matters of the public record," and thus adopting an approach that is "strictly historical, trying to understand the writings of the early Christians from the standpoint of the professional historian who uses whatever evidence happens to survive in order to reconstruct what happened in the past."[22]

Issues

Opting for a theological approach to NT introduction stands within a long, well-established tradition, and yet it clearly represents one among several options. If the history of the discipline of NT introduction teaches anything, it is that there is no single conception of the task, but there are some recurring, fundamental issues that anyone attempting to write a NT introduction must face. The following may be mentioned:

1. Scope

At the conclusion of his 1982 comprehensive review of the current state of the discipline of NT introduction, Kümmel identified the fundamental methodological problem as follows: Should NT introduction focus exclusively on the twenty-seven canonical NT writings or should it treat other relevant Christian literature?[23] While the latter is certainly a commendable goal, especially if one is seeking to treat the origin and history of early Christianity, is it a requirement? Calling for the NT writings to be treated alongside other early Christian, non-canonical writings certainly broadens the scope for comparison, thereby enabling readers to see things about the NT writings that would not otherwise be visible. However, treating NT writings as "equals" among other Christian writings can easily mask the *historical reality* that these twenty-seven writings emerged as canonical for a complex set of reasons and were consequently regarded by the church as authoritative in ways that their counterparts were not. Furthermore, deciding to eliminate the distinction between canonical and non-canonical writings is by no means a theologically neutral decision. It is rather a function of competing views of the church and ecclesiastical authority and the corresponding role Scripture plays within each. No one saw this better than W. Wrede who insisted that restricting oneself to the twenty-seven canonical writings meant placing oneself "under the authority of the bishops and theologians of those centuries."[24] "Anyone," he wrote, "who does not recognize their authority in other matters—and no Protestant theologian does—is being consistent if he questions it here, too."[25]

With such compelling claims to broaden the scope of NT introduction to include all early Christian writings until around 200 CE, scholars found it necessary to justify limiting their investigations to the twenty-seven canonical writings. For Adolf Jülicher, this was justified because the twenty-seven canonical writings had exercised greater historical effect (*Wirkungsgeschichte*).[26] In his review of Jülicher's introduction, Wrede acknowledged the "practical necessity" of such limitation.[27] H. J. Holtzmann, by contrast, insisted that such limitation was justified by the canonical status of the NT writings which alone could give internal coherence to a NT introduction.[28] In a similar vein, Kümmel insisted that because of their inclusion in "the canon demarcated by the early church, the NT writings possess a special character which has been recognized in faith by Christians."[29] Giving even more precision to the ecclesial argument, Marxsen proposed that the NT writings "as actualizations of the unique revelation that preceded them"[30] have "at least implicitly a special theological quality,"[31] and one can concentrate on them since they are the "earliest writings . . . those that stand nearest in time to the once-for-allness of revelation."[32]

Several things are clear from these arguments for limiting the scope of NT introduction. First, the criterion of apostolicity, i.e., composition by an apostle or someone directly linked to the apostolic circle, which once figured prominently in demarcating these writings as uniquely normative, no longer carries the same weight. Second, the recognition that the other two criteria for canonicity—orthodoxy and universality—have a different valence. If, as Marxsen argues, the NT writings are "actualizations of the unique revelation that preceded them" and in fact most faithfully represent the commonly shared faith of the first Christians, even with all their variety they emerge as the most compelling witnesses to early Christian faith. As Köster himself says of Irenaeus, Origen, and Eusebius, their primary question was: "which writings were used by the true believers from the beginning and have thus demonstrated their *theological* power as sources which sustained the life of the churches?"[33] In this case, orthodoxy means not so much formal adherence to early creedal confessions, at least not in an artificial sense, but fidelity to and consonance with what was widely believed, taught, and practiced by early Christians. While universality may have meant widespread acceptance and actual usage in the major geographical centers of early Christianity, it can come to have another dimension: which writings exercised *perennial* influence both inside and outside the church? Seen this way, the criterion of "effective influence" has both a practical and theological component. To ask which writings have actually figured most prominently in shaping later Christian thought and practice is also to ask about ecclesial discernment. Which writings has the universal church, under the influence of the Spirit, found to be theologically cogent? These several considerations are aptly summarized by Udo Schnelle:

> Even though in principle the academic discipline "Introduction to the New Testament" reserves the right to extend its investigation beyond the canonical boundaries, it still makes sense . . . to limit its specific subject matter to the twenty-seven books of the canon, both on pragmatic grounds and due to the influence that the concept of the canon has had in history. In the church, a normative status is attributed only to these twenty-seven books, and in the broad spectrum of theology, only they play a significant role. The concept of canon determines the contemporary use of early Christian literature.[34]

2. Arrangement

Closely connected with the question "Which writings?" is the related question "What order?" At its core, the decision is a simple choice between what might be called the canonical principle and the historical principle. It is not simply a decision whether the scope is limited to the twenty-seven writings or to the wider circle of early Christian writings. Even if one decides to limit the investigation to the twenty-seven canonical writings, one must decide whether to treat them more or less, in their canonical order, or to rearrange them according to some perceived scheme of chronological development. Kümmel opts for the former, treating first the narrative books (the Synoptic Gospels and Acts in one section, the Gospel of John in another); secondly, the letters, first the letters of Paul, then Hebrews and the Catholic letters; and thirdly, the Apocalypse. Marxsen illustrates the latter: first, the Pauline letters; second, the Synoptic Gospels and Acts; third, the pseudo-Pauline letters, including Hebrews; fourth, the "Church Epistles"; fifth, the Johannine writings, including the Gospel of John and the three Johannine epistles; and sixth, the Apocalypse.

The latter scheme, or the many variations thereof, can be defended on the grounds that a historical, i.e., chronological ordering principle, is more sensible. Thus, Schnelle writes, "The historical orientation of 'Introduction to the New Testament' suggests a *structure* that begins with the undisputed Pauline letters as the oldest writings of the New Testament."[35] Several things make this a problematic decision, most notably the notorious difficulty of reliably dating the NT writings. Granted, Paul's writings are probably the earliest (though possibly James is as early), but beyond that, how confidently can we date individual writings? We are on the firmest ground with 1 Thessalonians, 1 & 2 Corinthians, Romans and Galatians, but from there on the ground gets shakier. Furthermore, what appear to be neutral "historical" decisions reflect theological bias. When Kümmel suggests that NT introduction can play a vital role in helping to develop a theological critique of the canon and thereby help provide "an answer to the decisive question of what constitutes 'the heart of the New Testament' (*Mitte des Neuen Testaments*),"[36] he opens up the controversial discussion of the "canon within the canon." Since interpretors often assume that earlier is better, and therefore more reliable, beginning with Paul can easily have the effect of giving the Pauline writings, especially the "big four"—Romans, Galatians, 1 & 2 Corinthians—pride of place within the NT canon. There is no need to document how pervasive is the practice of effectively disparaging or ignoring those writings of the NT that are perceived to be late and/or derivative. Arguing for greater fluidity between NT and non-canonical Christian writings, Wrede observed the common practice among historians of doctrine and biblical theologians of using "the later New Testament material only rarely or not at all in their descriptions of faith in the post-apostolic age," citing as the most striking case Harnack's refusal to utilize the Gospel of John in his *History of Dogma*.[37]

To opt for the canonical principle in deciding how to order the writings also reflects a theological bias, but it is more explicit. If one takes the concept of canon as a theological given, as an expression of ecclesial discernment informed by the Holy Spirit, one can be up front in making this claim, even while recognizing that the current canonical Table of Contents is by no means value neutral. Placing Matthew before Mark, separating the Synoptic Gospels from John, detaching Acts from Luke, to say nothing of the ordering of the Pauline letters, the General Epistles, and the decision to place the Apocalypse last, are all decisions loaded with theological bias. It is better to be up front about the theological implications of the canonical principle than assuming it too is value neutral. That the current canonical ordering is the "received text" for Catholics, Orthodox, and Protestants and that this is the de facto arrangement readers of the NT directly confront both in private and liturgical use is another reason for retaining it, or something close to it, in a NT introduction.

In arguing for a canonical or quasi-canonical arrangement, one might retrieve the ancient notion of the twofold division of the NT writings into "Gospel" and "Apostle," apparently introduced by Marcion, perhaps as a Christian counterpart to "law and prophets" of Jewish writings.[38] When Irenaeus referred to the "Gospel," he meant, in the first instance, the apostolic faith and, by extension a section of the canon rather than an individual writing, a distinction also reflected in the Muratorian Canon's reference to "the third book of the Gospel, according to Luke." We thus have more sufficient grounds for starting with what the ancient church regarded as individual witnesses to the "Gospel" embodied in Jesus Christ.[39] While the distinction between "Gospel" and "Apostle" may be problematic in many respects, it at least suggests a way of seeing the four Gospels as primary witnesses to Jesus Christ in a way the (Pauline) epistles were not, even though they may have been chronologically later than Paul.

3. Relation to Other Texts

As we have already noted, serious disagreement exists over whether NT introduction is obligated to treat non-canonical Christian writings. Even if we decide that the scope of treatment is limited to the twenty-seven canonical writings, that does not necessarily mean that other Christian writings need to figure in the treatment of the canonical writings. But decisions must also be made about three other sets of writings, most notably (1) the Jewish Scriptures, either in the form of the Hebrew Bible or the Septuagint; (2) other Jewish writings including major figures such as Philo and Josephus and those variously included among the Jewish "apocrypha and pseudepigrapha"; and (3) the extensive group of writings from non-Christian, non-Jewish Greek and Roman writers during the Hellenistic-Roman period, so-called "pagan" literature. In each case, the question is not whether an NT introduction will treat these writings, either as a group or individually, but how one conceives the NT writings in relation to them and how, therefore, they will be utilized as comparative or illustrative texts in the treatment of the NT writings.

The relationship between the Jewish Scriptures and New Testament has been a long-standing question directly affecting how we read both sets of writings, not only as distinct sets of canonical texts to which Jews and Christians relate respectively, but also how Christians, who regard the Jewish Scriptures as the Old Testament, read the two testaments in light of each other. Christian readers do well to remember the theological bias against the Jewish Scriptures that set in as early as Marcion and perhaps reached its nadir with J. S. Semler who, in distinguishing between Holy Scripture and Word of God, proposed that the capacity for moral improvement should serve as the criterion for judging whether a biblical writing revealed the Word of God, and ultimately concluded, "Since we are not made morally better by any of the twenty-four books of the Old Testament, we are not able to persuade ourselves that they are divine."[40] But if we refrain from the sort of radical surgery that Marcion performed on a number of the NT writings, we confront writings which, taken as a whole, might be said to constitute a set of midrashic expositions of the Jewish Scriptures. It is surely a mistake to assume that each author/writing construes these Scriptures uniformly, and responsible treatment of each writing within a NT introduction will surely take into account both the diversity and complexity of the ways NT writers read and appropriate Scripture.

While Philo and Josephus and Jewish apocryphal and pseudepigraphical texts figure less centrally as the primary reference base for NT writings, they are by no means irrelevant. Especially those that clearly antedate the NT writings and reflect the ideological matrix out of which central Christian beliefs were shaped must be taken into account fully. Such prominent topics as Jewish Messianism, problematic titles such as the Son of Man, and Jewish apocalyptic so directly affect the way a broad range of NT writings and individual texts are understood that they require full, critical treatment. How such comparative texts are incorporated into the discussion depends heavily on how one construes the early Jesus movement, and any treatment that ignores the historical complexities of its birth as a Jewish reform movement within Palestine and its growth within both a Palestinian and Diaspora setting is bound to be distorted. Especially to be avoided are assumptions that the lines of interaction were one-way, that is, from Jewish to Christian, or that Christians were always "borrowing" Jewish conceptions and reshaping them to suit their purpose. The Johannine Apocalypse illustrates the problem. Rather than assuming a fixed, relatively well defined tradition of Jewish apocalyptic out of which the Johannine apocalypse emerged and seeing this Christian text as a prime representative of modified Jewish apocalyptic, one must recognize the generative influence on the broader apocalyptic tradition of the Johannine Apocalypse itself.

If Köster is right in claiming that NT introduction has for all practical purposes failed to take into sufficient account the results of the History-of-Religions School,[41] this increases one's responsibility to that vast field of texts and traditions often incorporated under the heading "Graeco-Roman paganism." Here, too, bias is often at work, although in a different direction, as some NT scholars remain reluctant to concede that Hellenistic-Roman outlooks and traditions exercised formative influence on early Christian beliefs and behaviors to the extent that Jewish traditions did so. More is involved here than the willingness to cite parallels from Greek and Roman authors to illustrate that Christian beliefs and behaviors were far from distinctive but rather had much in common with pagan beliefs and practices. One must be willing to see early Christianity as reflected in the NT as an integral part of the larger matrix of Graeco-Roman religions, even as was the case with Judaism, and correspondingly open to the possibility that Christian theological formulations are both worked out within this dynamically charged context and show the effects of having been formulated within such a context. This means that explanations of Christian theological formulations cannot be self-referential, either in terms of the NT and early Christian writings, or even in terms of the Jewish Scriptures; they must be developed with the widest lens possible.

As for non-canonical Christian literature, if anything, the scope should be broadened. While Christian writings through 200 CE may serve as the comparative base, much can be gained by tracing the "historical effects" of the NT writings over the course of Christian history. If, as Bernard McGinn reminds us, "the history of interpretation of a text is an integral part of its meaning,"[42] broadening the frame of Christian reference can only enhance our understanding of what the NT writings "mean."

4. Pedagogical Implications

Naturally, how each of these issues is resolved (or addressed) has profound pedagogical implications. Those teaching introductory survey courses are well aware of critical choices that have to be made not only in terms of lecture content but assigned readings:

(1) Are the twenty-seven canonical writings the primary "text" of the course, or do they constitute a subset of early Christian literature? In reading (or teaching) them, does one privilege them as canonical?

(2) Even if the twenty-seven writings are the primary focus of the course, in what order are they introduced and how are they weighted?

(3) If non-canonical texts are used as comparative texts, which texts are used, and to what purpose?

(4) What reading strategies are to be adopted? Underneath this question is the more basic question, What is the primary subject matter of the NT writings? Do they tell us primarily about the beliefs and behaviors of early Christians? Do they serve as historical sources through which we can trace and reconstruct the origin and development of early Christianity? Do they serve as revelatory texts—divine revelation through which ultimate truth claims are

being mediated? While these construals of the subject matter may be interrelated, they nevertheless represent discrete strategies.

What "Theologically" Means

It is one thing to argue that the discipline of NT introduction has theological implications, quite another that the conception and execution of such a work should be theological. One might engage in historical investigation of the NT writings and thereby upset cherished notions about apostolic authorship or presumed divine authority that attaches to these writings yet do so with little or no attention to the explicit theological claims they make. One might even be prompted to do historical analysis of the NT writings by theological motives, such as the desire to challenge the presumed authority of decisions made by earlier councils and church officials or justify one's preference for one writing or set of writings over another. But this does not necessarily constitute a theological treatment of these writings. What, then, does it mean to propose that one can write a *theological* introduction to the New Testament?

Part of the difficulty of providing a simple, straightforward answer is the inherent ambiguity of the term "theology" itself. As everyone knows, the term derives from two Greek words—*theos*, "god," and *logos*, "word" or "speech," thus designating thought or speech about God or the gods. In early Greek thought, a *theologos* is thus someone who discourses about the gods.[43] But as Hendrik Boers observes, the use of the term "theology" in the sense of "disciplined thinking about matters concerning the divine" occurs primarily as "a development of Christianity, and a gradual one at that," reaching its most fully developed form in Scholasticism, where it comes to be understood as a "coherent, logical, necessary system of thought."[44] While the practice of "disciplined thinking about matters divine" was certainly to be found in pre-Christian Greek thought, using the term "theology" to designate such practices was primarily a Christian development.

What makes "theology" an especially elusive term now are the many valences it has acquired in its use by Christian scholars over the past few centuries. Boers rightly reminds us that "'theology' is at the same time the most pervasive feature of New Testament interpretation, and the most elusive" (7). Tracing the way different scholars, such as Bultmann, Kümmel, and Bonsirven understood theology as they each sought to construct a "New Testament theology," Boers discovers "fundamental disagreements among (them) on what constitutes a theology of the New Testament, formally as well as materially" (12). Seen one way, the NT writings are a miscellany of religious texts containing "nothing that could in any real sense be called a theology" (10), yet over the centuries the church could in retrospect discover a theology lurking beneath their surface. Recognizing the seemingly irresistible fluidity of the term, Boers proposes his own working definition: "A coherent, logical, necessary system of general ideas in terms of which every element of our experience concerning matters relating to God can be interpreted" (13).

While the evolving scholarly discussion of the discipline of NT theology has its own logic and does not directly pertain to the related discipline of NT introduction, it is nevertheless relevant because the two disciplines are so closely related, even interrelated. Distinctions introduced especially by J. P. Gabler and William Wrede have been especially influential, requiring at least some attention, however briefly.

Gabler

As Boers notes, Gabler formulated three fundamental distinctions that were to prove extraordinarily influential in subsequent thought: the distinction "(1) between religion and theology, (2) between biblical and dogmatic theology, and (3) between biblical theology in a broader and in a narrower sense" (24). Of these, the most fundamental was the first, the distinction between religion and theology, which Gabler acknowledges had already been made earlier.[45] Worth noting is the context of religious controversy and division that prompted Gabler's address. Lamenting the widespread presence of such religious division, Gabler is eager to account for it as well as to move beyond it. He thus sees one of the "most serious" causes of discord as the "neglected distinction between religion and theology."[46] Acknowledging his dependence on Tittmann,[47] Gabler provides this classic formulation of the distinction:

> . . . religion is passed on by the doctrine in the
> Scriptures, teaching what each Christian ought to
> know and believe and do in order to secure happiness
> in this life and in the life to come. Religion then, is
> every-day, transparently clear knowledge; but
> theology is subtle, learned knowledge, surrounded
> by a retinue of many disciplines, and by the same
> token derived not only from the sacred Scripture
> but also from elsewhere, especially from the domain
> of philosophy and history. It is therefore a field
> elaborated by human discipline and ingenuity. It is
> also a field that is advanced by careful and
> discriminating observation that experiences various
> changes along with other fields.[48]

In his view, religious discord occurs when "some people apply to
religion what is proper to theology" (136), by which he presumably
means that ordinary, every-day folk should operate in a simple,
straightforward domain—the world of ordinary religion—content
to be unbothered by the much more technical discussions and distinctions of academic theologians. "Religion for the common man,"
he insists, "has nothing to do with this abundance of literature and
history (utilized by theology)" (136). One effect of such a distinction
is to lodge theology, both biblical and dogmatic theology, even though
they are separate disciplines, squarely within the context of the
university. In doing so, it gives social and political legitimacy to
both, and in Gabler's view, especially legitimates biblical theology
as a fully separate discipline that can pursue its work independently,
though in the ultimate service of dogmatic theology. Also worth noting is the way Gabler applied this distinction to the contents of the
NT itself—what one finds there is Christian religion in a fairly fixed
form, but what later developed, from the early church fathers forward, was theology, an ineluctably changeable enterprise since with
each age it had to correlate current philosophical and historical
knowledge with the teachings of Scripture. Religion was fixed, theology changeable: ". . . the sacred writers are surely not so changeable that they should in this fashion be able to assume these different types and forms of theological doctrine" (138).

Once this distinction is recognized and granted, Gabler is then
able to distinguish between biblical and dogmatic theology, both of

which would later be called second-order disciplines, yet each operating with different materials and in different modes. As he says,

> There is truly a biblical theology, of historical origin, conveying what the holy writers felt about divine matters; on the other hand there is a dogmatic theology of didactic origin, teaching what each theologian philosophises rationally about divine things, according to the measure of his ability or of the times, age, place, sect, school, and other similar factors. Biblical theology, as is proper to historical argument, is always in accord with itself when considered by itself—although even biblical theology when elaborated by one of the disciplines may be fashioned in one way by some and in another way by others. But dogmatic theology is subject to a multiplicity of change along with the rest of the humane disciplines; constant and perpetual observation over many centuries shows this enough and to spare (137).

Even though Gabler speaks of the task of biblical theology as "conveying what the holy writers felt about divine matters" (137), it was by no means for him simply a descriptive task. It was, in the fullest sense of the word, a constructive task. The biblical theologian must recognize, first, that even though "all the sacred writers are holy men . . . armed with divine authority" (139), different forms of religion are reflected in the Scriptures, most notably, those of the Old and New Testaments. Even within each testament, however, one finds different construals of religion, depending upon their chronological era, the biblical author, and literary form. Recognizing this diversity means acknowledging that Scripture contains "opinions not of a single man nor of one and the same era or religion" (139). This said, the biblical theologian faces two tasks: (1) the search for "sacred ideas" particular to individual authors or certain parts of Scripture and (2) the search for "universal ideas" that transcend particular times, persons, and situations. The former involves primarily philological, grammatical analysis that is attentive to the changes language undergoes through different periods as well as a particular writer's stylistic peculiarities. But it requires more than philological comparison. It is hermeneutical (although

Gabler does not use this term) since it involves identifying characteristic ideas and underlying meanings, and discerning broader
patterns of meaning that come to expression through the language,
all with a view to "drawing out the true sacred ideas typical of each
author" (141). The ultimate goal of such exegetical analysis is to
determine which ideas are of temporary applicability, "restricted
by God's own intention to a particular time, place, and sort of man"
(142), and which relate to "the unchanging testament of Christian
doctrine, and therefore pertain directly to us" (142). Such "ideas" as
the Mosaic rites or Paul's advice about women wearing veils will be
seen as having particular rather than universal applicability, as
indeed is the case with what is found in the "great part of these
books" (142). Through this process of sorting out, one will be able to
determine what is "truly divine"—the universal ideas that pertain
to the doctrine of salvation—and "what perchance is merely human"—the particular ideas of limited temporal and geographical
applicability. Thus emerges Gabler's twofold conception of biblical
theology—"true" biblical theology in the broad sense of faithfully
representing the "religions" reflected in Scripture, and "pure" biblical theology in the narrow sense of those ideas and teachings that
were universal and unchanging, "purified" of those elements that
were only applicable in their immediate historical context.[49]

Especially worth noting is that, for Gabler, what we would call
historical-critical exegesis is done finally in order to separate historically contingent elements of Scripture from those universal ideas
that were of consequence to Christians in every time and place—to
separate, as it were, the historical husk from the eternal grains of
truth embedded in Scripture. The ultimate goal of historical-critical exegesis is not historical reconstruction but theological interpretation. It enables the biblical theologian to get at the true, enduring Word of God.[50] The biblical theologian's work is completed
when this thoroughly constructive exegetical, hermeneutical, syn-
thetic task is completed, and then "biblical theology, pure and un-
mixed with foreign things" (142), can serve as the basis for the dogmatic theologian's constructive work. Properly done, biblical theology becomes the constant, unchanging foundation that dogmatic
theologians can take into account as one among several sources,
along with philosophy, history, and literature, as they construct their
ever changing systems.

In Gabler's view theology resides somewhere deep within Scripture, but theology does not yield its treasures easily. Even then, theology is what the biblical theologian constructs rather than something intrinsic to biblical religions. The "sacred ideas" may lie behind biblical texts, but they are not to be identified with the words of the biblical text, at least not in a straightforward, simple sense. His distinction between a particular form of human expression and an underlying universal truth was to have far-reaching effect in the history of biblical exegesis. In his view, NT writers accommodated "to the ideas or the needs of the first Christians" (142-43) by using historically particular forms of expression to express God's truth. As Sandys-Wunsch rightly observes, for Gabler "what is historical is secondary to what is true; however much it may accompany and even transmit the truth, the historical remains the rind on the orange and not the fruit itself" (147). Moreover, for him "Providence has ensured that parts of [the Bible] are trans-historical, that is, exempt from the limitations of the particular times in which they were written" (147).

Wrede

More than a century passed by the time William Wrede published his lectures under the title, "Concerning the Task and Methods of So-Called New Testament Theology" (1897).[51] By that time, thanks to Gabler, biblical theology had become a well-established theological discipline in its own right, and Wrede could insist that "New Testament theology has its goal simply in itself, and is totally indifferent to all dogma and systematic theology" (69). He could also insist that NT theology had no obligation to "serve the church" (72-73). Since he conceived NT theology as a "purely historical discipline" (69) and believed that "anyone who works to engage scientifically in New Testament theology [must] be capable of interest in historical research" (70), he argued that "investigation of historical reality has its own laws" (73). While he does not say so explicitly, Wrede is clearly convinced that historical investigation as he conceives it will directly challenge ecclesiastical claims, especially those that rest on history.

Wrede's lectures are focused exclusively on the discipline of NT theology, not NT introduction, although he recognizes the latter as a discrete, legitimate discipline whose primary aim is to survey "the content of individual documents, (indicate) their special features, and (discuss) disputed questions" (94). Yet his critique of his contemporaries' construals of the NT writings, especially when they purported to treat the theological dimensions of those writings, is so trenchant that it cannot be ignored. Moreover, both his conception of what the NT contains and what it is ultimately about, as well as his theory of theological inquiry, bear directly on any serious effort to deal with theological issues within a NT introduction. Köster's two-volume introduction bears vivid testimony to the lasting effects of Wrede's seminal essay.

Especially pertinent for our purposes is his critique of doctrinal concepts. While the object of his devastating critique are, in the first instance, NT theologies, such as those by B. Weiss[52] and Beyschlag,[53] Holtzmann,[54] and Schleiermacher,[55] it has implications for other scholarly genres including NT introductions, commentaries, and other monographs that attempt to summarize the theology of particular authors or writings. In fact, his characterization is an apt description of much that still occurs in these various scholarly genres:

> (One) sets out to reconstruct as exhaustively as possible the thoughts of every individual writer—i.e., his "doctrinal concepts." Related authors or writings are grouped together, but treated separately within the groups. In the case of Paul, the doctrinal concepts of different periods are sometimes further distinguished. The individual parts of the whole, are, so far as possible, arranged in a historical way. The individual doctrinal concept is obtained by working out what the main characteristic ideas of this writer are and arranging accordingly what has to be said on this and every other point. In each case, the individual concepts of a writing are carefully, meticulously analyzed and maybe defined by combining all the passages which contain a reference to them.[56]

Wrede concedes the value in this approach for grasping a writer's particularity, but raises four strong objections. First, a number of NT writings, such as 1 & 2 Peter, Jude, and James, are occasional writings, often brief, yielding only snippets of the author's larger thought world. This even applies in the case of Paul. What is expressed in these writings as responses to specific situations, Wrede insists, cannot necessarily be regarded as characteristic of the author/writing. Second, NT writings are devoid of "doctrine" in any meaningful sense. One can only speak of doctrine, in Wrede's view, "when thoughts and ideas are developed for the sake of teaching," which happens "only rarely in the New Testament" (75). Revealing his understanding of what the NT contains, Wrede insists:

> Most of it is practical advice, direction for life, instruction for the moment, the stirring up of religious feeling, talk of faith and hope for believers and hopers. Ideas, notions, and creedal statements play a part here, but are touched on in passing or presupposed, rather than consciously developed. Where there is deliberate development this normally happens under the control of some practical impulse or purpose. New Testament theology makes doctrine out of what in itself is not doctrine, and fails to bring out what it really is (75).

For Wrede, efforts to extract "doctrines" from NT writings effectively flatten the historical dynamics reflected in the writings as well as the considerable differences among writers and writings. He concedes that Paul, while no "theologian or systematician in the modern sense," is "a Christian thinker, and reflects like a theologian," which means that "his epistles do contain a strong theological element" (76). The authors of other writings, however, such as Acts, the Apocalypse, and the Pastorals, "are not theologians, however many elements of theology are found [there]" (76).

His third objection: the miscontrual of biblical "concepts." While admitting that the NT contains such concepts, Wrede is critical of efforts to catalogue them comprehensively. Far more important for Wrede is to identify those that are "normative and dominant, and hence the characteristic and indicative ones" (77). Especially objecting to the tendency to "squeeze as much conceptual capital as possible from every single phrase and every casually chosen expression used by an author" (77) as is often done in word studies, Wrede contends that it is far preferable to identify a "few decisive conceptions of the author, so that the main lines of its meaning can be given" (77). Excesses of well-meaning systematizers who attempt to be microscopically comprehensive prompts one of Wrede's more memorable characterizations: "One might with some justification call New Testament theology the science of minutiae and insignificant nuances" (78).

A fourth objection: New Testament theology is wrongly seen "as a succession of individual doctrinal concepts, or so to speak a conglomeration of clear little biblical theologies" (81). What is needed instead is to "show . . . the special character of early Christian ideas and perceptions, sharply profiled, and help . . . to understand them historically" (83). Far more important to Wrede than some artificial comprehensiveness is the capacity of the NT theologian to seize on characteristic, truly significant features of early Christian religion, and to present them in ways that retain their historical specificity as well as reflect their dynamic quality as deriving from a vital, living religion. Historical realism should not, in Wrede's view, be sacrificed on the altar of comprehensive systematization.

One of Wrede's fundamental disagreements with Holtzmann has to do with whether one concentrates on the NT writings themselves or their subject matter, or, more specifically, whether one treats the "history of literature" or the "history of early Christian religion and theology" itself. Obviously, Wrede opts for the latter, insisting that what he really wants to know is *what was believed, thought, taught, hoped, required and striven for* in the earliest period of Christianity; not what certain writings say about faith, doctrine, hope, etc." (84).

In deciding what was truly significant in early Christianity, the NT theologian must draw sharp distinctions among early Christian writings, evaluating each writing critically to determine whether it reveals truly significant conceptions. Does the writing "show signs of an individual mind that, even though we could not put a name to it, we could clearly regard as epoch-making or even moderately outstanding in the history of religions?" (85). Does it advance "with one-sided power so much as a single conception that was significant for the whole development in a way that makes us say: the idea has become normative or established through this writing, or has even been created by it?" (85-86). Judged by these rigorous standards, the majority of NT and early Christian writings fail miserably, in Wrede's view. Clearly eliminated are 1 Peter, Luke-Acts, Mark, and Matthew "so far as they do not merely codify the tradition" (85), 1 Clement, James, the Didache, the Pastoral Epistles, 2 Peter & Jude, the Epistle of Polycarp, and the Shepherd of Hermas. "However valuable (these writings) may be for edification, and though they may be treasured as sources, a historical judgment must say that they contain simply average Christianity" (86). Consequently, these writings "are of no interest to New Testament theology" (86). Almost, but not quite clearing the bar, are Ephesians, the Johannine Apocalypse, Hebrews and Barnabas. What, then, passes through Wrede's narrow sieve? The preaching of Jesus, Paul (as reflected in the genuine letters), the Johannine writings, and possibly Ignatius. While recognizing fully the independence of Johannine theology, Wrede insists that the author of the Johannine writings "was not so rich and creative a spirit as Paul's" (89).

Once this evaluative sifting of the documents occurs, one is then able to present NT theology as it developed historically. Wrede's projected scheme includes the following sections or stages: (1) Jesus' preaching; (2) the faith of the early church; (3) Paul; (4) faith and theology on Gentile soil, including treatment of (a) the relationship between Christianity and Judaism; (b) the significance of the OT for the Gentile church; (c) ethics; and (d) Gnosis; (5) Johannine theology; and (6) Ignatius.

In his concluding remarks, Wrede forthrightly admits that "the name New Testament theology is wrong in both its terms" (116). "The New Testament," he writes, "is not concerned merely with theology, but is in fact far more concerned with religion" (116). The term "New Testament" is inappropriate since the scope of investigation reaches well beyond the NT canon and encompasses early Christian literature up to Ignatius. The term "theology" is a misnomer since "the appropriate name of the subject-matter is: early Christian history of religion, or rather: the history of early Christian religion and theology" (116).

Even though Wrede's proposal has the effect of redefining radically the conception of NT theology as the "history of early Christian religion and theology," it raises fundamental questions about how any NT scholar should deal with the NT writings. Several of his insights are worth bearing in mind:

1. He insists on obliterating the distinction between canonical and non-canonical writings. Given the scope of his vision, this was a necessary distinction. Yet it is not a necessary distinction if, as Holtzmann argued, the concept of canon itself justifies limiting one's inquiry to the twenty-seven canonical writings and, in fact, is the only thing that gives such an undertaking internal coherence.

2. By emphatically questioning the existence of "doctrine" in any meaningful sense of the term in the NT writings, and even more so by challenging the way NT scholars ordinarily extract doctrines, or even individual theologies, from these writings, Wrede forces a sharpening of the method of theological inquiry and analysis. Especially salient is his insistence on identifying characteristic, genuinely significant ideas within an author or writing, and giving shape to them in a way that captures their distinctive contribution to early Christian thought and reveals why they had lasting influence.

3. Closely related is his trenchant critique of "comprehensive cataloguing" of texts around central ideas and the corresponding tendency to collect minutiae. Anticipating James Barr's later critique of the "theological dictionary,"[57] Wrede rightly cautions against squeezing too much out of too little.

4. His radically stringent evaluation of NT (and early Christian) writings in terms of their theological cogency forces the question of what counts as theological insight. If Paul is admitted to the company of Christian theologians, however tentatively, and John is included as a close second, then the case for admitting other NT authors, especially those of considerable length, such as the Synoptic Gospels, Acts, Hebrews, and the Apocalypse, is at least open for discussion. While it may be more difficult to make the case for the smaller writings, especially the Catholic epistles, Wrede's emphatic rejection of them as substantive theological treatises at least invites a reopening of the discussion of what "theological" means.

5. One benefit of Wrede's thoroughgoing historical approach is to give due weight to occasionality and context, thereby reminding us of the symbiotic relationship between praxis and doctrine. Questioning the common assumption that "the early Christian outlook was produced purely by the power of thought" (100), Wrede rightly contextualizes such theological notions as Paul's doctrine of justification by faith:

> Paul would never have formed his characteristic
> doctrine of justification by faith had he not taken in
> hand the task of converting Gentiles. The doctrine
> had a practical origin and practical purpose. It was
> not the other way round, as though the praxis were
> developed from a doctrine which had been created
> by religious thought and experience (100).

Recent Perspectives

Obviously much has happened in biblical scholarship during
the century following Wrede. NT theology as a separate scholarly
discipline within biblical theology developed momentum as major
theological syntheses appeared, including those by Bultmann,[58]
Stauffer,[59] Richardson,[60] Conzelmann,[61] Jeremias,[62] Kümmel,[63]
Goppelt,[64] Caird,[65] and Berger,[66] to name just a few. Yet, by the end
of the twentieth century some scholars began to notice that the conversation between biblical theologians and systematic theologians
had virtually stopped and that in many quarters biblical scholarship had grown increasingly specialized and decreasingly interested
in explicitly theological questions. The last several years, however,
have seen numerous calls for a theological reinvigoration of biblical
scholarship, and signs of renewed interest in theology among biblical scholars abound.

By proposing that "biblical interpretation should concern itself
primarily with the theological issues raised by the biblical texts
within our contemporary ecclesial, cultural, and socio-political contexts," Francis Watson echoes the sentiments of increasing numbers of biblical scholars even as he admits that "to argue for the
primacy of theology within biblical interpretation is to adopt a minority position."[67] An equally strong call for biblical scholars to engage Scripture theologically comes from Stephen Fowl who is convinced that the "discipline of biblical theology, in its most common
form, is systematically unable to generate serious theological interpretation of scripture."[68] Arguing that "Christian interpretation of
scripture needs to involve a complex interaction in which Christian
convictions, practices, and concerns are brought to bear on scriptural interpretation in ways that both shape that interpretation
and are shaped by it,"[69] Fowl builds on the pioneering work of
Brevard Childs, one of the earliest voices of reform whose critique

of the biblical theology movement represented a turning point in the debate, yet Fowl pushes well beyond it.[70] Similar recognition of the deep divide separating exegetes and systematic theologians also prompted Frances Young and David Ford to collaborate in an "exercise in practical hermeneutics," a focused theological reading of Second Corinthians.[71]

Beginning in 1986 an international group of Pauline scholars, gathered under the auspices of the Society of Biblical Literature, began an in-depth reexamination of Pauline theology that resulted in the publication of four volumes of essays between 1991-1997.[72] Especially relevant for our purposes is their operating ground-rule that attempts to get at each letter's theology should be made independently of the other letters. One letter, in other words, should not be read in light of another letter or the rest of the Pauline corpus, at least not initially. One useful distinction that emerged from the Pauline Group's discussion is the difference between talking about the "theology *of* a letter" and the "theology *in* a letter."[73] In his work on 1 Corinthians, Victor P. Furnish employed his broadly conceived working definition of theology that focused less on "some end product" and more on the "task": theology as "critical reflection on the beliefs, rites, and social structures in which an experience of ultimate reality has found expression."[74] Drawing on the fundamental distinction that underlay Bultmann's grand theological synthesis— the distinction between "the kerygma itself and the interpretation of that to which the 'theological thoughts' of the New Testament give expression,"[75] Furnish distinguishes between the gospel as event and its proclamation, on the one hand, and Paul's theological discourse that seeks to explain and unfold the truth of the gospel. Thus, in analyzing 1 Corinthians, Furnish focuses on the *process* of Paul's theological reflection, as something that "can only be found as one follows and engages the dynamics of his argument, including the movement back and forth between proclamation and exposition."[76] In formulating this dynamic understanding of theology, at least in its Pauline form, Furnish acknowledges his indebtedness to Schubert Ogden, an exemplary instance of productive conversation between a biblical theologian and a systematic theologian. Following Furnish's lead, I too will look to Ogden for guidance in formulating my own understanding of theology to be used in my theological introduction to the NT. But before doing so, I should note one other current example of renewed theological interest among biblical scholars.

The Cambridge University Press launched the series *New Testament Theology* in 1991 under the editorial guidance of J. D. G. Dunn. In the editor's preface to the series, Dunn observes the relative paucity of resources available to students interested in the theological aspects of NT writings. By producing a series of volumes dedicated to exploring the theology of individual NT writings or groups of writings, Dunn hopes to fill this gap. "The volumes," he writes, "seek both to describe each document's theology, and to engage theologically with it, noting also its canonical context and any specific influence it may have had on the history of Christian faith and life."[77] This broadly conceived understanding of theology naturally provides considerable latitude to each author, and individual volumes have succeeded at various levels in undertaking their task. They have not, however, in every case escaped the hazards of which Wrede warned. Nor have they operated with any uniform understanding of theology. Instead, the volumes, in different ways, illustrate Boers's observation mentioned earlier that theology continues to be used in widely different senses.

Several of Ogden's essays offer suggestions that can help us develop a more focused understanding of theology.[78] As a systematic theologian, Ogden works with a clearly defined sense of the division of labor that exists between biblical and systematic/dogmatic theologians. He sees "exegetical theology" as a branch of "historical theology," whose primary purview is to ask, "What has the Christian witness of faith already been as decisive for human existence?"[79] For him, "the study of Scripture is nothing other than historical study, continuous at every point from data to methods both with the study of other Christian traditions and thence with the comprehensive understanding of the entire human past" (9). While fully recognizing the unique role Scripture plays in Christian tradition, Ogden observes that "by far the largest part of the Christian past may be plausibly regarded as the history of scriptural interpretation" (10). In contrast to historical theology, systematic theology asks, "What is the Christian witness of faith as decisive for human existence?" (10). The third form of theology—practical theology—is more broadly construed than is often done, asking, "What should the Christian witness of faith now become as decisive for human existence?" (13).

Given this conception of the taxonomy of theology, Ogden introduces the distinction between saying and doing. Noting that theology, understood etymologically, is often understood as thought and speech about God, he proposes broadening our understanding of theology to include "doing": "the speech proper to theology may very well comprise *doing* along with *saying* . . . and theology must be understood accordingly as not only what is thought and said about God but what is done about God as well."[80] Even with this broadening of the definition of theology that moves it from being merely a cognitive discipline to one that in some sense involves action, Ogden prefers to think of theology in a restrictive sense. Not everything Christians think, say, and do relative to their Christian faith and witness deserves to be called theology, only those activities that reflect "more or less critically on the validity of it all" (422). Thus, "what it is to do theology properly so-called is not done at all unless and until one engages in just such critical reflection" (422). Further,

> . . . instead of referring to all that Christians think, say, and do about God on the basis of their experience of Jesus, (theology) is quite reasonably used to refer to either the process or the product of a certain kind of critical reflection—namely, the kind that is required to validate the claims to validity that Christians either make or imply in expressing their experience (423).

The wider circle of Christian reflective and practical activity Ogden prefers to call "witness":

> For what is called "theology" in the broader sense of all that Christians think, say, and do about God I prefer and will use the term "witness." Thus, in my terms, what it is to do theology proper is adequately understood, not simply as bearing witness, but only as critically reflecting on witness with a view to validating its claims to validity (423).

Here Ogden echoes Gerhard Ebeling:

> It is also a doubtful proceeding to use the concept "theology" in such a wide sense that any talk of God and any religious statement whatever may be designated as theology.[81]

It is, of course, common for systematic theologians to distinguish between first-order and second-order discourse, the former referring to the primordial language of religious people, the latter to the reflective language used by theologians in analyzing "first-order" statements. As George Lindbeck puts it, "Technical theology and official doctrine . . . are second-order discourse about the first-intentional uses of religious language."[82] The pressing question is whether NT discourse, or even all biblical discourse, should be understood exclusively as first-order discourse, or whether it in some inescapable sense can rightly be thought of as theological. For all of his restrictive claims about the majority of NT writings, Wrede was willing to see Paul and John as doing theology, a concession that informed Bultmann's grand synthesis that featured Paul and John primarily. But if Bultmann is right that *the theological thoughts (of the New Testament writings)* are to be *conceived and explicated as thoughts of faith, that is: as thoughts in which faith's understanding of God, the world, and man is unfolding itself,*[83] is there no sense in which this can be said of each of the twenty-seven writings? I think there is. One need not agree with Marxsen that all the NT writings are proclamation in order to appreciate his basic claim that the NT writings, taken as a whole, are pervasively theological. To characterize all the writings as kerygmatic is to oversimplify both their content and purpose. As Marxsen well knew, many types of "first-order" statements are embedded in the NT: creedal statements, hymns, kerygmatic summaries, and prayers, to name only a few. If form and redaction criticism have taught us anything, it is an appreciation for the way the NT writings, in a wide variety of ways, engage in traditioning—receiving earlier traditions, both written and oral, expanding them, reinterpreting them, and recasting them for new situations. Nor was this a mindless process, as if the tradents were mere conduits through which traditions were conveyed. Just as Paul critically reflected on the Christ event and its kerygmatic formulations, and expounded their "truth" in various ecclesial settings, so do many, if not all of, the NT writings that Wrede relegated to "average Christianity." For all the bad press Luke-Acts has received at the hands of biblical critics since Baur, it can no longer be excluded from the theological pantheon. As Conzelmann showed, Luke deserves the name theologian without qualification.[84]

If we are now in a position to ask whether all of the NT writings are theological treatises, can we move the discussion forward by developing a way of thinking about theology in the NT writings which, on the one hand, does not do serious injustice to their subject matter, but, on the other hand, enables us to get at their theological claims and message(s) without producing a "grey monotony" of doctrinal belief?[85]

A Proposal

Taking seriously Ogden's proposal that we can speak of theology as something we think/say and do, and Furnish's extension of Ogden's proposal that theology, at least in its Pauline form, can be thought of as both process and product—as an activity of critical reflection through which the NT writers explained the Christ event, both as something they experienced and something they believed and preached—I propose that theology be thought of in three modes: in a cognitive mode—as something one has or believes; in a critical-reflective mode—as something one does; and finally in a practical mode—as something one lives, in various behavioral forms, including individual and corporate ethics, liturgical performance, and the many other embodiments of Christian witness.

The advantage of using such a three-pronged understanding of theology in introducing the NT writings is that it allows us to take seriously the many types of faith-claims found in them and even to present them as "message," and do so in a manner reminiscent of conventional NT theologies. Heeding Wrede's advice, and even remembering Gabler's distinction between the surface level of the text (the historical form of the text's expression) and the underlying ideas through which the Word of God gets conveyed, we should avoid the collecting-summarizing syndrome that renders richly textured theological issues into neatly organized theologies or even theological subsections, thus X's Christology, eschatology, ecclesiology, etc.

By allowing the possibility that Bultmann's definition of theology can extend beyond Paul and John, we can even ask how "thoughts in which faith's understanding of God, the world, and (humans) is unfolding itself" are present in all the NT texts.

Combined with a concern to render properly the "product" of the NT writer's theological work is the equally important, and in many senses, inseparable task of attending to the "process" through which those writers arrived at their theological visions. This I prefer to call "theological sense making," or in Ogden's phrase "doing theology"—that complex web of mental, physical, spiritual, and social activities through which believers critically reflect on the Christian witness and its practical implications. Rather than limiting this activity to professional theologians, I prefer to broaden it to include all believers, at least in principle, and certainly to those authors and editors who produced the NT. While the kind of critical reflection in which systematic theologians engage may be of a differ order than that of ordinary believers, it is a difference in degree more than in kind. One way to think of the canonical process may be as a sifting process through which those writings that represented authentic critical reflection and constructive theological thought came to be regarded as normative in a way that others were not. Canon, on this definition, thus demarcates those writings that exhibited "second-order" reflection in ways that qualified them to become normative for Christian belief and practice.

Just as important, however, is the practical component—lived theology. By being equally attentive to the behavioral aspect of theology, we can explore the NT writings for what they reveal about both beliefs and behaviors. This emphasis on "behavioral theology" is resonant with Stephen Fowl's call for Christian believers to "embody Scripture."[86] This may take the form of trying to describe the ethical demands expressed in the NT writings, but it may also require getting at behaviors that are part of the contexts in which the writings were produced.

A Model for Thinking About Doing Theology

Once we have parsed the different aspects of doing theology, we can conceive of it as a dynamic process that individuals and communities of faith engage in when four things come into play: (1) the interpreter, either the individual or community of faith, (2) a sacred text, (3) a tradition of beliefs and practices, often consisting of elaborations of a sacred text, and (4) a context. If we think of a tetrahedron whose bottom three points correspond to Nos. 1, 2, and 3, and the top point as No. 4, and at its center the cluster of experiences and convictions that drive and shape the interpreter(s), we can say that theology is done when all four of these interact with one another, most often precipitated by a specific catalyst. The catalyst may be a simple question, a personal or community crisis, or a wide range of other situations or events that trigger the doing of theology. To separate the four components creates artificial distinctions, since the lines are often fluid between text and tradition, even as they are between the interpreter and context. But granting these fluid boundaries, each point is fixed enough to think of it as a discrete part of the process. We may say, then, *that Christian theological reflection results when interpreters, either an individual believer or a community of faith, engage in conversation with a sacred text and tradition, broadly construed, in order to make sense of, and give formal expression to, their experience and understanding of "God at work in Christ" within a specific context.*

What difference does it make to employ this model of "theological sense-making" as an analytical tool for getting at the theological dimensions of the NT? Most obviously, it provides a way of seeing the process through which NT writings became "products" of critical theological reflection. In particular, it highlights the critical role that Scripture interpretation plays within this process, emphasizing the pervasively midrashic quality of much NT writing. However, it does so in a way that moves beyond simple construals of the "Christian use of the Old Testament." By distinguishing between text and tradition, we are able to think of early Christians engaged in theological sense-making as they are in conversation with Scripture on the one hand, and various traditions, most notably the Jesus tradition, in whatever form they had it at their disposal, on the other hand.

Furthermore, it enables us to distinguish between what Furnish calls process and product. As one might expect, the different genres of NT writings pose certain problems. It is much easier, for example, to analyze the way Paul does theology in 1 & 2 Corinthians, or other letters, where there is a strong occasional element, than it is, for example, in the Gospels, whose social-historical situations are much less obvious. In those cases where a NT writing, for whatever reason, obscures one of the four "theological nodes," we should say so. This in itself may be revealing if for no other reason than, reminding us of the yawning gaps that the NT writings sometimes reveal.

There is yet another advantage, a practical advantage at that, especially useful in contexts where the NT is being introduced to seminary students and other Scripture interpreters. My proposed model replicates what occurs in every interpretive act, ancient or modern, and this invites modern interpreters to see NT authors/ editors "doing theology," or engaged in "theological sense-making," and themselves as engaged in a process that is qualitatively similar. Creating such an affinity between modern interpreter and ancient author need not blur the canonical line. It rather shows modern readers a process, as well as the products of theological reflection, that provides normative guidance for the church's life of faith. Among other things, it makes it more difficult simply to transfer scriptural belief and practice into a modern setting, instead inviting interpreters to see both the complexities and possibilities of engaging in critical theological sense-making.

Some Operating Assumptions

1. A theological NT introduction can be justifiably limited to the twenty-seven canonical writings, at least in its initial focus. Since it is a theological introduction, it can operate with a sense of canon not only on theological, but historical and practical grounds as well.

2. Each NT writing may be read as an autonomous theological text. This develops Marxsen's insight that the NT writings may be seen as "expanded witness to God's action in Christ." In contrast to Ogden and other systematic theologians, I regard the NT writings as more than "first-order" witness but as themselves examples, to different degrees, of critical theological reflection. Here I take seriously the principle articulated by the SBL Pauline Theology Group that each writing should be read on its own terms, at least

initially, and every effort should be made to discern and construe its "theology" in ways that are appropriate both to its genre, its known context, as well as its larger canonical context.

3.   The task of a theological introduction to the NT is to enable the reader, especially the beginning reader, to see each writing as a specific instance of "doing theology"—theological praxis, if you will. This entails at least four obligations:

a.   Accounting for the shape (literary form) of the text.

b.   Exposing, in so far as possible, the process of "theological sense-making" that gave birth to the text, and doing so by analyzing the conversation of the author/community with text and tradition within a specific social context.

c.   Articulating the writing's theological message, understood as its revelatory claims and insights. This should be framed as comprehensively as possibly, yet with every effort to capture significant particularities. This entails the writing's distinctive contribution to the larger scriptural witness. How this is framed will vary from writing to writing, but in every case it is critically important to distinguish content and meaning—i.e., the surface level of meaning from the theological truth claims that are being expressed through the words of the text. This may take the form of sketching the author's "theological vision" that informs the writing, or it may take other forms. Either way, it should be more than a simple summary of the writing's content or an extended paraphrase of its argument.

d.   Tracing the writing's theological impact on the life of the church and the broader culture: doctrinally, liturgically, ethically, and socio-historically. The "history of Scripture interpretation" will be especially useful here, but not simply to rehearse such history, but rather to show the theological cogency of the writing. Here we operate with the assumption noted by B. McGinn, that the "history of interpretation of a text is an integral part of its meaning."[87]

4.   A theological NT introduction must retain its role as a critical discipline. Not only should it identify and present the theological claims of the NT writings, and do so in a comprehensive, even sympathetic fashion, but it also has the obligation of evaluating those claims in their own right, in light of the broader biblical context.

Endnotes

1. Hendrikus Boers, *What Is New Testament Theology?: The Rise of Criticism and the Problem of Theology of the New Testament* (Philadelphia: Fortress, 1979), 10.

2. *Einleitung in das Neue Testament*, (Leipzig: Deichert, 1897-1899), 263.

3. So, Helmut Köster, "New Testament Introduction: A Critique of a Discipline," in Jacob Neusner (ed.), *Christianity, Judaism, and Other Greco-Roman Cults. Part I: New Testament* (Leiden: Brill, 1979), 1, esp. 7.

4. Werner G. Kümmel, *The New Testament: The History of the Investigation of Its Problems*, trans. S. McLean Gilmour and Howard C. Kee (Nashville: Abingdon, 1972), 69.

5. Ibid., 63-69.

6. See Köster, "Critique," 2.

7. Kümmel, *History of Investigation*, 68.

8. Köster, "Critique," 3.

9. Ibid., 6.

10. Ibid., 7

11. Ibid., 5. This is by no means a new proposal, since Gustav Krüger in *Das Dogma vom Neuen Testament* (Giessen: Curt von Münchow, 1896) had called for a similar broadening of the task of NT introduction (see Kümmel, *History of Investigation*, 303). In a similar vein, William Wrede, arguing that NT theology should be conceived as a historical discipline, also insisted on eliminating the distinction between the NT writings and other early Christian writings ("The Task and Methods of 'New Testament Theology,'" in Robert Morgan, *The Nature of New Testament Theology* [London: SCM, 1973] 70-73). See Udo Schnelle, *The History and Theology of the New Testament Writings*. Trans. M. Eugene Boring. (Minneapolis: Fortress, 1998), 7.

12. Köster, "Critique," 5.

13. Helmut Köster, *Introduction to The New Testament Volume 2: History and Literature of Early Christianity* (New York: de Gruyter, 1982), xix.

14. Ibid.

15. Willi Marxsen, *Introduction to the New Testament: An Approach to its Problems*. Trans. of the 3rd German edition (1964) by G. Buswell. (Philadelphia: Fortress, 1968), 8.

16. Ibid., 8-9.

17. Ibid., 11.

18. Luke T. Johnson, *The Writings of the New Testament: An Interpretation*. Revised edition. (Minneapolis: Fortress, 1999).

19. Eduard Schweizer, *A Theological Introduction to the New Testament*. Trans. O. C. Dean, Jr. (Nashville: Abingdon Press, 1991), 10.

20. Werner G. Kümmel, *Introduction to the New Testament*. Revised edition. Trans. Howard C. Kee (Nashville: Abingdon Press, 1975), 28.

21. Bart D. Ehrman, *The New Testament: A Historical Introduction to the Early Christian Writings*. 2nd ed. (New York: Oxford University Press, 2000), xxi.

22. Ibid., 14.

23. Werner G. Kümmel, "Einleitungswissenschaft, II. Neues Testament," *TRE* 9 (1982) 469-82, esp. 479. Also see his earlier essay, "'Einleitung in das Neue Testament' als theologische Aufgabe," *EvT* 19 (1959) 4-16, reprinted in E. Grässer et al., eds., *Heilsgeschehen und Geschichte* (Marburger Theologische Studien, 3; Marburg: Elwert, 1965), 340-50.

24. Wrede, "Task and Methods," 71.

25. Ibid.

26. Adolf Jülicher and Erich Fascher, *Einleitung in das Neue Testament* (Tübingen: J.C.B. Mohr [Siebeck], 1931), 2.

27. GGA 158 (1896) 529. Cited in Kümmel, "Einleitungswissenschaft," 479.

28. Heinrich J. Holtzmann, *Lehrbuch der historisch-kritischen Einleitung in das Neue Testament*. 3rd ed. (Freiburg: J.C.B. Mohr, 1892) 11.

29. Kümmel, *Introduction*, 29.

30. Marxsen, *Introduction*, 9.

31. Ibid., 2.

32. Ibid., 13.

33. Köster, "Critique," 7.

34. Schnelle, *History and Theology*, 12.

35. Ibid., 13.

36. Kümmel, "Einleitungswissenschaft," 480.

37. Wrede, "Task and Method," 185 n. 10.

38. John Knox, *Marcion and the New Testament: An Essay in the Early History of the Canon* (Chicago: University of Chicago Press, 1942) 2-3.

39. According to Knox, "The title of the Gospel section of the first catholic NT was not the "Gospels" but (precisely as in the Marcionite canon) the "Gospel"—the "Gospel according to Matthew, Mark, Luke and John" (*Marcion*, 141).

40. Johann S. Semler, *Abhandlung von freier Untersuchung des Canon* (4 vols.; Halle, 1771-75) 3.26. Cited in Schnelle, *History and Theology*, 4.

41. Köster, "Critique," 6.

42. B. McGinn, "Revelation," in Robert Alter and Frank Kermode, eds., *The Literary Guide to the Bible* (Cambridge, MA: Harvard University Press, 1987), 528.

43. See Plato *Republic* 379A; Aristotle *Metaphysics* 1000^a9.

44. Boers, *What is New Testament Theology?*, 16.

45. Gabler's classic formulation was contained in his inaugural address given at Altdorf in 1787. An English translation and commentary are provided by J. Sandys-Wunsch and L. Eldredge, "J. P. Gabler and the Distinction Between Biblical and Dogmatic Theology: Translation, Commentary, and Discussion of His Originality," *SJT* 33 (1980), 133-58. References to Gabler's address are taken from this article.

46. Ibid., 136.

47. C. C. Tittmann, *Progr(amm) de discrimine theologiae et religionis* (Wittemberg, 1782); cited in Ibid., 136, n. ii.

48. Sandys-Wunsch & Eldredge, "Gabler," 136.

49. See Boers, *What is Theology?*, 32.

50. Later, F. C. Baur would practice historical-critical exegesis, also motivated theologically, but primarily in the service of historical exegesis. For him this was quite legitimate given his conviction that God's Spirit could be traced in universal history. Even though Gabler operated with a clear sense of historical differentiation between the several biblical eras, for him historical-critical exegesis served theologically constructive rather than historically constructive ends.

51. Translated by Robert Morgan and included as chapter 2 in his *The Nature of New Testament Theology: The Contribution of William Wrede and Adolf Schlatter*.

SBT 2nd series, 25. (London: SCM, 1973), 68-116, 182-93. References to Wrede's essay are from Morgan's translation.

52. *Lehrbuch der biblischen Theologie des Neuen Testaments*, 5th edition. (Berlin: Hertz, 1873). English translation of the 3rd edition, *Biblical Theology of the New Testament* (Edinburgh: T. & T. Clark, 1882-83).

53. *Neutestamentliche Theologie*, English translation *New Testament Theology* (Edinburgh: T. & T. Clark, 1895-96).

54. *Lehrbuch der neutestamentlichen Theologie* (Freiburg: Mohr, 1897).

55. *Brief Outline of the Study of Theology* (Edinburgh: T. & T. Clark, 1850).

56. Morgan, "Wrede," 73-74.

57. *The Semantics of Biblical Language* (Oxford: Oxford University Press, 1961; reprinted London/Philadelphia: SCM/Trinity Press International, 1991).

58. Rudolf K. Bultmann, *Theology of the New Testament* (2 vols.; trans. Kendrick Grobel; New York: Scribner, 1951 [vol. 1, 1st German ed., 1948] and 1955 [vol. 2, 1st German ed. 1951/53]).

59. Ethelbert Stauffer, *New Testament Theology* (Trans. John Marsh from the 5th German ed.; London: SCM Press, 1955).

60. Alan Richardson, *An Introduction to New Testament Theology* (New York: Harper, 1958).

61. Hans Conzelmann, *An Outline of the Theology of the New Testament* (Trans. John Bowden from the 1968 German 2nd ed.; New York: Harper & Row, 1969).

62. Joachim Jeremias, *New Testament Theology: Part One: The Proclamation of Jesus* (Trans. John Bowden from the 1971 German ed.; London: SCM, 1971).

63. Werner G. Kümmel, *The Theology of the New Testament According to Its Major Witnesses: Jesus, Paul, and John* (Trans. John E. Steely from the 1969 German ed.; Nashville: Abingdon Press, 1973).

64. Leonhard Goppelt, *Theology of the New Testament: Volume 1: the Ministry of Jesus in Its Theological Significance* (trans. John E. Alsup from the 1975 German ed.; Grand Rapids: W. B. Eerdmans Publishing Co., 1981); *Theology of the New Testament: Volume 2: The Variety and Unity of the Apostolic Witness to Christ* (trans. John E. Alsup from the 1976 German ed.; Grand Rapids: W. B. Eerdmans Publishing Co., 1982).

65. George B. Caird (completed and edited by L. D. Hurst), *New Testament Theology* (Oxford: Clarendon Press, 1994).

66. Klaus Berger, *Theologie des Urchristentums: Theologie des Neuen Testaments* (2nd ed.; Tübingen/Basel: Francke Verlag, 1995).

67. Francis Watson, *Text, Church and World: Biblical Interpretation in Theological Perspective* (Grand Rapids: Eerdmans, 1994) vii. In his subsequent book *Text and Truth: Redefining Biblical Theology* (Grand Rapids: Eerdmans, 1997), Watson advances his argument by calling for an "interdisciplinary approach to biblical interpretation which seeks to dismantle the barriers that at present separate biblical scholarship from Christian theology" (p. vii).

68. Stephen E. Fowl, *Engaging Scripture: A Model for Theological Interpretation* (Malden, MA: Blackwell Publishers, 1998), 1.

69. Ibid., 8.

70. Besides Brevard S. Childs's *Biblical Theology of the Old and New Testaments* (Minneapolis: Fortress, 1993), see his essay "Toward Recovering Theological Exegesis," *Pro Ecclesia* 6 (1997), 16-26.

71. Frances M. Young and David Ford, *Meaning and Truth in 2 Corinthians* (Grand Rapids: Eerdmans, 1987).

72. Jouette M. Bassler, ed., *Pauline Theology: Volume I: Thessalonians, Philippians, Galatians, Philemon* (Minneapolis: Fortress, 1991); David M. Hay, ed., *Pauline Theology: Volume II: 1 & 2 Corinthians* (Minneapolis: Fortress, 1993); David M. Hay and E. Elizabeth Johnson, eds., *Pauline Theology: Volume III: Romans* (Minneapolis: Fortress, 1995); E. Elizabeth Johnson and David M. Hay, eds., *Pauline Theology: Volume IV: Looking Back, Pressing On* (SBLSym, 4; Atlanta: Society of Biblical Literature [Scholars Press], 1997.

73. The two essays illustrating this distinction appeared in the second volume (Hay edition): Gordon D. Fee, "Toward a Theology of 1 Corinthians" (37-58) and Victor Paul Furnish, "Theology in 1 Corinthians" (59-89).

74. This formulation appears in Furnish's earlier essay, "Paul the Theologian," in Robert T. Fortna and Beverly R. Gaventa, eds., *The Conversation Continues: Studies In Paul and John in Honor of J. Louis Martyn* (Nashville: Abingdon, 1990) 25. It is developed in his 1993 article, "Theology in 1 Corinthians," see esp. 59.

75. Furnish, "Paul the Theologian," 20.

76. "Theology in 1 Corinthians," 62.

77. Jerome Murphy-O'Connor, *The Theology of the Second Letter to the Corinthians* (Cambridge: Cambridge University Press, 1991), x.

78. "Doing Theology Today," in John D. Woodbridge and Thomas Edward McComiskey, eds., *Doing Theology in Today's World: Essays in Honor of Kenneth S. Kantzer* (Grand Rapids: Zondervan, 1991), 417-36. Especially worth noting is his collection of essays Schubert M. Ogden, *On Theology* (San Francisco: Harper & Row, 1986). Of special interest are "What is Theology?" (1-21), "On Revelation" (22-44), "The Authority of Scripture for Theology" (45-68); "Prolegomena to Practical Theology" (94-101).

79. "What is Theology?," 8.

80. "Doing Theology," 420.

81. Gerhard Ebeling, *Word and Faith* (Trans. James W. Leitch; Philadelphia: Fortress, 1960), 93.

82. George A. Lindbeck, *The Nature of Doctrine: Religion and Theology in a Postliberal Age* (Philadelphia: Westminster Press, 1984), 68.

83. Bultmann, *Theology* 2.237.

84. Hans Conzelmann, *Theology of St. Luke*. Trans. Geoffrey Buswell from the 1957 German 2nd ed. (New York: Harper & Row, 1960)

85. Wrede, "Task and Methods," 76.

86. *Engaging Scripture*, 3; see also the book he co-authored with L. Gregory Jones, *Reading in Communion: Scripture and Ethics in Christian Life* (Grand Rapids: Eerdmans, 1991).

87. See note 42.

Freedom and Law:
Toward a Theological Proposal

Reinhard Hütter
DUKE UNIVERSITY DIVINITY SCHOOL
DURHAM, NC

Introduction

My goal is to rethink freedom and law theologically. This project grows out of a deep concern about the dual crisis of freedom and law that characterizes both church and society in their late modern manifestations.

Let me offer five theses: *First:* In late modernity, we no longer know what freedom is, other than the self-assertion of our own contingent wills. *Second:* We no longer know what law is, other than the random and contingent assertion of an alien rule over our own will. *Third:* We no longer know how freedom and law are mutually dependent or why they must be so. *Fourth:* The effects of the first, second, and third theses are devastating for Christian faith as well as for contemporary society: in the churches a supersessionist antinomianism effectively practices a Marcionite disregard for and contempt of law as found in Scripture and the Christian tradition. The effects of this supersessionist antinomianism on contemporary mainline Protestantism are witnessed in the disintegration of Christian moral consensus and the rise of private preference and public utility as the sole criteria for judging the right and wrong of human agency. *Fifth:* In late modern society, we find a primarily negative freedom combined with an increasing legislated and bureaucratic regulation of civil society. While in the private sector license reigns under the label of free self-realization, an increasingly fine net of legal regulations covers civil society. Both *license* and *legalism* are on the rise together. The astounding increase of litigation in our late modern societies mirrors the collapsed interrelationship between freedom and law.

Although some definitions might be expected at this point, those definitions need to be postponed, else their premature deployment contribute to the problem. Most of the standard definitions tend to reduce the scope of freedom either to political freedom, freedom of choice, or a combination of the two. In similar ways, either the moral law or public legislation comes into focus, or "law" is simply reserved for its use in the hard sciences. *By contrast, I pursue concepts of freedom and law that are characteristic of humans as persons created by and called to a life in communion with God. In this fundamental and original sense freedom and law are positive terms. At the same time their moral and political implications and their emancipatory and disciplinary connotations are not excluded from the scope of inquiry.*

The Modern Aporia: Freedom as *Ungrund*[1]

The very way I perceive the crisis of freedom and law forces me to take the bull by its horns and question modernity's *sanctum sanctorum*—freedom. Let me explain: The crises of freedom and law as they are haunting late modernity are far from being accidental—they arise necessarily from the contradictory structure of freedom as autonomy. Modernity characteristically thinks that freedom is constitutive of the subject. This would not necessarily be a problem if a fundamental teleological structure were in place to orient human freedom ontologically to the highest good for its genuine realization. In such a framework law could easily serve as a normative guide on the way to the highest good.[2] Yet part of the modern project was to fundamentally critique and widely abandon integrative teleological assumptions.[3] However, without teleology law cannot occupy a constructive role in relationship to human freedom. Rather, law turns into freedom's competitor and thus endangers the subject's constitution as free. This antagonism between law and freedom begged for a resolution, and Immanuel Kant succeeded in providing it with the help of the concept, quite revolutionary in its day, of autonomy.[4]

Two things had to be achieved: Freedom had to be secured and the reality of law had to be accounted for. And so Kant derived the concept of the law from reason's practical capacity: the law is nothing other than reason's neccessary law. And in order for reason to be fundamentally practical in nature and thus to be able to legislate itself, an original and antecedent freedom needed to be postu-

lated.[5] This was Kant's ingenious move.[6] Yet in Kant's establish-
ment of autonomy, two modern abandonments become manifest.
Not only did the project of modernity abandon the Aristotelian-
Thomist teleology; it also abandoned the central Christian way of
thinking freedom and law through the mode of reception.[7] Right up
to the Enlightenment, part of the unquestioned consensus of Protestant and Catholic Orthodoxy was that freedom in its original splendor before the fall was *created* and thus fundamentally *received* freedom; therefore, freedom could be partially or completely lost.

By contrast, the ethics of autonomy ceases to think human freedom as genuinely received freedom.[8] This fundamental shift has
immediate and severe consequences. As soon as freedom is understood as constitutive of autonomy, the difference between uncreated
and created freedom becomes irrelevant, and consequently freedom
must turn into the *Ungrund*, the "unoriginate origin." Yet as this
Ungrund, freedom takes on the air of the absolute and wills itself
alone as unoriginate origin. The turn to self-will amounts to an er-
satz teleology, one that quickly denigrates into will to power. And
this denigration from teleology, to subjective will, to will to power,
eventually undermines the very law of reason that freedom was
originally meant to enable. An autonomy that cannot account for
the reception of freedom must ultimately decline into those substi-
tutes that today reign under the name of freedom: individual sovereignty, will to power, and/or license.

Freedom: Reception, Person, and Community

In other words, a flaw is hidden in the origin of modern autonomy—the failure to account for freedom's own *reception*. A received freedom can never turn into the *Ungrund*. Rather, being received conditions the very nature and shape of freedom. Received
freedom is always received as shaped freedom. The shape of this
freedom is itself received in the reception of law. Therefore freedom
and law are always received together in one bestowal.[9]

Here we have the beginning of an answer for this flaw. Yet a
new set of questions arises in light of this answer: Can the theme of
freedom and law be appropriately treated with reference only to
the individual? Would such individualism not inevitably be cap-
tured by the *aporia* of modernity's way of conceiving freedom? Yet if

we simply switch our focus from the individual to the community, would we indeed escape the problem, or simply turn to a communitarian form of the modern *aporia*?[10]

The concept of humanity that is both inherently communal and individual is the *person*.[11] And the community in which persons are called to full personhood in the most fundamental sense, that is, to a life with God, is the *church*.[12] By seriously engaging this train of thought, a further horizon of theological reflection opens: Can the theme of "freedom and law" be dealt with sufficiently if we remain on the level of anthropology (and even extend it into ecclesiology)? Or is it necessary to expand the inquiry into the doctrine of God, into an investigation of the nature of divine freedom—and law?

Shirking the expansion of the inquiry to the doctrine of God will only reaffirm the reductionist immanentism of modernity and the resulting oscillation between individualism and communitarianism. In contrast, allowing the doctrine of God to frame the inquiry lets freedom and law be understood through the truth that fundamentally connects humanity with the world because it first and foremost connects humanity with God. Consequently, approaching the theme of freedom and law comprehensively requires nothing less than a rigorously systematic theology of freedom and law. At its center stand three theses: (1) Freedom and law can only be recovered together instead of one at the cost of the other. (2) Freedom and law belong together as the original created unity of human life before God. (3) The concept of "reception" has to play a crucial role in rethinking the inherent interrelationship between freedom and law.[13]

What difference would it really make to conceive of freedom in the one way or the other? Let us turn to two paradigmatically divergent examples.

Two Alternative, Comprehensive Accounts of Freedom as *Ungrund*

1. A Post-Kantian Speculative Account: F.W.J. Schelling

The great secret of Kant's critical philosophy was freedom. It was part of Kant's wisdom and the cornerstone of his transcendental approach to postulate freedom without attempting to think freedom itself. Precisely this, thinking freedom itself, became the central challenge of the speculative efforts of German idealism, especially of Fichte and Schelling. Schelling's famous and impenetrable treatise *Of Human Freedom*[14] is a particularly interesting example because of its comprehensive and rigorous post-Kantian philosophical investigation into the problem of freedom. Moreover, representing the beginning of Schelling's later philosophy, this particular text epitomizes a highly charged transitory point in modern thought from which the entire post-Hegelian constellation—from Marxism to the existentialist notion of finitude and temporality as the ultimate horizon of being (Kierkegaard, Heidegger, Sartre)—received its decisive impetus. As Slavoj Žižek most recently argued, Schelling's late philosophy also anticipates the deconstructionist "decentering" of the self-presence of logos in most recent philosophical discussions.[15] Ultimately, Schelling's deep influence on Paul Tillich's thought had a significant, albeit mostly hidden, influence on modern Protestant theology in America.[16]

Schelling's *Of Human Freedom* offers a paradigmatic case for freedom thought not through the fundamental concept of *reception*, but rather through the concept of *indifference*. Freedom then comes to possess the human, who is, in Sartre's famous phrase, "condemned to freedom." Schelling's theory of freedom gives a metaphysical account of the *malum morale* that actually works as modernity's last theodicy. It rests on the semblance of a Trinitarian account of God, yet one with a fundamental theological flaw. Schelling's doctrine of God is such that God's own identity is constituted by an *unvordenkliche* act of self-determination for the good that is the eternal realization of God's freedom. Always already overcome in this primal act is a *Grund*, a divine potentiality that nevertheless remains present in God's existence as the very background of that which has been overcome in God's eternal self-determination. Underlying both potentiality (*Grund*) and realized existence of God is an abyss (*Ungrund*) of sheer indifference. This abyss divides itself into two equally eternal beginnings so that life, love, and personal existence arise. All of this can only occur by the indifference of the abyss giving itself up into the two beginnings, the *Grund* and God's existence. Schelling thus considers the unoriginate origin of freedom as the indifference of the absolute *Ungrund*, the abyss.

Human freedom now is conceived as the enactment of a fundamental choice, an original act of self-determination—not unlike that of God. Yet the crucial problem is that while God's fundamental self-determination for the good, that is, for who God *is*, is eternally established and the "ground" always already overcome in God, the human is poised in a structurally similar, yet substantively different position. The absolute indifference of the abyss is now reproduced on the level of an original human situation as the perfect equilibrium between the will of the ground and the will of God. It is the position of a mountain peak which is so steep and narrow that one has to fall in the one direction or the other. It is a balance constituted by nothing but the fundamental choice between two perilous options; and as Heidegger pressed Schelling on this point, it therefore is constituted by nothing.

In order to be anything but nothing, the freedom of an absolute self-determination from a perfectly indifferent position must rather be thought itself as *the reception of freedom*. Yet that would require a fundamentally different way of thinking God in relationship to freedom than Schelling did in his theodicist and only quasi-Trinitarian account. Might it be that a fully fleshed out account of human freedom via the concept of reception calls for an explicit reflection of God's triunity?

With this question in mind we need to turn to the most speculatively daring recent account of God's trinity, at the hidden center of which again sits the very theme of freedom.

2. A Trinitarian Account: Robert Jenson

Jenson's *Systematic Theology*[17] draws upon the best of the ecumenical tradition and the fathers in order to develop a rigorous theological account of the Gospel of Jesus Christ, a "metaphysics" of the Gospel. Furthermore, he is acutely aware of the modern problematic of freedom and its self-precipitary tendency toward nihilism in short of the Schellingian problematic of indifference as the unoriginate origin of freedom.

Jenson's Trinitarian account of freedom includes God's triune identities and the economy of salvation inasmuch as the former encompasses the latter. At its very center stands the Spirit as freedom. Here freedom is thought as a distinct divine identity that antecedently includes both the freedom of an original *giving oneself* (and therein being Father) and an original *reception* (and therein being Son). Yet the Spirit as freedom is not just the communal reality of giving and receiving in which Father and Son are free for one another. Rather, the Spirit as freedom is the identity of God's own future that always liberates anew the Father for the Son and the Son for the Father in mutual love. While there is an antecedent source of giving of freedom in the Father, it is outweighed by an infinite receiving of freedom that is the Spirit's identity. God ultimately both gives and receives his own freedom, and the latter only fully occurs in the eschatological inclusion of a redeemed creation. Thus in Jenson's work a dynamic notion of reception emerges in his way of thinking divine freedom. Divine freedom is a self-reception that occurs in the course of infinitely receiving freedom to be for the other in love, originating in the fundamental giver and thus origin of freedom, the Father.

This account of divine freedom does not, of course, immediately translate into created freedom but constitutes the correct theological horizon in which created freedom needs to be thought. Yet there remains one lacuna in Jenson's Trinitarian account of freedom. While developing an account of divine mandates in the course of his doctrine of creation, Jenson does not think the "law" (analogically conceived) explicitly in relationship to divine freedom. Because he does not develop an account of the *lex aeterna* as God's "law of freedom in love," i.e., no account of "eternal law" as the Spirit's law, he ultimately cannot relate God's Torah, the mandates of heaven, to God's triune identity. At this point, Jenson does not overcome the problematic inheritance of a non-Trinitarian thinking of Torah/law; thus the specter of the nominalist danger of Torah/law as God's contingent will for humanity in radical separation from the goal of deification/communion with God continues to lurk on the horizon in Jenson's otherwise pathbreaking account. Only if Torah/law itself is thought in relation to the "law of God's freedom" and thus as rooted in the triune life, can it truly participate in the teleology of the economy of salvation.

Theological Consequences

As these two accounts show, post-Kantian modernity forces theology to think freedom "from the beginning," in other words: to occupy the conceptual space of the unoriginate origin in order to prevent its use for a speculative account of human freedom as unoriginate origin.[18] Therefore, an account of divine freedom needs to be given before human freedom can rightly be conceived, i.e., the fundamental distinction between uncreated and created freedom needs to be thought and unfolded.[19] Yet how can we think divine freedom without falling into the trap of thinking the unoriginate origin, yet by nevertheless occupying the conceptual space that has been created since the unoriginate origin was first thought? Thinking divine freedom theologically cannot begin aprioristically with a speculative account of divine freedom, lest it is posited as a mere *potentia absoluta* that will be nothing but a synonym for the necessity of sheer random willfulness. Rather, thinking divine freedom needs to begin where divine freedom is encountered, where divine freedom reveals itself as what it is in communicating itself by calling to freedom and thus by setting concretely free. Thus, a theological reflection on divine freedom has to *begin* with the economy of salvation (the election of Israel, her calling into being that is her calling to freedom and the calling of humanity through Israel's Messiah into that freedom of communion that is at the same time the fulfillment of Israel's promises). It must then *lead to* theology proper, i.e., to a Trinitarian account of divine freedom—and thereby occupy the conceptual space of the unoriginate origin. Only after and in light of such an account of divine freedom is it possible to think human freedom as created, and more specifically as received freedom. Yet the question might arise whether such a robustly theological way of reconceiving created freedom will do justice to the phenomenon of "freedom" at all. Can such an account of freedom be true at all without justifying itself in light of this or that philosophical theory of freedom? There is significant conceptual support for this approach in a recent landmark study pressing for a radically theological account of truth.

Conceptual Confirmation: Marshall, *Trinity and Truth*[20]

Rather than simply offering conceptual support for the systematic structure of my proposal, Marshall's central thesis actually implies that it *has* to be done this way. In the course of a rigorous argument Marshall shows that the best available considerations of recent analytic philosophy of language support the necessity of a radically non-apologetic approach to the truth-claims of Christian beliefs: "[I]f central Christian beliefs are to be held true at all, they must have unrestricted epistemic primacy. A Christian view of things will be one which orders the whole open field of possible sentences or beliefs so as to achieve at least consistency with a christological and trinitarian center; in this way it will match epistemic priorities to its truth commitments, and so hope to come up with a plausible interpretation of the whole field."[21]

If Marshall is right, then a fundamental and comprehensive theological account of freedom and law must "begin with the beginning" in order not to leave conceptually unoccupied the modern space of the unoriginate origin. It also must start by thinking freedom theologically "from the inside out," that is, it must grant epistemic primacy to the central Christian beliefs, and that is the triune identification of God and the economy of salvation it implies.

Marshall's way of solving some fundamental issues around the question of the truth and justification of beliefs thus resolves the question of the primary framework of reference and justification for a comprehensive theological account of "freedom and law." Would it need to be a certain philosophical conceptuality and approach, be it phenomenological (Scheler), analytic (Dennett, Inwagen), idealist (neo-Fichtean, neo-Hegelian), or process (Whitehead)? Would it need to draw conceptually from a scientific anthropology (Plessner et al., with Pannenberg's anthropology as the paradigmatic model)? Would it need to implement, in other words, the epistemic dependency thesis, "according to which the primary criteria for deciding about the truth of Christian beliefs . . . must not themselves be distinctively Christian"?[22] Yet drawing upon any of these conceptualities as the justificatory framework for the inquiry would imply a choice between rival and often incompatible accounts. However, this moment of choice would immediately weaken any apologetic approach by revealing a fundamental point that Marshall drives so convincingly home: the justification of beliefs rests on other beliefs. And thus the justification of the choice of philosophical conceptuality would rest on other beliefs that beg justification and so forth.

In short, Marshall's argument shows why it is not only to be expected but wholly appropriate in light of the most rigorous account of truth that analytic philosophy has to offer that the central Christian beliefs—here, the doctrine of the Trinity—are found to have explanatory power with the rest of reality—here, freedom and law.

And the Law?

A theology of freedom will ultimately always result in antinomianism if it is not supplemented by a nuanced and comprehensive theology of the law.[23] Yet the latter is what modern Protestantism, especially in its increasing subscription to Enlightenment suppositions, is lacking. This is a double shortcoming. On its theological side it has its root in the increasing failure to think the law as framed by a comprehensive economy of salvation in which *Torah* continues to matter. On its conceptual side, closely interwoven with the theological aspect, it is the increasing habit to think the law in a fundamentally non-analogical way. Its strictly univocal use in most of Protestant theology (to be precise, predominantly for its Lutheran strand) as restraining, enforcing, and convicting could only bring into the strongest relief its fundamental opposition to the Gospel as liberating and life-giving. This construal prevents thinking of the law so that it allows for a constructive understanding of Israel's Torah-obedience and Torah-joy. Therefore, it must conceptualize Christian freedom (and *a fortiori* freedom as such in modernity as secularized Christendom) in ultimately antinomian ways. In short, a non-analogical concept of law can no longer capture its fundamental *Torah* aspect, the crucial insight that created freedom is destined for a life with God that has a definite *Gestalt*. A non-analogical concept of law must result either in legalism (implementing the Torah-aspect in the framework of a univocal concept of law; thus supporting the "3rd use of the law") or in antinomianism (by rejecting the Torah aspect of the concept of law as formative for Christian life).

This development is, of course, primarily relevant only for the church and the Christian way of life. Yet it has clear repercussions for the church's understanding of Israel as well as a non-supersessionist self-understanding in relationship to Israel and Israel's Torah. Moreover, the non-analogical, significantly narrowed understanding of "law" in the late-modern public is at least one cause of the false opposition of freedom and law. This freedom can only be conceived negatively, and this "law" can only reflect the arbitrary will of a political majority continuing an ultimately contingent legal tradition (as exemplified in its possibly clearest form in the more recent works of Richard Rorty).

The following ten theses offer the contours of a comprehensive theology of law that grows from the theology of freedom as sketched up to this point, presupposes an analogical concept of law, and addresses the modern individualist *aporia* of autonomy by fundamentally accounting for the priority of community in thinking about both freedom and law:

1. It is not just ten rules for decent behavior that Israel receives in the Decalogue. Rather, its preamble unequivocally claims Israel and in so doing constitutes the form of Israel's irrevocable way of life with the God who raised it from Egypt. As Frank Crüsemann has argued, this way of life, being always directed to its source, constitutes the form of Israel's freedom. For Israel the nature of "positive freedom" is thus irreversibly defined: freedom is "life with God" and is actualized in the course of continuously mediating God's commandments by continuously receiving them. Practicing the form of this freedom is therefore practicing its ongoing reception. In Psalm 119 we can find a paradigmatic witness to this mode of continuously receiving freedom's form as a way of life with God. Israel's life of faith, as witnessed by the Scriptures, documents most clearly that this continuous receiving only occurs in community, a community shaped by practices of memory, worship, and discipleship.

2. Yet since this way of life depends on a source that is intrinsically beyond its reach, it inevitably leads to its own crisis.[24] Were it not for its prophetic indictment, this crisis would not necessarily be visible by itself. It emerges in full clarity only in light of its resolu-

tion. While "the law is holy, and the commandment is holy and just and good" (Rom 7:12), it cannot achieve its own end, or fulfill its comprehensive reception. This fulfillment remains God's own eschatological act imparting the messianic gift of reception in the form of God's own self-giving. In Christ's life, death, and resurrection, this mode of reception is fundamentally fulfilled "for the many" and offered to all nations as gift and as example. Ultimately, it is for Christ's sake that the law is continuously present in the church. Without God's law continuously being taught, we do not understand what it means that Christ fulfilled God's law *pro nobis*, that Christ is the gift of fulfillment, and that we always remain in need of Christ's fulfillment of the law.[25] In other words, only in light of its ongoing presence does Christ remain "the unsurpassable exegesis of the law" as well as its ongoing fulfillment.[26]

3. In Christian *catechesis*, the Decalogue circumscribes the practices in which creaturely freedom is genuinely received and therefore continuously practiced, and continuously practiced and therefore genuinely received. The fundamental mode of reception is faith, for the first commandment can only be fulfilled by faith. Yet faith is nothing else than the receiving of Christ. If it is not active, living faith, it is always something other than genuine faith. Therefore, genuine creaturely freedom exists only insofar as it is fully received in the form of—and thus as being formed by—God's commandments in faithful enactment.[27]

4. If genuine freedom is always received and formed by its reception,[28] then humans cannot realize freedom on their own; nor can they successfully think freedom as self-originating origin without continuously perverting freedom. Nor can humans give themselves the law in the course of whose practice genuine freedom is realized.[29] Since the law that is the partner of genuine freedom can only be received, it cannot be purely human law. It rather needs to be the gift of the One whose creatures humans are. And if it is to be received as the Creator's gift, it needs ultimately to be reflective of the Giver (*lex aeterna*).[30]

5. In contrast to antinomian Protestantism, there is no displacement of the revealed law in Aquinas, Luther, Melanchthon, or Calvin. Because they presuppose the law's paradigmatic fulfillment in Christ, they are able to practice a differentiated reception of the

law that still deserves to be seriously considered. In its fundamentally contingent reception (*Decalogue*), the law remains authoritative as the revealed summary of the *natural law*. In contrast, the understanding of Israel as a contingent political reality finds its equivalent in the "*human law*" (Aquinas) or the "*Sachsenspiegel*" (Luther). Finally, the understanding of Israel as God's holy people (*purity law and sacrificial law*) is not abandoned, but rather, through baptism and the Lord's Supper, the holiness of Israel is fulfilled in Christ.[31] Though this traditional way of differentiation is far superior to displacing the law in a roundabout way in liberal Protestantism, it might very likely not be the last word on this matter.[32]

6.   The antinomian displacement of the law, in contrast, undercuts the notion of freedom as gift that is realized as reception and thus continuously connected to the only possible source of genuine freedom.   The law's critical function continues to press that genuine freedom is utterly dependent on God's redeeming and restoring self-giving in Christ. Yet at the same time, this freedom is enacted in a way that continues the mode of reception through the form it takes in practicing God's precepts or commandments.

7.   Genuine freedom, therefore, presupposes communal practices of ongoing reception that include practices of remembrance, instruction, interpretation, discernment, discipline, and discipleship.[33] The enactment of genuine freedom presupposes and requires the existence of distinct communities in which these practices of reception concretely occur.

8.   These communities can neither be conceived as aggregations of like-minded individuals for limited purposes nor, as is now occurring, as a panacea for the loneliness, isolation, and inner emptiness of the late modern individual. These communities cannot arise as another thing to be done, achieved, put into place, and managed but can only be received as the result of a continuing conversion.

9.   If freedom's form and fulfillment, the redemption from its "fall" into individual sovereignty, will to power, and license, is to be received "on the way," if it is to be learned by participating in the practices of reception, then the self's late modern problematic of ceaselessly oscillating between the daydream of Promethean freedom and the nightmare of the eclipse of freedom is irresolvable on its own terms.[34]

10. Because freedom is fallen, "positive freedom" (as the freeing of freedom in and through the practices of its reception) must ultimately also be able to account for the rudiments of "negative freedom" (as protected by a "law" that equally recognizes the fundamental dignity of all human beings *qua* human beings).[35] What is crucial is not understood in most liberal theory—"negative freedom" itself rests upon the freeing of freedom as its ongoing reception—lest "negative freedom" is deconstructed as a decisionist fiction.[36] In order to avoid this deconstruction, the law of "negative freedom" must itself be received. Yet this reception depends internally on the reception of that law that is both the fulfillment and form of genuine freedom. In other words, political liberalism depends on resources that are intrinsically beyond its grasp.

Toward a Comprehensive Theology of Freedom and Law

The task is to move toward a comprehensive theology of freedom and law. *First*, thinking "freedom" along the lines of a Trinitarian, economic, and anthropological account of "reception" (analogically conceived) in turn creates the theological space for an integral, yet differentiated theology of law.[37] *Second*, the ensuing theology of law rests on a fundamentally analogical concept of law that will help in overcoming some of the problems of distinguishing "law and Gospel" that have haunted Protestantism from its beginning. *Third*, the task of integrating "person" and "community" in the "law of freedom" addresses the problems inherent in the modern apotheosis of the subject (including intersubjectivity) as well as in its post-modern pulverization. *Fourth*, no satisfying account of the intrinsic relationship between the reception of freedom and the reception of the law can be given without attending to the desire and love of the good, in other words, without that teleology that directs both freedom and law in their positive nature. Even more so, Christ must be understood as the embodiment of this fundamental reception.

Yet finally, the "so what" question: What are the implications of this proposal? What difference does its trajectory make? Let me conclude my remarks with three tentative suggestions. First, a perspective for overcoming the impasse between license and legalism opens up. In its original form the law gives shape to that relationship of persons whose embodiment is genuine freedom, that is, positive freedom. Second, there is a way to situate the negative freedom of modern liberalism. Negative freedom and its liberal entourage of rights are rooted in an antecedent reception of positive freedom. Thus negative freedom is parasitical upon a positive account of freedom and its concomitant reception of law in order for negative freedom to be intelligible at all in its protective and emancipatory function. Third, positive, genuine freedom only exists in communities in which freedom and law are ongoingly received, which raises crucial questions for the church. Which are the practices in and through which this reception occurs? Do we understand the importance of these practices rightly and do we let ourselves sufficiently be drawn into them and be shaped by them? These are only some of the implications of my inquiry. In light of the disastrous outcome of the modern misunderstanding of freedom, including the present technological, scientific, and economic take-over of the planet, I am simply suggesting a fundamental reconsideration of the ways we conceive of freedom and law.

Endnotes

1.   Cf. my "(Re-)Forming Freedom: Reflections 'after *Veritatis Splendor*' on Freedom's Fate in Modernity and Protestantism's Antinomian Captivity," *Modern Theology* 17 (2001), 117-161; esp. 122-129.

2.   Cf. Alasdair MacIntyre, "Theology, Ethics, and the Ethics of Medicine and Health Care," *Journal of Medicine and Philosophy* 4 (1979), 437; and idem, "How Can We Learn What *Veritatis Splendor* Has to Teach?," in *Veritatis Splendor and the Renewal of Moral Theology: Studies by Ten Outstanding Scholars*," ed. by J.A. DiNoia, O.P. and Romanus Cessario, O.P. (Princeton: Scepter Publishers, 1994), 73-94.

3.   For the lasting problematic that arose from abandoning the teleological scheme in ethics, cf. Alasdair MacIntyre's account in his *After Virtue: A Study in Moral Theory* (Notre Dame: University of Notre Dame Press, 2nd ed. 1984). Yet the actual critique and abandonment of teleological thinking from the late medieval period on—I am primarily thinking here of the rise of nominalism—is a complex history. After all, in the period called modernity we find some remarkable attempts of mediation between universal mechanics (i.e., early modern non-teleological natural science) and teleology in Leibniz, Wolff, and Kant. In Hegel's system, modern teleological thinking reached a unique culmination. Yet none of these attempts had significant (if any) influence on the way natural science emerged—especially from the middle of the nineteenth century on, that is, after the final demise of Hegelianism. Cf. Robert Spaemann and Reinhard Löw, *Die Frage Wozu? Geschichte und Wiederentdeckung des teleologischen Denkens* (Munich: Piper, 2nd ed. 1981).

4.   Jerome B. Schneewind, *The Invention of Autonomy: A History of Modern Moral Philosophy* (Cambridge: Cambridge University Press, 1998), 483-530. While I agree in large parts with Schneewind's reconstruction of Kant's ethics, I do not agree with

the skeptical implications that Schneewind's characterization of autonomy as Kant's "invention" suggests. Cf. my engagement of Schneewind in "God and the Search for Moral Truths," *Christian Century* 115 (1998), 1147-1151.

5.   Cf. Immanuel Kant, *Critique of Practical Reason*: "This kind of credential of the moral law—that it is itself laid down as a principle of the deduction of freedom as a causality of pure reason—is fully sufficient in place of any apriori justification, since theoretical reason was forced *to assume* at least the possibility of freedom in order to fill a need of its own" (*Kritik der praktischen Vernunft (KpV)* 5:48; cf. the course of the argument up to 5:50). The quote is taken from Immanuel Kant, *Critique of Practical Reason*, trans. and ed. by Mary Gregor. Introduction by Andrews Reath (Cambridge: Cambridge University Press, 1997), 42.

6.   This, of course, is the all too roughly summarized outcome of a very complex development of Kant's thought on the matter of freedom. Cf. Henry E. Allison, *Kant's Theory of Freedom* (Cambridge: Cambridge University Press, 1990) for a detailed account of the precise contours of Kant's emerging account of freedom.

7.   In Kant's mature thought freedom comes to occupy a conceptual space in relationship to the concept of God that makes it impossible to think of freedom as created and, as such, received. Cf. the well-known remarks in the preface to Kant's *Critique of Practical Reason*: "Now, the concept of freedom, insofar as its reality is proved by an apodictic law of practical reason, constitutes the keystone of the whole structure of a system of pure reason, even of speculative reason; and all other concepts (those of God and immortality), which as mere ideas remain without support in the latter, now attach themselves to this concept and with it and by means of it get stability and objective reality, that is, their possibility is proved by this: that freedom is real, for this idea reveals itself through the moral law" (*KpV* 5:4; translation quoted from *op.cit*).

8.   For a superb reconstruction of the "ethics of autonomy," cf. Dieter Henrich, *"Ethik der Autonomie,"* in idem, *Selbstverhältnisse: Gedanken und Auslegungen zu den Grundlagen der klassischen deutschen Philosophie* (Stuttgart: Reclam, 1982, 1993), 6-56.

9.   Cf. my "(Re-)Forming Freedom," 145-147.

10.   There is no communitarian solution to the modern aporia of freedom for, as Ronald Beiner rightly observes, "the withdrawal into particularistic communities merely confirms what defines the problem in the first place. . . . To affirm community as such is to abstain from judgment about the substantive attributes of a given community. Communal autonomy, like individual autonomy, abstracts from judgments of substance" (*What's the Matter with Liberalism?* [Berkeley: University of California Press, 1992], 31). Cf. Stanley Hauerwas, "Communitarians and Medical Ethicists: Or, 'Why I Am None of the Above,'" in idem, *Dispatches from the Front: Theological Engagements with the Secular* (Durham: Duke University Press, 1994), 156-165.

11.   Cf. here especially Philip A. Rolnick, "Persons, Purpose, and Grace," in Robert K. Johnston, L. Gregory Jones, and Jonathan R. Wilson (eds.), *Grace upon Grace: Essays in Honor of Thomas A. Langford* (Nashville: Abingdon Press, 1999), 181-198 and Robert Spaemann, *Personen: Versuche über den Unterschied zwischen "etwas" und "jemand"* (Stuttgart: Klett-Cotta, 1996).

12.   This obviously is a claim that requires a range of warrants and specifications. For a beginning, cf. theses 6-8 further down. On the ontology of personhood that bridges between divine and human personhood and the church as "communio" of persons, cf. John D. Zizioulas, *Being as Communion: Studies in Personhood and the Church* (Crestwood: St. Vladimir's Seminary Press, 1985, 2nd ed. 1993) and for an instructively critical engagement of Zizioulas, cf. Miroslav Volf, *After Our Likeness:*

The Church as the Image of the Trinity (Grand Rapids: William B. Eerdmans, 1998), 73-123.

13. "Reception" distances this approach from the largely non-Trinitarian metaphysical commitments of process theology as well as from the modern way of construing the "law of freedom" via subjectivity (and later intersubjectivity) and its postmodern deconstruction.

14. Friedrich Wilhelm Joseph Schelling, *Philosophische Untersuchungen über das Wesen der menschlichen Freiheit und die damit zusammenhängenden Gegenstände*, hg. von Thomas Buchheim (Darmstadt: Wissenschaftliche Buchgesellschaft, 1997). (Page references in the text refer to the German edition). English translation: *Of Human Freedom*, with a critical introduction and notes by James Gutmann (La Salle: Open Court, 1936).

15. Slavoj Žižek/F.J. von Schelling, *The Abyss of Freedom / Ages of the World* (Ann Arbor, University of Michigan Press, 1997).

16. For Schelling's impact on Tillich but especially also for Schelling's conceptual superiority to Tillich's interpretation and adaptation of his thought, cf. Philip Clayton, *The Problem of God in Modern Thought* (Grand Rapids: W.B. Eerdmans Publishers, 2000), 467-471.

17. Robert W. Jenson, *Systematic Theology, Volume I: The Triune God* (New York: Oxford University Press, 1997); *Volume II: The Works of God* (New York: Oxford University Press, 1999).

18. This is an insight that has deeply shaped the work of Hans Urs von Balthasar in ways that separate him from the Thomisms of the 19th and 20th centuries. See especially his *Apokalypse der deutschen Seele: Studien zu einer Lehre von den letzten Haltungen*. 3 vols. (Freiburg: Johannes Verlag Einsiedeln, 1st ed. 1932-39, 3rd ed. 1998).

19. Cf. Hans Urs von Balthasar, *Theodramatik II / 1: Der Mensch in Gott* (Einsiedeln: Johannes Verlag, 1976), 220-288.

20. Bruce D. Marshall, *Trinity and Truth* (Cambridge: Cambridge University Press, 2000).

21. *Ibid.*, 140.

22. *Ibid.*, 50.

23. Thomas Aquinas's integration in the *Summa Theologiae* stands here as the great ecumenical example in the Western tradition that, almost as soon as having been achieved, was abandoned.

24. Jer 31:31-34 can be read as a text in which this problematic intensifies in a dramatic, yet ultimately promising, way.

25. Cf. Luther's *Fifth Disputation Against the Antinomians* (1538), *Weimarer Ausgabe, D. Martin Luthers Werke: Kritische Gesamtausgabe*. (Weimar: H. Bohlau, 1884) vol. 39/I, thesis 61 and 62, where Luther states that God's law, which we do not fulfill, reflects God's own goodness, and precisely because God's law is good and perfect, it condemns us.

26. I owe this expression to R. Kendall Soulen. Cf. his important and thought-provoking reflections in idem, *The God of Israel and Christian Theology* (Minneapolis: Fortress Press, 1996), 156-177.

27. In his exposition of the Decalogue in the *Large Catechism*, Luther does not use any "law" language—precisely because it remains open how the Decalogue is received, whether in faith as freedom's form (and therefore not as *"alia lex"* but as freedom received in obedience to and communion with God) or without faith (as an *"alia lex"* for the sake of human life under the condition of sin). George Lindbeck put

it exactly the right way when he observed regarding the logic of the Decalogue in the *Large Catechism*: "As Luther perceived it, Christian tradition has confused two fundamentally different senses of the concepts of 'precept' (his usual word for 'commandment') and therefore also of 'obedience.' . . . His innovative method of unmasking the confusions was to call precepts 'doctrine' or instructions in the performance of practices, which, when well learned, are intrinsically satisfying. As fallen creatures, to be sure, we do not spontaneously experience the practices in which the commandments instruct us as intrinsically good, but God's goodness gives us the confidence that that is what they are. We thus need not hesitate to train ourselves in them, even without faith or desire. . . . The practices God commands can to some degree be satisfying in themselves, quite apart from rewards and punishments, even when performance is as inadequate as it always is for human beings, and even when true faith and love of God and neighbor is lacking" ("Martin Luther and the Rabbinic Mind," in Peter Ochs (ed.), *Understanding the Rabbinic Mind: Essays on the Hermeneutic of Max Kadushin* [Atlanta: Scholars Press: 1990], 156f).

28. Wilfried Joest, *Gesetz und Freiheit: Das Problem des Tertius Usus Legis bei Luther und die neutestamentliche Parainese* (Göttingen: Vandenhoeck & Ruprecht, 2nd ed. 1956), 203 fn. 62.

29. Kant saw this in a limited sense. According to Kant, we encounter the law and interpret it as both co-constituted and received.

30. Here occurs the "either-or" between Aquinas and Scotus, that is, between intellectualism and voluntarism in the conception of the law. Cf. Jerome B. Schneewind, *The Invention of Autonomy: A History of Modern Moral Philosophy*, (Cambridge: Cambridge University Press, 1998) for an account that uses this "either-or" to map the inner tension in the way modern natural law emerged in Europe in the course of, and after, the wars of religion.

31. This is the case for gentile Christians. For members of Israel joining "the way," Acts 15 mirrors the seriousness of the question of the ongoing life according to the Torah for Jewish Christians in the very early Christian communities. This burning ecclesiological (!) question unfortunately disappeared with the disappearance of Jewish Christians in the following centuries and the increasing antagonism between church and synagogue. Only in light of the Holocaust and a renewed Jewish-Christian dialogue did this question surface again. For an excellent discussion, cf. the symposion on "Jewish-Christians and the Torah," *Modern Theology* 11 (1995), 163-241.

32. For a fascinating new exegetical initiative in this area, cf. Markus Bockmuehl, *Jewish Law in Gentile Churches: Halakhah and the Beginning of Christian Public Ethics* (Edinburgh: T&T Clark, Ltd., 2000).

33. Stanley Hauerwas has pressed this insight in his recent work. Cf. especially "The Truth about God: The Decalogue as Condition for Truthful Speech," in idem, *Sanctify Them in the Truth: Holiness Exemplified,* (Edinburgh: T&T Clark, 1998) 37-59, and *The Truth About God: The Ten Commandments in Christian Life*, with William H. Willimon (Nashville: Abingdon Press, 1999).

34. For a description of the oscillation between modernity's daydream of Promethean freedom and the postmodern nightmare of the eclipse of freedom, cf. my "(Re-)Forming Freedom," 122-129.

35. I am indebted to Judge Laurie Ackermann for coming to this insight. Belonging to the new South African supreme court, he was part of the juridical committee that approved the new constitution of South Africa.

36. It is by no means accidental that political liberalism continues to be haunted by the specter of Carl Schmitt. If negative freedom is not continuously protected by the ongoing reception of genuine freedom, it becomes vulnerable to the kind of deconstruction that Carl Schmitt's work represents.

37. In light of the dominant twentieth-century contruals of Luther's theology and ethics, somewhat revisionist readings of Luther and the Protestant tradition will need to come into play here. See my essay "The Twofold Center of Lutheran Ethics: Christian Freedom and God's Commandments," in Karen L. Bloomquist and John R. Stumme (eds.), *The Promise of Lutheran Ethics* (Minneapolis: Fortress Press, 1998), 31-54; 179-192; and also "(Re-)Forming Freedom," 138-145.

The Fact of Death and the
Promise of Life in Israelite Religion

Jon D. Levenson
HARVARD UNIVERSITY DIVINITY SCHOOL
CAMBRIDGE, MASSACHUSETTS

Among both Jews and Christians today, it is commonly believed that adherence to the doctrine of the resurrection of the dead is a point of difference between these two related communities. Judaism, it is widely believed, regards death as natural, irreversible, and in accordance with God's final will. Christianity, on the contrary, affirms (at least in its classical forms) not only that God raised Jesus from the dead but also that in so doing, he gave a proleptic anticipation of his resurrection of all the dead in the eschatological era.

In fact, the classical rabbinic tradition, from which the familiar modern forms of Judaism, even the most liberal, derive, held a different view, one much closer to the Christian position. The rabbis saw the belief that God would raise the dead at the end of time as an indispensable element of their own religious life. The first great law code of rabbinic Judaism, the Mishnah, thus relegates those who deny that the resurrection of the dead is in the Torah itself to the category of those "who have no portion in the world-to-come," i.e., the category of rank heretics.[1] The rabbis also structured the affirmation that God "revives the dead" into the statutory liturgy and thus required that it be made every day—weekday, Sabbath, and festival, even in the house of mourning in which death's sting is still fresh and death's cruel finality seems so real.

Note the scope of the rabbis' demand in the version of the Mishnah cited above. They ask for assent not only to the doctrine of a resurrection but to a belief that it can be found in the Torah, i.e., the Pentateuch. It is not necessary to examine here the strained exegeses that the Talmudic tradition developed to validate this bold claim. Even the rabbinic tradition itself did not argue that these were the only possible readings of the verses they pressed into service in defense of their claim, and the medieval Jewish Bible commentators who pursued the "plain sense" (*peshaṭ*) of the text were even less likely to read them in this way. The first inclination for scholars practicing historical criticism is to dismiss the rabbinic interpretation as tendentious and anachronistic. To us, the rabbis, like the early Christians and, for that matter, religious people in all communities and times, simply retrojected their own central and tenaciously held belief in an eschatological resurrection into the scriptures— scriptures in which the finality and irreversibility of death is, in fact, everywhere the belief. In the minds of most critical scholars, the actual view of the Hebrew Bible is nicely stated by the wise woman of Tekoa to King David, "We must all die; we are like water that is poured out on the ground and cannot be gathered up" (2 Sam. 14:14). To some modern people, this sad observation is, in fact, greeted with a certain joy. Those displaying the characteristic modern skepticism about the traditional doctrines of resurrection, whether in the Jewish or the Christian form, sometimes find in the Hebrew Bible a resource for a religious justification for their own naturalism. In this approach, the Hebrew Bible is interpreted to support the idea that death is natural, irreversible, and, most importantly, altogether in accordance with God's will—until, that is, the idea of resurrection mysteriously appears late in the biblical period, in Hellenistic times.[2] As Lloyd Bailey puts it, "mortality as the Creator's design for humans seems to be the basic perspective of the O[ld] T[estament] literature."[3] If so, then the suspicion that many modern people have that resurrection is a vestige of childish, pre-scientific thinking is not so heterodox after all; one can hold the suspicion and still be in continuity with the Jewish or the Christian traditions on this key point. For there was a time when the religion of Israel did not know of the now eminently orthodox doctrine of resurrection. The wise woman of Tekoa was not only wise but ahead of her time as well.

There is, to be sure, a large measure of truth in this, but it is a truth based mostly on the familiar modern phrasing of the question, "Will I have life after death? Will I be resurrected from the grave?" To this question, the wise woman's observation constitutes the answer most characteristic of the Hebrew Bible: Death, sadly, is universal and final. It comes to all of us; it is the last word in our existence. The problem with this way of posing the question is that it misses another equally characteristic feature of the Hebrew Bible, the highly social and familial construction of personal identity so characteristic of the communities that produced that set of scriptures. To summarize briefly, in ancient Israel, identity tends to be more communal than individual. As Robert Di Vito puts it, "ancient Israel is an 'aggregate of groups rather than . . . a collection of individuals,' and, apart from the family, the individual is scarcely a viable entity—socially, economically, or juridically."[4] To that list of three adverbs, we must surely add another—"religiously." For the idea that their God had promised them national greatness and a land of their own was very ancient among the Israelites, long preceding the late monarchic and exilic articulation of the idea characteristic of the late Pentateuchal sources. The prime enemies of that promise to the collectivity, the lethal threats to Israel's survival, in those sources are the barrenness of her would-be matriarchs and the loss of the promised sons. These are themes that suffuse the book of Genesis and not just its demonstrably late sources. They also reverberate through the rest of the Hebrew Bible. Amazingly, the biblical writers tell us, against all odds and the dictates of a cruel nature, these assaults on the promise of life, though real and the source of enormous grief (all of it justified), are turned back. God grants fertility and restores the doomed son, either literally or through a new birth. In addition, one must note the ubiquitous biblical promise of life as a reward for careful and faithful obedience to God's commands. This appears most memorably in the Deuteronomic injunction to Israel to "Choose life—if you and your offspring would live—by loving the LORD your God, heeding His commands, and holding fast to Him" (Deut 30:19-20). Whether the idiom is Deuteronomic, Priestly, or Sapiential, the promise of life to those who observe God's directives suffuses the Hebrew Bible (e.g., Lev 18:5; Prov 3:1-2, 13-18; 4:22; 8:35-36).

The problem, then, with that all too familiar and characteristically modern way of phrasing the question—"Will I have life after death? Will I be resurrected from the grave?"—is not only that it is individualistic and cannot accommodate the more social and communal construction of the self in ancient Israel. It is also that this phrasing gives no hint of the idea that the "I" in question lives under a promise of life and is, in fact, ideally subordinated to a regimen that promises abundant life.

Between this promise or offer of life and the equally ubiquitous fact of death in the Hebrew Bible, there is, as theologians say, a "tension." How can the same God who creates human beings mortal and decrees their death also promise them life as a consequence of their obedience to his commands, or even as a gracious gift made despite their failure to obey? By way of answer, let it first be noticed that within its ancient Near Eastern context, this tension is not so extreme as it seems to us, for "life" in that context has a much wider semantic range in the Hebrew Bible than it does for us. It includes, for example, power, skill, confidence, health, blessing, luck, and joy.[5] Thus can the factitive verb "to bring to life" (ḥiyya) mean simply "to cure, to make healthy,"[6] as we should expect in a culture in which the division between sickness and death was less clear than it seems to us and fewer victims of serious illness survived. For this reason, when ancient Israelite texts speak of "life," they usually mean not deathlessness, but a healthy, blessed existence. That such an existence must come to its inevitable end therefore in no way implies a defeat of God's promise of "life," so understood. Thus can Abraham or Job die "at a good ripe age, old and contented," whatever complaints they had against God now long in the past (Gen 25:7; Job 42:17).

The opposite of "life" in this understanding includes not only weakness, disease, depression, and the like, but also a humiliating death, especially one that is violent or premature.[7] It is this form of death, and not mortality in general, that Hezekiah, for example, prays that God spare him (Isa 38:1-3). When he does, that king quite naturally speaks as one who has been given life and spared "the pit of destruction" to which his sins had doomed him (vv 16-20). That he will still die at the end of his fifteen-year reprieve, symbolized by the miraculous retreat of the shadow on his father's sundial, does not qualify his joy in the least nor suggest to him that his sins were still working their toxic magic after all. Ancient Israelites had no reason to complain if they lived to a normal old age, such as the psalmist's three score and ten, and were spared the "trouble and sorrow" of which the same psalmist complains and were granted the "favor of the LORD" for which he petitions (Ps 90:10, 17). Anyone so favored could, like Abraham and Job, die "old and contented"—and without recrimination that the fact of death, the inevitable return of the shadow on the sundial, had undermined God's ubiquitous promise of life.

Further mitigation of the tension between the inevitability of death and God's promise of life comes from the highly social and familial construction of personal identity highlighted above. In a culture in which identity is so deeply embedded in family structures—is, indeed, inseparable from them—life is largely characterized by the emergence of new generations who stand in continuity and deference to the old. Barrenness is here the functional equivalent of death in more individualistic cultures, and the return of fertility functions like resurrection: it replaces death with life. It is thus not surprising that the blessings and curses of covenant in the Torah offer abundant fertility to those who observe God's commands, but threaten those who violate them with sterility and the death (or loss by other means) of children (e.g., Lev 26:9, 22, 29; Deut 28:11, 32, 41, 53-57, 62-63). These blessings and curses are addressed to the entire nation, not to individuals within it. That the individual Israelites will all surely die does not in the slightest impair the promise of life and fellowship with himself that YHWH has extended to the House of Israel. Here again, the fact of death and the promise of life stand in no great tension, for the two move on different planes, the individual and the national, respectively. Indeed, one might speculate that the stronger the consciousness of national identity became in ancient Israel, the less keen was the sting of individual misfortune, including the misfortune of an untimely death or the loss of descendants. In any event, the experience of undeserved adversity did not necessarily impel an ancient Israelite to accuse the Deity of injustice or unfaithfulness to his own pledged word. It could, of course, but it did not have to. For the unfulfilled promise (or threat) might come to fulfillment later, or even in a later generation.[8] In Wisdom Literature, the failure to recognize the time lag between unjust events and God's inevitable and reliable justice is, in fact, characteristic of the fool (e.g., Ps 92:7-8). The wise person, by contrast, knows that God's justice comes at its own unfathomable pace and may arrive only in a future generation. But arrive it surely shall.

Seen within the universe of ancient Israelite belief, then, the promise of life so prominent throughout the Hebrew Bible is not inconsistent with the brute fact of human mortality that is equally prominent therein. The God of Israel can without contradiction both offer life to his faithful and decree that all shall die. Still, even within the cultural universe of ancient Israel, I submit, a tension between the fact of death and the promise of life does remain. Or, to phrase the same point slightly differently, the arrangement in which *both* of these are affirmed is inherently unstable, and we should not be surprised to find a different model of simultaneous affirmation appearing in the post-exilic period. The new model is one in which people necessarily die but are subsequently revived and, if found worthy, granted eternal life. This later model is, of course, what has come to be known as the resurrection of the dead.

To understand the intrinsic instability of the pre-exilic settlement, let us first revisit the crucial point that "life" (*ḥayyim*) in biblical Hebrew has a wider semantic range than its English equivalent. If "life" can mean health and well-being, and "to bring to life" (*ḥiyya*) can signify simply "to cure, to make healthy," then the biblical promise or offer of life inevitably comes into contact with another ancient Israelite affirmation, also of high frequency and venerable antiquity—the affirmation that YHWH is Israel's healer:

> See, then, that I, I am He;
> There is no god beside Me.
> I deal death and give life;
> I wound and I will heal;
> None can deliver from My hand. (Deut 32:39)

Within the older understanding of death and life, the third line in the excerpt above (v 39c) means simply that God is the sole source of both death and life, as of both illness and health in the fourth (v 39d). He alone decrees both the end and the beginning of life, just as he decrees both disease and its remedy. "I deal death and give life," in short, need not imply resurrection, as the wording (especially the word order) might imply to the today's reader. But the same observation cuts the other way as well: if life is somehow equivalent to healing, and death to wounding, then why cannot the sole and unchallengeable Deity who heals lesser wounds also heal the graver malady that is death? In other words, if the semantic range of "death" in biblical Hebrew includes both disease and biological cessation,[9] is there any reason—again, strictly within the cultural universe of ancient Israel—to think that God could heal disease but could not reverse death? For it is not only the case that what we call "disease" the ancient Hebrew could call "death." The reverse is also the case: what we call "death" they could and did describe as "disease." Death, in short, could be seen as the most severe of illnesses and characterized (in this understanding) not by non-existence but by debilitation and physical fragility. As Aubrey R. Johnson puts it, "death, in the strict sense of the term, is for the Israelite the weakest form of life."[10]

This, it seems to me, explains the first remark of the deceased Samuel to Saul when the latter has had the necromancer of Endor summon him from the underworld. "Why have you disturbed me and brought me up?" asks the prophet (1 Sam 28:15). To us, this might seem comical. Surely, after years in the Underworld, the old man should be happy to return, however briefly, to the world of the living and not see this as a disturbance. In fact, however, he returns as a spirit only (*'elohim*), though one incarnated as an old man wrapped in a mantle (vv 13-14). Samuel is now neither a disembodied soul at peace with himself nor a fully realized person returned to his flesh, but, to put it in familiar language, a ghost annoyed at having to expend his precious energy in his brief appearance in the world of the living. The dead man still *exists*, but he is not *alive*. He exists in a state of permanent weakness, and any disturbance can only add to his discomfort. Most modern people would call that state "severe illness," but ancient Israel could call it "death" and see it as characteristic of Sheol, the dark, dank, lonely and profoundly depressing subterranean abode of the dead.[11]

Many biblical texts do indeed tacitly assume the accuracy of the Wise Woman of Tekoa's observation that "We must all die; we are like water that is poured out on the ground and cannot be gathered up" (2 Sam 14:14). But we must not overlook the fact that others presume the reverse. I am thinking of psalms, for example, that praise YHWH for bringing the psalmist up from Sheol (e.g., Ps 30:4). The obvious objection that the psalmists in question were never "really" dead only betrays the modern definition of death of the one who voices the objection. For in the psalmist's mind, the adversity he had experienced—illness, false accusation, enemy attack, or whatever—had truly brought him into the terrifying domain of death, from which his God's faithfulness and justice marvelously rescued him.[12] A major ingredient in the marvel and in the psalmist's ecstasy, it seems to me, is that such rescues from death are exceedingly rare, the Wise Woman of Tekoa's observation being the rule, not the exception. Even rarer are those instances in which someone who is "really" dead returns to life, as do the boys whom Elijah and Elisha resurrect in parallel narratives (1 Kgs 17:17-24; 2 Kgs 4:8-37). Were resurrections not thought to be rare—were they, that is, the ordinary course of things—the mother of the child Elijah resurrects would hardly have had occasion to affirm, as she does in the last words of the narrative, "Now I know that you are a man of God and that the word of the LORD is truly in your mouth" (1 Kings 17:24). Resurrection in ancient Near Eastern culture was thought to be a miracle, and miracles, as C.S. Lewis writes, "are, by definition, rarer than other events," and "it is obviously improbable beforehand that one will occur at any given place and time."[13] But this is very different from saying that death is universal, absolute, and irreversible, even at the hands of the God who is acclaimed as healer and deliverer of the afflicted.

This train of reasoning gives us another insight into the relationship between the fact of death, on the one hand, and the promise or offer of life, on the other. Earlier, we saw that these are not in logical contradiction in the Hebrew Bible after all, since "life" there can mean simply a long life span or one that ends in peaceful and honorable circumstances. The association of death with disease suggests another way of understanding the simultaneous acceptance of these two seeming opposites. Death is the ordinary human fate, and it is ordinarily irreversible, just as serious disease in the ancient Near Eastern world was ordinarily incurable. In a world without antibiotics, steroids, and effective surgery, few victims recovered from illnesses that are today readily curable, or at least controllable. Consider Naaman, the leprous Aramean general whom Elisha, the Israelite man of God, cures in the chapter after the one about his resurrection of the Shunammite boy. Surely Naaman had visited the best healers in Damascus in a futile quest of a cure for his affliction. His response when the man of God has healed him is strikingly reminiscent of the response of the mother of the boy whom

Elijah resurrected: "Now I know that there is no God in the whole world except in Israel." (2 Kings 5:15; cf. 1 Kgs 17:24). In the ordinary course of events, lepers remain lepers, and the dead remain dead.[14] But the God who "heals all your diseases" and "redeems your life from the Pit," as the Psalmist says (Ps 103:3-4), is not constrained by the ordinary course of events, and the exceptional case is still a reality with which to reckon. Indeed, its very status as a rare exception commends it to the Israelite mind as an act of God, a supernatural intervention into the dreary course of nature that is marked by incurable disease and irreversible death.

The pre-exilic worldview of which I am speaking is, to be sure, different from the worldview of those later Jews and Christians who held a doctrine of the resurrection of the dead. It does not do justice to the difference to say, as many do,[15] that in the pre-exilic period, death was thought to be irreversible, appropriate, and in accordance with God's will, whereas in the later period (among those who believed in resurrection) God was thought to rescue from death. A better way of stating the point, I maintain, is to say that what had been a rare exception in the early period became in the late one the basis for a general expectation. This is the apocalyptic expectation of a universal resurrection in a coming dispensation in which all God's potentials would be activated in a grand finale of stupendous miracles very much at odds with the natural course of history. One central aspect of the eschatological inversion is that the previous exception becomes the norm, as all opposition to God's saving power melts before his triumphant might—death emphatically included. It is not that human nature, suddenly and on its own, becomes invulnerable to death. Rather, God would at long last grant the rescue from adversity for which Israelites had always prayed, saving those who had hoped in him against all hope.

The burden of the preceding discussions is that there are tensions within the older Israelite notion that the "life" that God offers has to do with longevity and happiness, rather than with deathlessness or resurrection. Happiness, in this understanding of things, requires and includes health, and the health that is thus promised may result from God's curing a fatal illness. This includes the fatal illness that the ancient Israelites (and we as well) call death and that we (unlike them) instinctively consider final and irreversible.

Similar tensions, only stronger, characterize the other understanding of the promise of "life" in pre-exilic Israel that I developed above. My reference here is to the collective, or national character of that promise in the Hebrew Bible: It is the people of Israel and not individual Israelites who are granted the eternal covenant that, among other things, prevents their annihilation, fertility thus being the rough functional equivalent of resurrection in a more individualistic culture. The promise of a bright future after affliction, whether tendered in Pentateuchal sources or in the prophets, in no way implies that any given individual will have a future beyond his or her appointed life span. The promised future finds its fulfillment in the later generations of the chosen people.

The tension in this case inheres in the fact that a sharp distinction between the individual and the group usually cannot be drawn in this literature. When Robert Di Vito, whom I have quoted, writes that in the Hebrew Bible, "the subject is deeply embedded, or engaged, in its social identity,"[16] it must be noted that he is not denying the existence of a subject altogether. He is, rather, only differentiating the characteristic Israelite construction of personal identity from "salient features of modern identity, such as its pronounced individualism [which is] grounded in modernity's location of the self in the 'inner depths' of one's interiority rather than in one's social role or public relations."[17] And when Di Vito goes on to speak of Israelite identity as "comparatively decentered and undefined with respect to personal boundaries,"[18] I take him to be pointing to the pronounced fluidity that exists between the relationship of personal and collective identity in ancient Israel. It is this fluidity that explains how national or tribal ancestors can pre-enact the experience of their descendants, for example, and that leads to such longstanding disputes among exegetes as to whether the Suffering Servant of Second Isaiah is an individual or the nation or whether the first person singular in the Psalms refers to a lone speaker or to the community personified as such.[19] The very fact that these disputes have gone on so long raises the suspicion that the modern categories are inappropriate to the culture to which we seek to apply them. More importantly, it also suggests that promises of felicity that are directed to the nation at large may have been taken on occasion as applicable to individuals within it as well.

An analogy to the process I have in mind can be found in Ezekiel 18, the chapter in which the great prophet of the early exile protests against the notion of inherited guilt, epitomized in the popular saying, "Parents eat sour grapes and their children's teeth are blunted" (v 2). Ezekiel's retort—"The person who sins, only he shall die" (v 4)—is often taken as a denunciation of the idea of collective guilt and a decisive advance for the opposing notion of moral and spiritual individualism. The prophet's focus, however, is not on contemporaneous individuals at all, but on *generations*, and his principal point is that the guilt of the ancestors which caused the destruction of the Judahite kingdom and the ensuing exile does not condemn their current descendants to endless misery. A righteous father, one who abstains from abuses like robbery or sexual relations with a menstruous woman, "shall live," he assures us (vv 5-9). Should he have a son who engages in such flagrant sins, however, "He shall not live!" Ezekiel insists. "If he has committed any of these abominations, he shall die; he has forfeited his life" (vv 10-13). But the latter's own son, if he "has taken heed and not imitated" his father's abuses, "shall not die for the iniquity of his father…he shall live!" (vv 14-19). The message is obvious:

> The person who sins, he alone shall die. A child shall not share the burden of a parent's guilt, nor shall a parent share the burden of a child's guilt; the righteousness of the righteous shall be accounted to him alone, and the wickedness of the wicked shall be accounted to him alone. (Ezek 18:20)

Another way of stating this is to say that in God's moral calculus, each moment carries equal weight. No one generation can condemn its descendants, or acquit them. It bears mention that Ezekiel's preaching is in opposition not only to the popular proverb he cites in v 2, but also to sources in the Bible itself. The affirmation in the Decalogue that God "visit[s] the guilt of the parents upon the children" (Exod 20:5; Deut 5:9) springs to mind immediately. More relevant to Ezekiel's situation, however, is the claim that the destruction of the Judahite kingdom and the Jerusalem Temple in the prophet's own time is owing to King Manasseh's sin two generations earlier (2 Kgs 21:11-15; 24: 3-4).

For our purposes, two points about Ezekiel 18 are especially interesting. One is that the language of God's approval or disapproval of a person's actions is the language of life and death, respectively. The righteous shall live; the wicked shall surely die, even when the misdeeds are not classified as capital offenses in the surviving biblical law codes. What Ezekiel is reporting is not case law or guidance for human courts, but God's ultimate verdict—a judgment of life and death, with no intermediate points. How, exactly, that judgment is realized in human affairs and procedures is left vague.

The more important point for our discussion lies in the scenario the prophet sketches after having laid out the case of the righteous father with the wicked son and the righteous grandson and stated the conclusion cited above (Ezek 18:20). Here Ezekiel moves away the problem of *generations* that has occupied his attention throughout the chapter and speaks, instead, of two *moments in the life of one person*:

> [21]Moreover, if the wicked one repents of all the sins that he committed and keeps all My laws and does what is right and just, he shall live: he shall not die. [22]None of the transgressions he committed shall be remembered against him; because of the righteousness he has practiced, he shall live. [23]Is it my desire that a wicked person die?—says the LORD GOD. It is rather that he turn back from his ways and live. (Ezek 18:21-23)

The reverse, the prophet goes on to say, is also the case. The treachery a once righteous person commits condemns him: "he shall die" (vv 24-25). In each situation, the national has become personal. The two generations have been consolidated into two moments in one life, a life imperiled by sin but graced by God's preference for life and by the availability of repentance, the return to God. We must not overlook the consequence of this consolidation. The idea that Israel, condemned to a sentence of death, shall, by the grace of God, recover in a future generation uncontaminated by the ancestors' violations[20] has been transformed into the notion that the recovery can occur in one individual's lifetime. He can escape a death sentence by returning to God and his commandments. Only then shall he live, but the possibility of life after a death sentence (and one that is eminently deserved) is real.

But how shall we take that happy verdict, "he shall live" (Ezek 18:28)? What does it mean in practice? The absolute and apodictic way in which he states the divine verdicts throughout chapter 18 makes it unlikely that Ezekiel, like figures in earlier Israelite religion, understands "life" as simply a life span that is of normal length and ends peacefully and in dignity. But does Ezekiel, then, really believe that the righteous and the repentant will never know death's sting? If so, then surely his examples of righteousness and repentance are purely and only theoretical, for no one, even in Ezekiel's accounting, has lived forever. And just as surely, the prophet's repeated insistence that God's ways are fair must fail (vv 25, 29). For the behavioral demands that God makes are rankly unrealistic if they always result in death, despite God's own preference for life. This question of the ultimate fate of individuals, though pressing to us, is simply not on Ezekiel's mind. That "the same fate is in store for all," as Qohelet would later put it (Qoh 9:2), "for the righteous, and for the wicked; for the good and the pure, and for the impure" does not seem to have occurred to the great prophet of the early exile. The latter, in common with the greater part of prophetic literature, still believes in a strict correlation of deed and consequence (though the correlation is not necessarily immediate or individualistic[21]).

But here Ezekiel unwittingly finds himself in a dilemma. If death is punishment for sin, but sin can be avoided or abandoned, and God's ways are just, then the natural death that is the universal human fate must not be the last word, and the righteous who shall live and not die must be granted life only *after* they go the way of all flesh. This is not, I stress, a conclusion to which Ezekiel actually arrives, but it is one to which the deep structure of his theology inescapably points. His is, in other words, a theology much closer to the later doctrine of a universal resurrection and last judgment than first seems the case.

Let us revert to the question with which we began. Is the notion of a resurrection of the dead to be found in the Hebrew Bible? At one level, the obvious answer is negative. With the exception of a very few special individuals like Elijah and perhaps Enoch, whom God takes directly to himself (2 Kgs 2:6-12; Gen 5:21-23), death is universal and inevitable in this literature. With the exception again of a very few individuals—special sons whom Elijah and Elisha revive, the man who comes back to life when his body touches the latter's bones (1 Kgs 17:17-24; 2 Kgs 4:8-37; 13:20-21)—death is never reversed. This is not just an empirical observation about biblical narrative. Biblical texts articulate the point explicitly (e.g., Ps 49:6-13) and offer theological explanations of how humanity rightly lost the opportunity for the immortality for which they long (Gen 2:25-3:24) and came to have their life span limited (6:1-4). This being the case, it is no cause for wonderment that those who identify Judaism with the Hebrew Bible are surprised to find that belief in resurrection occupies a prominent and central place in Jewish literature and theology and becomes, in fact, a normative and obligatory aspect of Judaism.

But I have been at pains to argue that the inevitability and irreversibility of death in the Hebrew Bible is only part of the story. The other part is the ubiquitous promise of life, sometimes conditional, sometimes not, offered by a God who enjoins his people, in the words of Deuteronomy (30:19), to "Choose life." Especially in the foundational texts in Genesis and Exodus, the survival of that people is continually under attack by infertility and genocide. And yet just as continually—and often miraculously—new life appears, and God's promise overcomes the power of death that had seemed invincible. That God has the power to heal the most hopeless diseases and even to bring people up from Sheol, restoring their vitality, is also well-attested in the hymnic and lament literature of the Hebrew Bible (e.g., 1 Sam 2:6; Ps 30:2-4). The revival of the recently deceased individuals who come into contact with Elijah or Elisha provides suggestive narrative examples of this theology at work.[22] Ezekiel's famous vision in the valley of the bones (Ezek 37:1-14) comes closer to the idea of resurrection, however, for the people revived there have long been dead; their bones are dry. This is, of course, only a vision, but a vision that was thought to communicate something that could not and would not become a reality would surely fail. If Ezekiel thought the revivification of the dry bones and their restoration into living people were impossible, he would hardly have chosen a scene in which that happens as the vehicle to awaken Israel's faith in the God who will restore them to their land.

We face, in sum, a more complicated situation than scholars have usually taken to be the case. In the Hebrew Bible, death is universal and usually not reversed, but God promises, offers, and prefers life and saves his people from annihilation. He even saves some individuals (in exceptional circumstances) from a death that is impending or one that has already occurred. My point is not that a full-fledged doctrine of the resurrection of the dead, when it arrives, changes nothing. It changes much. But it also reflects certain key features of the deep structure of the theology of pre-exilic Israel, a theology in which the fact of death and the promise of life are two elements of capital importance and the relationship between them is unstable. There is something profoundly true in the rabbinic claim that the resurrection of the dead can be derived from the Torah.

Endnotes

1. *M. Sanh.* 10:1 (*Mishnah Sanhedrin*)

2. See, e.g., Abba Hillel Silver, *Where Judaism Differed: An Inquiry into the Distinctiveness of Judaism* (New York: Macmillan, 1956), 265-84.

3. Lloyd Bailey, Sr., *Biblical Perspectives on Death* (Philadelphia: Fortress, 1979), 38.

4. Robert A. Di Vito, "Old Testament Anthropology and the Construction of Personal Identity," *Catholic Bibilical Quarterly* 61 (1999): 221. The words in the single quotes are from John Rogerson, "Anthropology and the Old Testament," in *The World of Ancient Israel: Sociological, Anthropological, and Political Perspectives. Essays by Member of the Society for Old Testament Study,* ed. R. E. Clements (Cambridge, UK: Cambridge University, 1989), 25.

5. See Christoph Barth, *Die Errettung vom Tode in den individuellen Klage- und Dankliedern des Alten Testaments* (Zurich: Theologischer Verlag, 1987), 28, and Robert Martin-Achard, *From Death to Life: A Study of the Development of the Doctrine of Resurrection in the Old Testament* (Edinburgh and London: Oliver and Boyd, 1960), 46.

6. See Barth, *Die Errettung,* 139, where he compares ḥiyya to the Akkadian expression *mita bulluṭu,* "to revive the dead."

7. See Bailey, *Biblical Perspectives,* 48.

8. See Joel S. Kaminsky, *Corporate Responsibility in the Hebrew Bible* (Sheffield, England: Sheffield Academic Press, 1995).

9. I have borrowed the helpful term "biological cessation" from Bailey, *Biblical Perspectives,* 39.

10. Aubrey R. Johnson, *The Vitality of the Individual in the Thought of Ancient Israel* (Cardiff: University of Wales Press, 1949), 69. See also Martin-Achard, *From Death*, 46, and Barth, *Die Errettung*, 102, 165.

11. On Sheol, there is a rich literature. See, e.g., Barth, *Die Errettung*, 76-91, and Nicholas J. Tromp, *Primitive Conceptions of Death and the Netherworld in the Old Testament* (Rome: Pontifical Biblical Institute, 1969), 129-51.

12. See Tromp, *Primitive Conceptions*, 137. There is much room, however, to doubt Tromp's distinction between "the domain of Death" (from which God could save) and the "domain of the dead" (from which there is "no possibility of return").

13. C. S. Lewis, *Miracles: A Preliminary Study* (New York: Macmillan, 1947), 104.

14. There are ample reasons to doubt that the disease traditionally translated as "leprosy" was, in fact, the one to which modern clinicians apply the term. Nonetheless, it is clear that Naaman suffered from a chronic and painful skin disorder.

15. See, e.g., Bailey, *Biblical Perspectives*, 4.

16. Di Vito, "Old Testament Anthropology," 221.

17. Ibid., 200.

18. Ibid., 220.

19. For examples, see Brevard S. Childs, *Introduction to the Old Testament as Scripture* (Philadelphia: Fortress, 1979), 314-16 and 519-20.

20. As in Num 14: 26-35.

21. See, e.g., 21:9, in which YHWH's sword falls on "both the righteous and the wicked."

22. This is not to gainsay the point made by Klaas Spronk, *Beatific Afterlife in Ancient Israel and in the Ancient Near East* (Neukirchen-Vluyn: Neukirchener Verlag, 1986), 72, that "[t]his revivification of recently deceased persons is more akin to the case of the very ill than to the final resurrection." It is important to recall, however, that at least in the earlier phases of the religion of Israel, that distinction between grave illness and death was blurry (if it existed at all). It is much to be doubted that the authors of these texts in Kings thought that if the individuals in question had been deceased for much longer, God would have been impotent to revive them.

The Radical Reconstruction of Childhood: Is There a Place for Theology?[1]

Bonnie J. Miller-McLemore
VANDERBILT UNIVERSITY DIVINITY SCHOOL
NASHVILLE, TENNESSE

My research and writing as a Luce Fellow has centered on the question of how to raise children faithfully as a feminist Christian in a complex postmodern society. In this single sentence, I juxtapose four elements that do not sit easily together—Christianity, feminism, children, and postmodernity. I am convinced, however, that much is gained from this juxtaposition. As a Christian feminist mother of three boys, my research naturally emerged out of my own personal frustrations with the limitations of mainline Christian and feminist views of children and, at the same time, my conviction that both Christianity and feminist theology have important insights to offer.

Whereas my personal frustrations are widely shared, my confidence in Christianity and feminism is less so. On a personal level, many people, regardless of class, race, or religious tradition, find that parenthood is a vocation under siege and that the formation of children is a task for which they are largely unprepared. In addition, on a social level, there is a growing public concern about children, but most people today seldom see Christianity as a credible or relevant resource, either in terms of congregational guidance or academic theological insight. When it comes to child rearing advice, feminists do not fare much better. It has been hard for feminists, both secular and religious, to avoid the pitfall of placing women's and children's needs against one another.

Dogged pursuit of my question has therefore required several steps common to fundamental practical theology, from descriptive, historical, and analytical investigation to more constructive efforts. In this paper, I attend to only one slice of this research. I turn to an area where I found myself both surprised and intrigued—my historical investigation of the cultural construction of children and the reconstructive theological efforts that this historical study invites.

The twists and turns of history reveal a stark need for much deeper theological reflection on how we think and talk about children today. The images and realities of childhood are under radical reconstruction and this reconstruction inevitably spills over into important moral and theological understandings.

Historical Roots of Child-Rearing Anxieties

An intense anxiety surrounds the question of how to bring up children today. Mainline congregations and academic theology have paid little attention to either this anxiety or to its historical roots, even though these roots are inextricably entwined around deep moral and religious quandaries.

The anxiety about raising children is a direct outcome of a series of "domestic revolutions," as historians Steven Mintz and Susan Kellogg call the far-reaching transformations in American family life of the last three centuries.[2] Profound alterations in demographic, organizational, functional, and social characteristics of the Western family have raised what might be called the "Child Question": What will become of children in a greatly changed world in which they no longer seem to fit easily or well?[3]

Economic Shifts: Children as Asset or Burden?

In 1999, on an elementary school field trip to a 4-H agricultural center, I listened as a woman explained the processes of dairy production on a farm in bygone years to two classrooms of third-grade children. She displayed an antique butter-churn and several other implements used to get butter from cow to table. Who, she asked, did they think churned the butter? Blank stares led her to hint, "Do you have chores?" "No" was the resounding chorus of about fifty eight to nine year olds. In the distribution of farm labor not all that long ago, as it turns out, children close to their age churned the butter. That children no longer see themselves as directly responsible for family welfare may seem like a small matter. But in actuality it exemplifies a sea-change.

One of the best known and widely debated theories about childhood is that of historian Philippe Ariès. He saw the "idea of childhood" as a "discovery" of the seventeenth century. Until that time, childhood was not considered a distinct developmental stage. Children were perceived largely as tiny adults or at least as adults in the making.[4] Scholars of all sorts have contested these claims, demonstrating a real appreciation for childhood prior to the modern period. Perhaps a poor English translation of Ariès's French term "sentiment" as simply "idea" has contributed to the confusion.[5] By "sentiment," he did not necessarily mean that childhood itself did not exist; rather childhood did not carry the emotional freight that it has acquired since that time. The debate over historical accuracy aside, however, Ariès was right on at least two accounts. Each historical period fashions its own unique attitudes toward children. And, equally important, a profound change occurred with the advent of modernity. Modernity raised new questions about a child's place in society that have plagued parents up to the present day.

What is it about the Enlightenment, the Industrial Revolution, and today's continued technological and social innovations that has displaced and continues to displace children? Why have the developments of the last few centuries made it harder and harder for families to deal with their responsibilities?

Although in pre-modern and early modern times children remained subordinates in a highly structured, patriarchal family, they had essential roles. As soon as they were old enough, they took their place in family industries, weeding and hoeing gardens, herding domestic animals, carding and spinning wool, making clothing, and caring for younger brothers and sisters. The seventeenth-century American family in general existed as a more cohesive whole, bringing together under one roof the labors of economic production, domestic life, social interaction, and political participation. As family historian John Demos puts it, "All could feel—could *see*—the contributions of the others; and all could feel the underlying framework of reciprocity."[6] While children may have had to submit to the sometimes arbitrary authority of harsh fathers or weary mothers, they knew where they stood in relationship to the family's well being. They were a part of the struggle to survive and thrive.

With the advent of industrialization, men became breadwinners and women largely became homemakers in ever more exclusive ways. Most accounts stop here. But what about children? With work and family split into public and private worlds, children, like women, lost their place as contributing members of household economies and, later in life, as insurance for aging parents. This shift occurred more slowly for girls and for working-class and slave children whose labor in textile mills and coal mines or as field and domestic workers initially made it possible for middle-class mothers and children to retreat to a private realm. Eventually, however, with emancipation, mandatory education, and child labor laws in the last century, the end result was much the same for almost all U.S. children. No longer participants in home industries or farmed out as servants and apprentices and eventually banned from factories, children no longer increased a family's chances of survival but instead drained limited resources. While appropriately freed from exploitative labor, their position in the family changed dramatically from asset to burden. Parents simply no longer expected children to be useful.

Today's parents resist the idea of children as workers. Yet, ironically, an inverse commodification of the child has become increasingly harder to resist. As if parents need any reminder of the costs, estimates of the expense of raising a child make regular news headlines. In 1980, not that long before my oldest son was born in 1986, children, it was reported, would cost parents between $100,000 and $140,000. This public pricing of children as a major family liability, something foreign less than a century ago, epitomizes the revolution that has occurred in daily life.

Psychological Overcompensation: Children as Emotionally Priceless and Yet Invisible

This sweeping historical change, however, does not necessarily mean that children were any less cherished. To the contrary. What would become of children now? From the nineteenth century until today, children became even more precious in a new way. Ironically enough, the more productively useless children became and the less valuable in the "real" world, the more emotionally priceless they became within the home.[7] With the benefits of children less obvious, their desirability and even presence in the family required fresh explanation. Almost as if overcompensating for expelling children from the adult world, debates about the nature and amount of attention adults should lavish on them have raged in the years since industrialization. New social science experts on the intricacies of child rearing, aided by theologians like Horace Bushnell on the true nature of Christian sacrificial love, happily offered variations on an answer. Children were to be inordinately and unconditionally loved in the private sphere of home and family—that is, loved without any limit on private parental excess or expectation of return on the child's part.

The early nineteenth century saw a glorification of motherhood often described as the "cult of womanhood," extolling the piety, purity, and passivity of wives and mothers. Every bit as captivating and virulent was the "cult of childhood" and the obsession with child rearing. The very idea that improper maternal love could permanently harm a child's development, dictating how they would turn out as adults, was virtually unheard of in the Middle Ages.[8] But by early modernity, children were idealized as precious, delicate, and in need of constant care. "Only the most careful and moral 'rearing,'" observes Demos, "would bring the young out safe in later life; anything less might imperil their destiny irrevocably."[9]

That the child was prized did not mean, however, that children assumed center stage. Throughout these domestic revolutions of the last several generations, children moved farther and farther from the center of adult activity and more and more into a separate, privatized realm of home and school. Children not only lost steady contact with parents; they lost contact with the wider world of non-family adults. The family's purpose itself became increasingly defined around personal desires, shifting progressively from the parent-child relationship to the couple.[10] The redefined family goals of emotional companionship and fulfillment did not fit all that well with one of the results of intimate love—children. In fact, it was not too hard to see the demands of raising children as an impediment to these goals. Long before the feminism of the mid-twentieth century, therefore, parenting and children began to lose their ascribed status in the larger scheme of adult life. Children were to "be seen but not heard." This English proverb was not recorded before the nineteenth century, according to one dictionary of quotations, even though it was familiar "with maids in place of children" since the 1400s.[11] Regardless of its exact origin, its familiar ring even today speaks a thousand words about the marginalization of "inferiors," women and servants certainly, but especially children in modern society. In the adult business of modernity, adults gaze upon children with adoration but children had better keep quiet.

Even the artifacts used by and for children reveal the need to create a separate, restricted place for them. In a fascinating study of changes in the material culture surrounding child rearing, historian Karin Calvert observes that "most children's furniture of the seventeenth century was designed to stand babies up and propel them forward" into adulthood and away from the precariousness of early childhood. By contrast, by the middle of the nineteenth century cribs, high chairs, and perambulators replaced the objects designed to assimilate children rapidly into adult society. These new inventions served instead as barriers, carefully establishing a child's special sphere separate from the adult realm. Infant furnishing was designed to "hold infants down and contain them in one spot."[12] These differences reveal a change in where parents saw danger. Before the nineteenth century, parents located life's major threat in childhood with its dangers of disease, sin, and death. The sooner parents could usher children through childhood the better. In the nineteenth century the danger moved to adulthood with its threat of worldly contamination. Childhood then emerged as a safe haven and the longer children remained there the better.

Even demographically, children have come to occupy an ever-shrinking place in adult lives. In the nineteenth century, only about twenty percent of families did not have children under eighteen years old. By 1991, at least forty-two percent of all families did not include children.[13] The one most common living arrangement in the U.S. in 1998 was unmarried people and no children, doubling in just a few decades from sixteen percent of all families in 1972 to thirty-two percent. In the twenty-first century, as more choose to postpone marriage or remain single and childless and as those who bear children live longer after their children leave home, a majority of households will not include children.[14]

It is the state of poor children, however, that most epitomizes the problem of the displacement of children from public view. The private sentimentalization of children and child rearing, it seems, has been inversely related to a collective indifference toward other people's children. The contradictions are grim. Some four-to-twelve-year-olds have almost five billion dollars in discretionary income from gifts, allowances, and chores, while a fourth of the nation's children live in poverty. Middle-class parents invest in private schools and educational tax-deferred funds while poor parents buy burial coverage for their child's premature death. The U.S. economy grew by approximately twenty percent in the 1980s as four million more children moved into poverty, making up the largest proportion of poor persons in the United States. As Daniel Patrick Moynihan remarks, "there is no equivalent in our history for such a number or such a proportion."[15]

Moral and Religious Quandaries: Children as Depraved or Innocent?

Hand in hand with these redefinitions of the child as productively useless but emotionally priceless and yet increasingly invisible was the redefinition of the child as morally and spiritually innocent. That is, childhood was also erased as a vital moral and religious phase of human development. In part, this was an inevitable consequence of who responded to the "Child Question." In all the fuss over what would become of children, social scientists more than church leaders and theologians began to provide the answers. In one of the most striking inversions of the last three centuries, largely secular ideas replaced fundamentally religious approaches to child rearing. The theologians who did continue to speak about children, such as Friedrich Schleiermacher or Bushnell, were mostly happy to comply with the ideas of philosophers and scientists on the child's nature. Beyond this, most theologians did not even try to address the topic at all.

Prior to the eighteenth century, parents may have treated the care of children casually, but attention to a child's moral and religious development was anything but casual. A parent's primary task was to suppress and control what was seen as a child's natural depravity. Children entered the world as carriers of "original sin," an affliction associated with pride, self, and above all, will. They, like adults, encountered daily temptations but without the aid of adult religious disciplines of self-scrutiny and self-regulation. Hence, religious advice-literature urged "breaking" and "beating down" of the will by the heads of households through weekly catechism, daily prayer and scripture reading, repeated admonitions, and sometimes intense psychological and even physical reprimand.[16]

By the end of the eighteenth century, fewer people accepted this portrayal. The child's mind is a blank slate, philosopher John Locke argued, upon which anything may be imprinted. The child is by nature social and affectionate, not sinful, Jean-Jacques Rousseau said. By the mid-nineteenth century the emphasis had almost entirely shifted (although certainly not within all circles). Children were now defined as morally neutral, even "innocent" and "sacralized." One of the most powerful illustrations of this shift appears in the evolution of children's portraits. In colonial representations, children of the upper class wear grown-up fashions and adopt regal stances, with hands on hips and one leg extended, designed to indicate their future adult status. By the mid-eighteenth century, such personifications of adultlike children were replaced by the endearing, soft image of the naturally innocent child. Children were endowed with an almost celestial goodness, pure and unsullied by worldly corruption. This "Romantic child," art historian Anne Higonnet declares, "simply did not exist before the modern era."[17]

This change marks a major shift in understandings of moral agency and accountability. In the pre-modern view of *imperfect children in a fallen world*, responsibility for human evil and failure was more evenly distributed among child, parents, community, church, and society. With the rise of *perfectible children in an imperfect world*, blame for problems increasingly moved away from the child. As one historian puts it, "As God's sovereignty lessened, parental responsibility increased."[18] As a child's moral duties shrank, maternal moral obligation expanded accordingly. Parents were obliged to protect children from social threats, of which there seemed to be increasingly more. Emotional nurture more than moral and religious guidance would bring about independence, self-initiative, and creativity, the skills that seemed necessary for success in a modernized society instead of obedience to authority. If children demonstrated selfishness or aggression, the reason was that they were being improperly cared for and not something inherent in their moral or spiritual nature.

Bushnell, the most prominent theologian to address child rearing in the nineteenth century, kindly offered religious justification for this shift. His book, *Christian Nurture*, deified the household and Christianized emotional nurture. A child is still born spiritually and morally disabled, but a faithful family environment offered a handy remedy. In fact, every act of parental care, every word and deed, mattered. Devotion to one's own children could itself be justified as salvific.[19]

But if child-rearing problems were no longer related so much to sin as to emotional needs, who cared any longer what theologians had to say? Gradually parents looked less and less to the church and more and more to secular experts. In an innovation unique to the twentieth century, all facets of childcare received attention in the laboratory centers attached to major universities, such as Yale, Cornell, and Minnesota. Child experts now included not only pediatricians, psychologists, psychiatrists, and educators but also sociologists and anthropologists.[20] Childcare manuals became the new "Bibles" for proper motherhood, climaxing in the mid-twentieth century with Dr. Spock. The best-selling 1968 edition of *Baby and Child Care* was released after 179 previous paperback printings of the original 1945 edition. The book sold millions of copies. Without using Freud's technical terms, Spock popularized Freudian assumptions about the absolutely crucial importance of the early years for a child's future.[21] This pattern of seeing faulty child rearing as the source of delinquency, poverty, violence, and other major social problems continues today. In Dr. Spock's world, the household required a kind of scientific engineering and ingenuity. Housekeeping became a matter of home economics and interior design; child rearing became a job that could be methodically mastered and even perfected.

In the past half-century, science became obsessed with a peculiarly modern question: Why do children turn out the way they do? Social scientific debates about nature and nurture largely replaced moral and religious debates about innocence and depravity. Judith Harris, author of the much-discussed *The Nurture Assumption*, claims that nature and nurture, what psychology used to call heredity and environment, are the "the yin and yang, the Adam and Eve, the Mom and Pop of pop psychology."[22] Parents in turn became more and more hung up about doing the right thing, having been led by science into believing that children and parents are perfectible, infinitely open to human design, rather than flawed and imperfect. Today many middle-class parents have taken the mandate to lavish the very best on one's own children to an extreme, intensely apprehensive about how one's own individual children will turn out. Significantly, this preoccupation is focused on fewer and fewer children: the number of children per household has dropped from 6.6 in 1890 to 1.9 in 1994.[23] Like a silent spiritual contagion, this preoccupation and the inevitability of failure has spread from mothers to fathers, single parents, stepparents, grandparents, and even siblings.

No wonder recent books challenging this obsession and taking an extreme opposite position sell so many copies. Harris's book itself argues that psychology has tricked us: peers matter, children socialize other children, but parents are basically not responsible. She concludes a chapter on "What Parents Can Do" with an especially gratifying section titled "The Guilt Trip Stops Here" that reads like a recipe to ease our heavy load. Similarly, education consultant John Bruer received all sorts of hype when he challenged the "myth" that the family environment during the first three years alters brain development.[24] Jerome Kegan likewise declared the idea that the first two years determine a child's development seductively false.[25] Do any of these books, however, offer satisfactory answers to the deeper moral and spiritual questions that have now arisen about what children need and adult responsibility for children? Unfortunately, questions about guilt, responsibility, and children can no longer be so easily resolved.

A Place for Theology?
Children as Moral and Religious Agents

We stand now in the midst of a major reconstruction in our understandings of children. This reconstruction is on the "same order of magnitude," Higonnet believes, as that which occurred with the romanticization of the child in the eighteenth century, a portrayal of childhood that has now run its course.[26] Just as the new construction of innocent childhood caused anxiety, resistance, and innovation in its time, so also does the reinvention of childhood today. Three negative images dominate contemporary views of children—the Hurried child, the Market child, and the Neglected or Endangered child.[27] Beyond assessing the problems of the child who must check a daily planner before deciding to play with a friend or the child bombarded by advertisements as the next big growth market, it is equally important to ask why these images have taken over. They are desperate, even if poor, cultural attempts to figure out where and how children will now fit into postmodern life. These views are particularly disturbing because they upset cherished nineteenth-century conventions of idyllic childhood, revealing the artificiality and limitations of the invention of childhood innocence. Moreover, they contest the sharp line drawn between adult and child worlds. They show the inevitable and sometimes severe consequences for children of adult actions in the so-called separate adult realm, and they insist that adults once again take children's lives more seriously, including their moral and religious struggles. Together these images point toward a more apt characterization of postmodern children. We have moved irrevocably beyond the sentimental toward some other vision, what Higonnet calls "Knowing children."

In place of the ideal of the innocent child, "Knowing" children call into question children's "psychic and sexual innocence by attributing to them consciously active minds and bodies."[28] The ideology of innocence meant that adults saw children as cute but less often as capable, intelligent, desiring individuals in their own right. Innocence allowed adults to picture children as passive, trivial, and even available to adult objectification and abuse. Absolute distinctions between adult and child especially stranded adolescents, as if they ought to metamorphose overnight from one to the other and spare adults the real complexity of human life. More than anything, however, the more realistic, less romanticized "Knowing child" mixes together sexual, moral, and spiritual attributes previously dichotomized. The "Romantic child," by contrast, was defined in terms of what an adult was not—"not sexual, not vicious, not ugly, not conscious, not damaged." The "Knowing child" presents a less simple alternative. As Higonnet remarks, children are as much about "difficulty, trouble, and tension" as they are about "celebration, admiration, and passionate attachment." This confronts adults with "many more challenges as well as many more pleasures than any idea of childhood has done before."[29]

The image of the "Knowing child" suggests an intriguing return of moral and religious questions. If the pre-modern family portrayed the child as *imperfectible in a fallen world* and the modern world saw the child as *perfectible in an imperfect world*, the postmodern child is perhaps the most morally and spiritually perplexing: *the imperfect, even potentially volatile, child in an imperfect, volatile world*. Recent events, such as child-on-child violence and school shootings, have raised serious questions about how to judge the moral and spiritual capacities of children and the responsibilities of adults. At the same time, children seem all the more vulnerable. By picturing children as innocent, blank slates, adults often abused their responsibility for earnest protection of children's physical, moral, and spiritual well being. Adults can no longer avoid their obligations to oversee children's moral and spiritual development by surrounding themselves with pictures of cuddly, unblemished, blissful infants.

In a word, a rich moral and religious complexity has returned along with the honesty and real ambiguity of children and parenting. How well do children really know what they need? Are their desires as susceptible as adult desires to the human temptation of wanting too much or wanting wrongly or destructively? "Can a child indeed choose to do evil?" as American religious historian Margaret Bendroth asks. "Perhaps," she concludes, "our own times suggest the need to revisit an old and still deeply anguished question."[30]

Such questions are complicated by an important critique of parents and Christianity that has dominated much thinking on children in the past two decades. Led by psychoanalyst Alice Miller and others who have avidly taken up her work, people have become acutely aware of the distorted use of children to meet adult needs as well as the dangers of religious justification for such abuse.[31] Drawing on her work, several others have spelled out in great detail how biblical and Christian images are used to justify abusive patterns.[32] However, in all this discussion a huge question stands unanswered. If "much Christian theology has been rooted in the threat of punishment," as Philip Greven argues,[33] why has Christian theology paid so little attention to creating a more child-friendly theology that sets new precedents for interactions with children? Can an alternative course be drawn from scripture and other Christian sources, to provide a better means of guidance and discipline? Do Christian understandings of sin and love inevitably lead to child abuse or can they be read in fresh ways to empower children and parents?

Reconstructive efforts are especially needed in three broad areas: notions of sin, redemption, and children; ideas about children's worth; and parenting as an important religious practice. In the remainder of this paper, I focus only on the first. I take up the other two at greater length elsewhere.[34]

Given the amazingly destructive role doctrines of sin have played in condoning the harsh and abusive treatment and discipline of children, why jump into this thicket at all? While we automatically react negatively to the idea of children as sinful or depraved, the history of the "depraved adultish-child" of pre-modern times and the "innocent childish-child" of modern times has shown the limits of both views. The reign of the cherished, romanticized child created its own set of problems every bit as troubling as belief in the sinful, corrupt child had done. A more complex understanding of sin and grace therefore helps us move beyond the unfortunate dichotomy of the last several centuries between child as villain and child as victim, or child as wholly depraved and child as wholly innocent. It especially explains the moral and spiritual complexity of the teen years without pathologizing them. Indeed, the theological concept gives children and adults a word and way to talk about betrayal of self, others, and God, an experience that they undoubtedly share.

Second, if one can talk about sin, restoration, and children, one can then reconsider the complexities of moral and spiritual development, a topic familiar to many pre-Enlightenment theologians, but largely depleted of significant meaning today. Prior to the turn to the Romantic child, many Christian theologians described the course of a child's spiritual formation in rich and varied ways. Although it comes as a surprise to our postmodern ears, these largely forgotten views add something missing in more recent psychological views. Romanticized views freeze children in a sort of static childhood innocence threatened by external forces. Current life cycle views in psychology divide development into stages of either increasing independence or increasing relationality—enlightening but limited typologies of human nature.

By contrast, classical Christian developmental schemes capture important dimensions of a child's evolving moral and religious struggles. They trace the dynamics of an incremental accretion of responsibility and make a place for human frailty, mistakes, and destructive failures. These failures are not occasions for despair or unrelenting guilt but rather occasions for deeper moral and religious awakening, compassion, remorse, reparation, and formation. This view contests the prevalent drive to perfect parenting and individual children. It suggests a different approach, one that includes a ready disclosure of shortcomings and the promise of reprieve. A theological framework also suggests that adults in religious communities have broader responsibilities for the formation of children well beyond their own biological offspring.

Finally, as this implies, historical notions of sin and children are far more complex and diverse than conventional negative stereotypes allow. Oversimplified conceptions need to be challenged and corrected. Not all allegations of evil in children are a form of religious contempt and abuse. In some cases, as Marcia Bunge demonstrates in her exploration of Hermann Francke, an important German Pietist of the eighteenth century, the idea of original sin and redemption actually fostered the more humane treatment of children in general. It motivated Francke to treat children with respect and kindness and, by leveling the playing field in which all are fallen, to extend such care to poor children in a deeply class-conscious society.[35] In a word, there is not a one-to-one correlation between ideas about original sin and harsh punishment of children. Augustine actually argues against physical reprimand, John Calvin does not advocate it, and even Jonathan Edwards, who calls children "young vipers," does not talk about corporal punishment or "breaking the will" of sinful children. Without denying the harm done in the name of Christianity and in the name of each of these figures by their followers, the weight of the theological tradition falls strongly on the side of the child.

In an edited volume, *The Child in Christian Thought*, two authors actually devise their own terms to capture the nuance with which important theologians, Augustine in early Christianity (354-430 C.E.) and Menno Simons as part of the Radical Reformation (1496-1561 C.E.), talked about children as sinful. In her work on Augustine, Martha Stortz suggests "non-innocence" as the best phrase to describe a third possibility that Augustine assumed between innocence and depravity. In Augustine's eyes, an infant is willing but not yet capable of causing or strong enough to cause harm, literally not harming or *"in–nocens."*[36] In a similar fashion but for a quite different Christian figure and period, Keith Graber Miller invents the phrase, "complex innocence" to capture Simon's understanding of the "absence of both faithfulness and sinfulness in children," an "'innocence' . . . tempered with the acknowledgement of an inherited Adamic nature predisposed toward sinning."[37]

Stortz does not skirt Augustine's highly ambiguous historical legacy. In the course of history, these same ideas were used to justify corporal punishment, as demonstrated by a later chapter in the same book on the harsh measures used by Jesuit and Ursuline missionaries in their work among the Huron Indians in Canada in the seventeenth century. Still, although Augustine's ideas led to later travesty, his own thinking was "remarkably nuanced." As Stortz describes it:

> He refused the romantic option of seeing children as completely innocent, born with a nature as pure as Adam's before the Fall. Equally he refused the cynic's view of infants as miniature demons in desperate need of discipline. Non-innocence fairly characterizes his attitude toward infancy. As they matured and acquired the abilities to speak and reason, children assumed a gradually increasing accountability for their actions.[38]

Similarly, Simons develops his own understanding of an intermediary position between innocence and guilt, even though he does so for almost opposite theological purposes—as part of a bigger argument against, rather than for, infant baptism. In the process of providing scriptural, theological, and practical arguments for the excellence of adult baptism, he distinguishes between "a *nature* predisposed toward sin and actual *sinning*, disallowing the former to obliterate childhood innocence and identifying only the latter as that for which believers have responsibility before God."[39] A child's "complex innocence" then entails the inborn tainted nature that becomes a graver cause for concern only as a child acquires the ability to discern and confess human frailty.

Allowing for sin, in turn, permitted Augustine and Simons to describe the incremental moves from non-innocence or complex innocence to increased accountability and culpability. Although Simons did not believe that moral and spiritual maturity always coincided with chronological markers, he held that parents had a serious obligation to watch for, recognize, cultivate, and celebrate the age of accountability. Augustine, by contrast, drew on common understandings of antiquity to create a quite sophisticated demarcation of the changing nature of sin and accountability through six stages from infancy to old age.

If a grasping insatiability characterized infancy, disobedience is the notable sin of the second stage of life in which children acquire language, perceive adult expectations, and learn the rules. In adolescence the non-innocence of infancy takes on an increasingly malicious form of "deliberate malice," most characteristically exemplified for Augustine in his own youthful foray with friends into a fruit garden, stealing pears prompted by nothing else than the "sheer delight of doing something wrong." Here we have not just grasping desire or even outright disobedience but the infringement of a "certain bedrock equity in the world of human society," a violation of basic human decency.[40] Stortz identifies this developmental understanding as one of Augustine's major contributions to contemporary considerations of children. Her words are worth quoting at length:

> Augustine . . . recognized boundaries between the various stages of the life cycle and found in each stage a level of accountability that was chronologically and experientially appropriate. In particular, he evaluated the first stages of the life cycle in terms of increasing levels of moral accountability. Although they were non-innocent, infants assumed little or no accountability: they had

neither language nor reason. It was fruitless to rebuke them because they could not understand language. With the acquisition of language and reason came greater accountability. He expected children to obey verbal commands and adolescents to understand the basic demands of human decency. These graduated levels of accountability implied graver consequences for transgressions. Looking back on a gang-stealing of pears, Augustine lamented the sins of his youth—but at least he knew when it was over![41]

In other words, the non-innocence of infancy, left unnoticed and untutored, is replicated, intensified, and amplified in the outright guilt of later stages of life.

Several general observations can be made from this brief foray into classic texts. Describing virtue, accountability, and guilt in children is a daunting task. We learn from Christian theology to do so nonetheless, but to proceed with fear and trepidation. Second, in this effort we do not get much help from scriptural accounts of Jesus' life. The New Testament simply does not make either child rearing or a child's religious formation a topic of discussion. The debates of church history about sin and baptism therefore have at least filled a gap in marking the child as a religious and moral being about to embark on a serious pilgrimage. Moreover, this view stressed the critical obligation of the Christian community for bringing children to voluntary commitments of faith and discipleship. Religious debates about children and sin then open up fresh avenues to discuss the radical understanding of parenting as a religious discipline and practice in its own right. As in Simons's worldview, discussions of sin and grace "utterly obligated parents and the Christian community to nurture children" in the faith.[42] Religious rituals must sanction the turning points of religious formation. Criteria for discipline must correspond to a child's gradual ability to speak, understand, discern, and incorporate good habits and virtues. In other words, people must take the environment, the social and family context, and parental example and guidance seriously *without* absolving children of gradual responsibility for their own actions or undercutting the richness of their own developing moral and religious sensibilities.

While many, many reasons lead children into trouble, the social sciences often picture the child as a victim of forces beyond her or his control, blaming parents and culture and choking out discussion of complicated questions about moral and religious formation. The tendency to attribute evil to either heredity or the environment sometimes robs the child of responsibility, will, and freedom, overlooks the complexity of parenting, and ignores the richness of religious traditions that have attempted to understand the inherent, although not inevitable, nature of human frailty and brokenness. While many people have focused on the destructive consequences of Christian views of children and the abuse performed in Christianity's name, we must continue to plumb the depths of an alternative course drawn from scripture and other Christian sources. As cherished conventions of childhood are upset and images of children and adult responsibilities multiply, articulating a fresh Christian reading on children and child rearing becomes more than a purely academic exercise. It becomes a matter of contributing to a reinvention that is already well underway and in need of a richer variety of perspectives, including perspectives that might address moral and spiritual questions that many secular approaches overlook.

Endnotes

1.   Material that appears in this chapter also appears in similar but more developed form in *Let the Children Come: Revisioning Children from a Christian Perspective* (forthcoming, Jossey-Bass, 2003). Used by permission of John Wiley & Sons, Inc.

2.   Steven Mintz and Susan Kellogg, *Domestic Revolutions: A Social History of American Family Life* (New York: Free Press, 1988), xiv.

3.   This question is obviously closely related to what has been called the "Woman Question" by Barbara Ehrenreich and Deirdre English (*For Her Own Good: 150 Years of the Experts' Advice to Women* [New York: Doubleday, 1978]): Shorn by industrialization of their status and function as important participants in public life, what were women going to do with themselves?

4.   Philippe Ariès, *Centuries of Childhood: A Social History of the Family Life*, Robert Baldick, trans. (New York: Vintage Books, 1962), 125, originally published as *L'enfant et la vie familiale sous l'Ancien Régime* (Paris: Librairie Plon, 1960).

5.   Hugh Cunningham, "Histories of Childhood," *The American Historical Review* 103: 4 (October 1998): 1197.

6.   John Demos, *Past, Present, and Personal: The Family and the Life Course in American History* (New York: Oxford University Press, 1986), 10, emphasis in the text. See also his *A Little Commonwealth: Family Life in Plymouth Colony* (New York: Oxford University Press, 1970).

7.   Viviana A. Zelizer, *Pricing the Priceless Child: The Changing Social Value of Children* (Princeton: Princeton University Press, 1994).

8. Cunningham, "Histories of Childhood," 1197. See James A. Schultz, *The Knowledge of Childhood in the German Middle Ages, 1100-1350* (Philadelphia: University of Pennsylvania Press, 1995).

9. Demos, *Past, Present, and Personal*, 35. See also Larry L. Bumpass, "What's Happening to the Family? Interactions between Demographic and Institutional Change," *Demography* 27: 4 (November 1990): 488; and "Is Low Fertility Here to Stay?" *Family Planning Perspectives* 5 (1973): 68-69.

10. Stephanie Coontz, *The Social Origins of Private Life: A History of American Families 1600-1900* (New York: Verso, 1988), 35.

11. Henry L. Mencken, *A New Dictionary of Quotations on Historical Principles From Ancient and Modern Sources* (New York: A.A. Knopf, 1942), 169.

12. Karin Calvert, *Children in the House: The Material Culture of Early Childhood, 1600-1900* (Boston: Northeastern University Press, 1992), 6-7.

13. Dennis A. Ahlburg and Carol J. De Vita, "New Realities of the American Family," in *Family in Transition*, 9th ed., ed. Arlene S. Skolnick and Jerome H. Skolnick (New York: Longman, 1997), 24; see also Ron Lesthaeghe, "A Century of Demographic and Cultural Change in Western Europe: An Exploration of Underlying Dimensions," *Population and Development Review* 9: 3 (September 1983): 431.

14. Tom W. Smith, "The Emerging 21st Century American Family," (Chicago: National Opinion Research Center, 1999), available on the Internet at www.norc.uchicago.edu.

15. Daniel Patrick Moynihan, "Social Justice in the Next Century," *America* 165: 6 (September 14, 1991): 136.

16. See Demos, *A Little Commonwealth*, ch. 2; Philip J. Greven, Jr., *The Protestant Temperament: Patterns of Child-Rearing, Religious Experience, and the Self in Early America* (New York: A.A. Knopf, 1977), ch. 9.

17. Anne Higonnet, *Pictures of Innocence: The History and Crisis of Ideal Childhood* (New York: Thames and Hudson, 1998), 15.

18. William G. McLoughlin, "Evangelical Child Rearing in the Age of Jackson: Francis Wayland's Views of When and How to Subdue the Willfulness of Children," in *Growing Up in America: Children in Historical Perspective*, ed. N. Ray Hiner and Joseph M. Hawes (Urbana: University of Illinois Press, 1985), 96.

19. Margaret Bendroth, "Children of Adam, Children of God: Christian Nurture in Early Nineteenth-Century America," *Theology Today* 56: 4 (January 2000): 502-503.

20. Mary Cable, *The Little Darlings: A History of Child Rearing in America* (New York: Charles Scribner's Sons, 1972), 186.

21. See A. Michael Sulman, "The Humanization of the American Child: Benjamin Spock as a Popularizer of Psychoanalytic Thought," *Journal of the History of the Behavioral Sciences* 9 (1973): 258-65.

22. Judith Rich Harris, *The Nurture Assumption: Why Children Turn Out the Way They Do* (New York: Free Press, 1998), 1.

23. Donald Hernandez, with David E. Myers, "Revolutions in Children's Lives," in *Family in Transition*, 9th ed., ed. Arlene S. Skolnick and Jerome H. Skolnick (New York: Addison-Wesley, 1997), p. 257.

24. John T. Bruer, *The Myth of the First Three Years: A New Understanding of Early Brain Development and Lifelong Learning* (New York: Free Press, 1999).

25. Jerome Kegan, *Three Seductive Ideas* (Cambridge: Harvard University Press, 1998).

26. Higonnet, *Pictures of Innocence*, 193.

27. For an analysis of the "market child," see Todd David Whitmore (with Tobias Winright), "Children: An Undeveloped Theme in Catholic Teaching," in *The Challenge of Global Stewardship: Roman Catholic Responses*, ed. Maura A. Ryan and Todd David Whitmore (Notre Dame: University of Notre Dame Press, 1997), 161-185. David Elkind first identified the "hurried child" in the early 1980s (*The Hurried Child: Growing Up Too Fast Too Soon* [Reading: Addison-Wesley Publishing Co., 1981]; 3rd edition published by Perseus Press, 2001). The "neglected or endangered child" is my own nomenclature for a view that has received the most attention in recent years from both conservative and liberal perspectives, and in far too many books to cite here.

28. Higonnet, *Pictures of Innocence*, 12.

29. Ibid., 224, 209.

30. Bendroth, "Children of Adam, Children of God," 505.

31. Alice Miller, *The Drama of the Gifted Child,* translated by Ruth Ward (New York: Basic Books, 1994); *For Your Own Good: Hidden Cruelty in Child-Rearing and the Roots of Violence*, translated by Hildegarde and Hunter Hannum (New York: Farrar, Straus, and Giroux, 1983); *Thou Shalt Not Be Aware: Society's Betrayal of the Child*, translated by Hildegard and Hunter Hannum (New York: Meridian, 1986).

32. See, for example, Philip Greven, *Spare the Child: The Religious Roots of Punishment and the Psychological Impact of Physical Abuse* (New York: Knopf, 1990); Donald Capps, *The Child's Song: The Religious Abuse of Children* (Louisville: Westminster John Knox Press, 1995); Jennifer L. Manlowe, *Faith Born of Seduction: Sexual Trauma, Body Image, and Religion* (New York: New York University Press, 1995); and Stephen Pattison, "'Suffer Little Children:' The Challenge of Child Abuse and Neglect to Theology," *T & S* 9 (1998): 36-58.

33. Greven, *Spare the Child*, 8-9.

34. Bonnie J. Miller-McLemore, *Let the Children Come: Revisioning Children from a Christian Perspective* (forthcoming, 2003, Jossey-Bass) and *Care of Children as a Religious Practice* (forthcoming, 2005, Jossey-Bass).

35. Marcia Bunge, "The Child in 18th Century German Pietism: Perspectives from the Work of A. H. Francke," in *The Child in Christian Thought*, ed. Marcia J. Bunge (Grand Rapids: W.B. Eerdmans, 2001), 247-78.

36. Martha Ellen Stortz, "'Where or When was Your Servant Innocent?' Augustine on Childhood," in *The Child in Christian Thought*, ed. Marcia Bunge (Grand Rapids: Eerdmans, 2001), 82.

37. Keith Graber Miller, "Complex Innocence, Obligatory Nurturance, and Parental Vigilance: 'The Child' in the Work of Menno Simons," in *The Child in Christian Thought*, ed. Marcia Bunge (Grand Rapids: Eerdmans, 2001), 194.

38. Stortz, "'Where or When was Your Servant Innocent?'" 100.

39. Miller, "Complex Innocence, Obligatory Nurturance, and Parental Vigilance," 201, emphasis in text.

40. Stortz, "'Where or When was Your Servant Innocent?'" 85.

41. Ibid., 101-2.

42. Miller, "Complex Innocence, Obligatory Nurturance, and Parental Vigilance," 194.